Research Methods in Luxury Management

This is one of the first textbooks to explore the research process within the specific context of luxury brand management. It adopts a case-rich approach, informed by original research, to guide the reader through the various stages of the research process, from conception to completion and application.

Beginning with a summary of past and present research in the field of luxury, the book then outlines the fundamental principles of research, paying particular attention to representativeness and contextualisation, before guiding readers through the intricacies of research design. Further topics include the nature of data in the field of luxury, the research challenges facing luxury practitioners, quantitative and qualitative research methods for luxury brand management specialists, analytical techniques, and guidance for presenting and applying research findings within the luxury environment. Real-world examples and case studies are provided in each chapter, and the book rounds off with some review challenges and problem-solving exercises to facilitate self-learning.

Research Methods in Luxury Management is essential reading for postgraduate and advanced undergraduate courses in luxury brand management, luxury marketing and luxury strategy. It will also be a useful tool for practitioners and problem-solvers within and beyond the luxury industry.

Michael J.G. Parnwell is Professor Emeritus of East Asian Studies at the University of Leeds, UK. His academic background is in development studies, sustainability and tourism, and he has taught research methods for over 20 years, including at Goldsmiths, University of London, the University of Leeds, the University of Hull and the Macau Institute of Science and Technology, and in Thailand, Vietnam and Cambodia.

Kelly Meng is the programme director for the MA in Luxury Brand Management at Goldsmiths, University of London, UK. Kelly has previously held senior managerial positions with leading international companies in the retail and luxury industries. Kelly is also author of *South African Business in China: Navigating Institutions* (Routledge, 2022).

Mastering Luxury Management

The luxury sector is a rapidly evolving and competitive global industry, requiring premium brands to be dynamic and innovative in their business and management decisions to remain relevant. This series meets the need for thorough yet practical and accessible textbooks that address the complexity of the luxury industry and the challenges facing its management.

Mastering Luxury Management is a valuable resource for luxury management courses, helping readers to acquire an in-depth understanding of contemporary theories and how they apply in practice, alongside recognising trends and developments that may shape the future marketplace. Individually, each text provides essential reading for a core topic. A range of consistent pedagogical features are used across the series, including international case studies that demonstrate practical applications in the luxury context.

Each text will be invaluable reading for advanced undergraduate and postgraduate students, in particular those studying for a Master's or MBA in Luxury Management or Luxury Brand Management, as they provide tools and strategies for a successful future career in luxury.

Strategic Luxury Management
Value Creation and Creativity for Competitive Advantage
David Millán Planelles

Contemporary Issues in Luxury Brand Management
Edited by Sylvie Studente and Eleonora Cattaneo

For more information about this series, please visit: www.routledge.com/Mastering-Luxury-Management/book-series/LM

Research Methods in Luxury Management

Michael J. G. Parnwell
Kelly Meng

Routledge
Taylor & Francis Group

LONDON AND NEW YORK

Designed cover image: Somboon Sitthichoptam

First published 2023
by Routledge
4 Park Square, Milton Park, Abingdon, Oxon OX14 4RN

and by Routledge
605 Third Avenue, New York, NY 10158

Routledge is an imprint of the Taylor & Francis Group, an informa business

British Library Cataloguing-in-Publication Data
A catalogue record for this book is available from the British Library

ISBN: 978-1-032-28117-9 (hbk)
ISBN: 978-1-032-28110-0 (pbk)
ISBN: 978-1-003-29537-2 (ebk)

DOI: 10.4324/9781003295372

Typeset in Bembo
by codeMantra

Access the support material: www.routledge.com/9781032281100

Contents

Figures

Tables

Boxes

Preface

It would have been hard to imagine, when their paths first crossed 17 years ago, that the authors would end up writing a book on research methods together. It would be fair to say that Kelly Meng's first impression of research methods was not altogether flattering or favourable. She found it daunting, uninteresting, almost pointless, and certainly did not appreciate its timetabling at 15.00 on a Friday afternoon! That dislike of methodology extended to her teacher, and she 'advised' everyone who would listen not to take the research methods modules – until she realised they were both compulsory. The teacher, meanwhile, had been teaching research methods for the best part of 30 years, not because he particularly wanted to but largely because none of his colleagues – all very competent researchers – had any inclination to contribute to the programme. When he retired in 2014, he thought he had seen the back of methods teaching for good. Obviously not!

It was only when Kelly embarked on her PhD research that the penny truly dropped, and the value of everything she had learned became readily apparent. And now, somewhat ironically, when she teaches her own students of luxury brand management, you can hear clear echoes of the intellectual principles and operational techniques that passed from teacher to student all those years ago. And she has come to appreciate that research methods is not something that is isolated from other forms of academic endeavour, a course that has to be taken, but is in fact a crucial element of and foundation for the whole process of knowledge generation and understanding.

Their paths crossed once again when Kelly introduced the Master's programme in Luxury Brand Management at Goldsmiths, University of London, in 2017. With as many as 60–70 students each year, and a need to organise workshops for the research-based dissertation, Mike Parnwell, now an emeritus professor at the University of Leeds and hoping to rediscover his identity as a 1960s hippy, was brought in to try to inspire students who hailed from most corners of the globe. This was an interesting challenge in its own right: Mike's career had focused on development, poverty and sustainability in South East Asia, and here he was instantly having to become a leading expert on luxury! But, having supervised or examined more than 80 PhD students, he at least knew a fair bit about postgraduate research.

This book is the product of convergent paths and congruent worldviews, and hopefully it is all the better for this. We come from different disciplinary backgrounds but share certain moral and philosophical perspectives on knowledge and on life. This is why we have presented a largely multidisciplinary perspective on luxury research, and why we look holistically at the luxury industry as a whole rather than focusing on luxury fashion, which most academics tend to do. Kelly has extensive experience of the luxury industry from a practitioner perspective, and so we have sought to ensure that the information contained in the book is of potential value to people working in the industry, as well as students who hope soon to take their place as luxury professionals. We have used examples from across the luxury industry and relating to a wide array of issues, in the hope that it will help make the discussion of methodology appear real and have relevance to present-day challenges. We are both deeply intrigued by the fundamental essence of luxury, but see problems looming on the horizon that, we hope, young (and not so young), intelligent, informed and motivated students will be willing and able to address. We hope this book may make a contribution to this endeavour, however modest.

Michael Parnwell
Kelly Meng
November 2022, London

CHAPTER 1

Research Methods in Luxury Management

Introduction and Overview

We will start this book with two opening paragraphs. Choose which one you prefer.

The luxury industry has experienced phenomenal growth since the turn of the 21st century, and this expansion has attracted the attention of a rapidly increasing number of academic researchers. The value of the personal luxury goods market[1] worldwide increased almost four-fold, from €76 billion in 1996 to €283 billion in 2021, after recovering strongly from a significant dip in 2020 (to €217 billion) resulting from the COVID-19 pandemic.[2] The luxury industry as a whole, which is dominated (48.3%) by sales of luxury automobiles, attained a total value of €1.14 trillion in 2021. In tandem with the rapid expansion of the luxury industry has been a proliferation of academic publications on the subject of luxury: in 2021, 869 articles were published on this topic, compared with 100 in 1996 and only 2 in 1990.[3] There are also now at least 51 Master's programmes in Europe alone that focus on aspects of luxury management, marketing or business (see Table 1.1). As the luxury industry has grown, so too has research interest in its dynamics and impact, be that the highbrow work of scholars and students, the systematic analyses of industry consultants, the more flowery storytelling of commentators and bloggers, or the attention-grabbing narratives of influencers and social media.

The phrase '*sortie du temple*' has been used[5] to describe a significant watershed in the history of luxury, occurring around the mid 1990s, which saw a shift in emphasis from rarity and exclusivity towards accessibility and ubiquity, from iconic *maisons* towards stock market-listed corporations, from meticulous artisanship towards mass production, and from local provenance towards global reach. The democratisation of luxury had commenced, and the essence of luxury was being challenged. The temple analogy is apposite: from its earliest origins, luxury had a close association with sacredness and divinity – only luxurious items and materials were deemed suitable as gifts of worship (Cabigiosu, 2020, 11). As time progressed, luxury goods and their skilled creators also took on an aura of 'sacredness' to those versed in the *art de vivre* (the art of living well) and wishing to flaunt their social superiority. But luxury had experienced *sortie du temple* moments even before the forces of globalisation threatened its aura of sanctity. For example, in 1950, the House of Dior transformed its business by introducing accessories, brand extensions and a licensing scheme that took ready-to-wear 'wholesale couture' to global markets (Okawa, 2020); and, in 1967, Yves Saint Laurent opened his first *prêt-à-porter* store, Saint Laurent Rive Gauche, which instantly became "the new sanctum of Paris youth culture" (The Museum at FIT, 2015) and an epicentre of the 1960s "youthquake" (Thomas, 2008, 8), in the process establishing a production and sales model that many other couturiers were soon to follow.[6] It is this

DOI: 10.4324/9781003295372-1

TABLE 1.1 Master's Programmes with a Focus on Luxury, 2022

Programme Focus	Number of Programmes
Luxury Management*	44
Luxury Marketing*	16
Luxury Business*	11
Country	
France	18
United Kingdom	13
Italy	8
Spain	8
Switzerland	4
Other countries	5
Modalities	
Full-time*	52
Part-time*	13
One-year	35
Two-year	16
On-campus*	48
Distance-learning*	11
Blended learning*	4
Total Number of Programmes	56

Note: * Indicates multiple counting.

Data source: masterstudies.co.uk (accessed 5 October 2022)[4]

constant evolution of both the meaning and character of luxury that makes it such an alluring subject in the pursuit of knowledge and understanding through the process of research.

These two paragraphs say essentially the same thing: that the luxury industry is growing rapidly; that its expansion has consequences; and that both the processes and impacts of change generate issues and challenges that researchers are interested in understanding, and perhaps also contributing to their amelioration. And yet the flavour of the two paragraphs is quite different. The first has a cold, factual, objective, quantitative feel to it; the second has an essential, subjective, cultural and qualitative touch. We have immediately landed on one of the fundamental dichotomies which influences how we see the world and, in the present context, how we view the world of luxury: a functional perspective that sees luxury as a business, and an aesthetic or emotional (romantic, even) perspective that focuses on the essence of luxury. And circulating within these two realms of luxury are people – designers, producers, marketeers, consumers, admirers, commentators, evaluators – who differentially attach value to these two perspectives in their pursuit of the finest things in life. Welcome to the world of luxury research!

> The concept of luxury, like a diamond, has many facets and multiple colors, which change on the basis of the perspective from which it is scrutinized.
>
> (Cabigiosu, 2020, 18)

Different people may view the gradual metamorphosis of luxury differently. Many will applaud its apparent robustness, dynamism and inventiveness, and will appreciate the way it has become more inclusive, accessible and geographically dispersed. Others will decry precisely the same processes, bemoaning the associated erosion of uniqueness, exclusivity, cachet, legacy, localism, craftsmanship and *savoir faire*: that luxury is selling its soul to the (global) market. The first paragraph of this chapter has an almost triumphant feel to it; the second seems quite nostalgic in nuance, conveying a sense of something lost and a fear for the future. And yet the phrase *sortie du temple* means stepping out of, rather than descending from, the 'temple' of tradition and cultural heritage; moving forward rather than remaining locked in the past. Take a million people and you may well find a thousand different perspectives on the character and trajectory of luxury, so diverse is the constituency and so complex the array of permutations affecting the industry today. The job of the researcher is to make sense of these complex and often contradictory and countervailing forces; to provide analysis and insight that contribute to a better and deeper understanding of the modern-day dynamics of luxury and the issues this gives rise to. The student researcher of luxury may well be drawn to this field through the allure of luxury and their interest in aspects of the industry's evolution, upon which they may adopt a position or stance, but the task of the researcher is not to paint a picture of luxury in the colours of their choosing, but to piece together an image based upon the fragments of an investigation, assembled as objectively as possible, which considers multiple angles, narrated in a plausible argument and supported by strong evidence.

The aim of this book is to introduce student researchers of luxury, principally at the Master's level, to the principles and practice of research. But we do not just want to produce yet another book on research methods which uses occasional examples from the field of luxury to illustrate its various points. Also, we do not want to produce a textbook which draws a circle around the student researcher and simply *assumes* that what they learn may have some relevance to and value in the field of luxury management. We will try as much as possible to integrate these two realms: the academic and the practical. What we come up with may not be to everyone's taste. There is a quite plausible argument that says academic research should be principally theoretical and should deal with big ideas and grand processes rather than the mundane minutiae of everyday life. Why go to university to learn how to manage a luxury brand when you can do this at vocational college, or even as an apprentice or intern? We respect this and certainly do not downplay the need for research to have a strong theoretical foundation. But our experience has shown that the majority of students who study for a postgraduate degree in the field of luxury brand management hope to enter the luxury industry at some point in the future (if they have not already), and so a strong case can be made to ensure that the training they receive, not least in the field of research, has some relevance both to their future employment and to the luxury brands to which they will take their skills and knowledge. We therefore need to strike an appropriate balance between the theoretical and the practical, and between the intellectual and the mechanical. We hope we have managed to achieve this in our book.

One way we have sought to make this discussion relevant to the realm of luxury is by engaging directly with industry professionals and practitioners, not least in exploring where and to what extent research fits into the industry's routine operations, and how well academic research currently functions to inform luxury research and practice. We have conducted our own research, admittedly rather modest in scale, and report the findings at the beginning and end of this book to provide a counterweight to our systematic exploration and elucidation of a research methodology that most students of luxury should find useful. Our approach is fundamentally multidisciplinary: in other words, it does not restrict itself to the philosophical approach and methodological conventions of a single academic discipline, based in no small measure on the fact that luxury studies is itself multidisciplinary in character, even though fields such as business studies or psychology may claim it for themselves. Our approach is also multisectoral, based on our belief that luxury extends far beyond its conventional focus on luxury fashion, and that it is all the richer for this.

In Chapter 2, we introduce luxury as a field of research, sketching its landscape and outlining its key landmarks. To achieve this, and at the same time to introduce our first research method, we present the findings of some meta-analyses and bibliographic citation studies which provide an overview of academic research on luxury and trace its intellectual evolution. The most comprehensive meta-analysis in the field of luxury to date, entitled "Mapping the Luxury Research Landscape: A Bibliographic Citation Analysis", was produced by Hannes Gurzki and David Woisetschläger in 2016. But, as we saw in the opening paragraph, the world of luxury research has been growing dramatically in recent years, and so we have sought to bring this study up to date by presenting a profile of luxury research from 2015, when Gurzki and Woisetschläger's research ended, to the present day. In the process, we also introduce some of the intricacies of a database-centred literature search, which is crucial for positioning a research enquiry within appropriate fields of the existing body of knowledge. In the second part of the chapter, we present the findings of a short survey of luxury industry professionals which was designed to garner information about how luxury brands undertake research, and what approaches to research are most frequently used. In so doing, we start the process of articulating the scholarly and practical aspects of research enquiry.

Chapter 3 aims to help the student researcher through the sometimes-daunting process of identifying a research topic as the starting point on their research journey. In addition to exploring a range of potential themes drawn from the multiplicity of issues, processes, challenges and controversies that define luxury today, we also go through some of the criteria that might influence their choice of topic, and many of the requirements that attach to postgraduate research – such as originality, criticality, positionality, representativeness and reflexivity – which the student researcher must consider when mapping out their research path. Put in other words, does their research allow them the opportunity to say something fresh and worthwhile about an aspect of luxury; to build an argument rather than passively follow those of others; to reflect on where they stand in relation to current debates and in relation to the nature of knowledge; and to ensure that their research enquiry reaches the right people and is able to speak with authority based on a sound methodology?

In Chapter 4, we discuss how research might be approached from a philosophical perspective before touching on theoretical frameworks and disciplinary conventions. In the process, we engage with the tendency towards dichotomous reasoning – quantitative/qualitative, deductive/inductive, realist/interpretivist and so on – which profoundly influences how we approach research and understanding and was our point of entry to the present chapter. We then move on to research design, commencing with the intellectual process of creating mental frameworks which help to define the parameters of a research investigation. We then explore the crucial stage of formulating research questions in a way that gives structure to the research and helps to identify the boundaries of a research investigation. Research is often built upon big ideas and broad concepts, but these can be challenging to explore unless they are broken down into tangible and manageable elements – a process that is referred to as *operationalisation*, which will be introduced in Chapter 4 but will be a recurring theme throughout this book.

Chapter 5 is dedicated to data: how we differentiate data and information, and the nature and forms that data take, drawing a distinction between primary and secondary data and looking at the character of both quantitative and qualitative data. We then go on to look at sources of data for luxury research, with a particular focus on social media. This leads on to a discussion of legal considerations when accessing and handling both primary and secondary data, and a wider discussion of the ethics of research. The chapter then touches on the important issue of data representativeness (something we consider to be particularly relevant to the field of luxury but is not always given the prominence it deserves in much academic research in this field) and the role of sampling, before finishing with an appraisal of the merits and demerits of using crowdsourcing as a means of obtaining data for research.

Having discussed the nature of data, Chapter 6 introduces an array of research methods that the researcher can use to obtain primary data for the purposes of their research investigation. We first draw a distinction between method and methodology. Before we introduce the principal quantitative and qualitative research methods, we present the results of another short survey into how, methodologically, academic researchers in the field of luxury tend to approach their research. We find an overwhelming focus on systematic, quantitative research, which appears to be slightly at odds with the predominantly qualitative approach that most luxury industry professionals tend to adopt and, arguably, the qualitative nature of luxury itself. The remainder of the chapter introduces the main research methods that students of luxury are most likely to encounter, ranging from surveys and questionnaires, through semi-structured interviews and focus groups, to case studies and different forms of observation. Each research method is explained with the help of examples from the field of luxury.

Chapter 7 explores the many approaches and techniques of research data analysis that the student researcher of luxury is likely to encounter at their level of enquiry. We start with the analysis of categorical data and the use of the Chi-square test before moving on to numerical data. Statistical techniques introduced include analysis of variance, correlation, regression and structural equation modelling. We complete the discussion with a look at the analysis of non-numerical data using content analysis and also introduce the software tool NVivo, which helps to organise non-numerical data for this purpose. Data analysis is a bit like Marmite[7] – you either love it or you hate it. The chapter is written with the latter clearly in mind, taking and illustrating each process step by step.

Chapter 8 looks at the presentation of research findings, both by students and by luxury industry practitioners, and the writing-up of research dissertations. The discussion touches on various aspects of dissertation structure and content and pays particular attention to how the so-called 'literature review' fits into the overall framework of a piece of research. We then look briefly at how practitioner research is typically presented to a wider audience, touching on similarities to and differences from the presentation of academic research. The chapter also offers some advice on reading and note-taking, time management, complying with word limits, the dangers of plagiarism and the principles of criticality. Chapter 9 continues this theme of the interfacing of academic and practitioner research by presenting the findings of a series of interviews we held with luxury industry professionals, asking where and how research fits into their routine activities. Our interviewees also kindly offered some words of advice to aspiring entrants into the luxury industry, which we present at the end of the chapter. Chapter 10 draws the contents of the book together in a few paragraphs which remind the reader of some of the challenges facing the luxury industry today and expresses the hope that graduates versed and immersed in the principles and practice of research may be well positioned to rise to these challenges and build a promising future for luxury in a rapidly changing world. We then present some review and problem-solving exercises which are designed to test students' grasp of the various techniques we have introduced in this book, and we also make some recommendations for further reading if students wish to develop and expand their skills in the field of luxury research.

Throughout the book, we have used a myriad of topical examples from various fields of luxury to illustrate the points being made and the techniques being introduced. We have also incorporated the findings of our own research into the role played by research in luxury management, and some of the challenges we face in seeking to ensure that the training students receive in completing a research dissertation has relevance to the skills the luxury industry needs. We hope that the style of writing and the way we have explained luxury research will be accessible to students from a range of backgrounds and with diverse capabilities and levels of prior exposure to the field of research.

NOTES

1   The personal luxury goods sector is made up of luxury fashion (31.5% by sales value in 2021), luxury watches and jewellery (21.8%), luxury leather goods (21.3%), prestige cosmetics and fragrances (19.4%) and luxury eyewear (6.0%) (Statista, 2021, accessed 7 October 2022).
2   www.statista.com/statistics/266503/value-of-the-personal-luxury-goods-market-worldwide/ (accessed 5 October 2022).
3   Data from the Web of Science database (accessed 7 October 2022; requires subscription).
4   www.masterstudies.co.uk/Masters-Degree/Luxury-Management/#main (accessed 5 October 2022).
5   Literally 'leaving the temple', a phrase used by Bain & Company to mark the first phase in the so-called democratisation of luxury, commencing around 1994 (D'Arpizio *et al.*, 2017, 6; see also Wei, 2022: www.luxurysociety.com/en/articles/2022/03/is-the-sortie-du-temple-of-bottega-veneta-imminent, accessed 7 October 2022).
6   The Museum at FIT, "Yves Saint Laurent's Rive Gauche Collection", 3 March 2015 (https://exhibitions.fitnyc.edu/blog-ysl-halston/yves-saint-laurents-rive-gauche-revolution/) (accessed 8 Oct. 2022).
7   Other brands of concentrated yeast extract are available.

CHAPTER 2

The Landscape of Luxury Research

In order to undertake research in the field of luxury, it is important to have a comprehensive understanding of this broad subject area. Accordingly, we will start this book by sketching out *the landscape of luxury research*, from its origins to its present status both as a field of academic study and as it manifests itself in luxury management. To achieve the former, we will make use of a small number of studies which have presented an overview of the field of luxury research as a whole. The most valuable of these studies, undertaken by Hannes Gurzki and David Woisetschläger in 2016, uses bibliographic citation analysis to identify the key contributors to, and clusters of, luxury research since it emerged as a field of interest following the publication of Thorstein Veblen's *The Theory of the Leisure Class* in 1899 (Gurzki and Woisetschläger, 2016). Their analysis was based on publications data up to and including 2015, and so, later in this chapter, we have attempted to bring this overview up to date by examining all academic publications in the field of luxury that were published up to the end of September 2022. In the process, we also introduce student researchers of luxury to important techniques of literature search using keywords. To balance the discussion with a view from the luxury profession, we also present the results of a short survey which sought to ascertain some of the practical uses to which research is put within the luxury industry itself. The chapter thus aims to set the scene for the discussion that follows by providing an overview of what 'luxury research' means, both as a field of academic study and in luxury management practice.

UNDERSTANDING LUXURY RESEARCH

A first step is to delineate luxury as a field of study, which in turn requires a clear definition of 'luxury'. But ask a thousand people to define luxury and to map out its boundaries and you will likely get at least a hundred different characterisations. Luxury is both tangible and ethereal: it is principally manifest in the 'luxury industry' with its constituent brands, designs, products and services, but it is also a socio-psychological essence which people breathe, feel and desire. The emergence of 'masstige' brands and 'accessible luxury' has added porosity to the definitional boundaries of 'luxury', and the so-called 'democratisation of luxury' has so significantly expanded the consumer market that it is impossible to characterise the 'typical' luxury client. Luxury is a relative concept which means different things to different people. From an academic point of view, it is also a multidisciplinary field of study (see Figure 2.1), meaning that it may

DOI: 10.4324/9781003295372-2

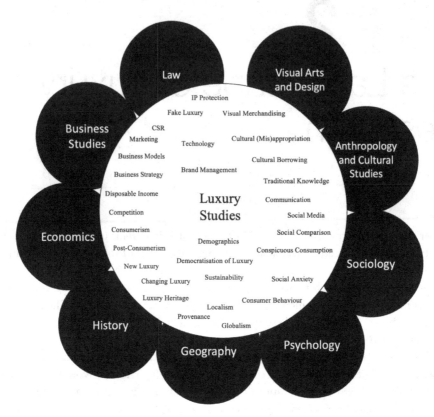

FIGURE 2.1 Luxury Studies within the Structure of Knowledge.

be a meeting point for intellectuals with a myriad of disciplinary identities, or that practitioners may draw their theoretical and methodological inspiration from a multitude of intellectual traditions and approaches. The academy is conventionally divided into subject areas which are referred to as disciplines – for example, physics, chemistry, biology and so on in the natural sciences; economics, politics, sociology, psychology and so on in the social sciences – and so a multidisciplinary field straddles two or more of these disciplinary areas. Luxury research may be undertaken by disciplinary specialists (e.g., in business studies or psychology), who use the luxury industry as a focal point or case study for their research, or by luxury specialists, who incorporate intellectual and methodological approaches drawn from multiple disciplines (e.g., visual arts and design or anthropology and cultural studies). Luxury studies are, arguably, too recent and too specialised a field of study to be considered a discipline in its own right.

An important first step in research is to identify *keywords* that help specify one's chosen field of interest. Researchers use keywords extensively in literature searches, and keywords can also be crucial in building an investigative framework for a piece of research, as we will explore further in Chapter 4. A keyword is a word (or phrase) that (typically in combination with other keywords) is central to delineating or defining a field of study. Naturally, 'luxury' would be an obvious initial keyword for any study in this area,[1] but to be useful it would typically need to be used in conjunction with other keywords which give direction to the sub-field of luxury that a researcher may be concerned with, such as luxury + marketing, luxury + consumer, luxury + snob or bandwagon, counterfeit + luxury, luxury + sustainability, and so on. Different people would choose different keywords according to their particular point of focus and interest, perhaps influenced by their own disciplinary specialisation or background. Identifying keywords is an intellectual process: one needs to know the field of luxury well enough, and have a clear enough picture of one's research objectives, to be able to specify keywords succinctly, efficiently and accurately. Keywords will typically be the starting point in literature and information searches using specialised databases (see below) or for search engine optimisation. We will return later in this book to the use of keywords in luxury research, but to start with we want to show how the choice of keywords significantly influences how luxury is defined and operationalised.

BOX 2.1

Meta-analysis

Meta-analysis is the first research method that we introduce in this book. Meta-analysis provides an analytical overview of a field of study based upon the core elements of all previous research studies in this field. This is quite helpful, because research is typically undertaken as an individual pursuit focused on a single or specific problem or topic. By convention, it will also cross-reference other pieces of research (citations), but the contribution to knowledge made by individual research studies is often fragmentary and quite narrowly focused. Meta-analysis allows the opportunity to draw together and consolidate the results of several cognate studies to produce a state-of-the-art synopsis of a particular research field. One challenge faced by meta-analysis is the heterogeneity of the various research studies and approaches under consideration: each may have a particular focus and methodology, the collation of which may require data standardisation or caveats about accuracy and utility.

Meta-analysis usually proceeds through five steps. The researcher(s) first formulates hypotheses or research questions relating to the topical theme in which they are interested. They then proceed to identify relevant sources – typically using bibliographic databases such as the Web of Science to find core texts, then exploring the bibliographies of these articles for further sources, and so on. This mass of sources then needs to be narrowed down to the most relevant and useful articles according to strict selection criteria developed by the researcher(s). Relevant information or data are then extracted from these sources and may be subjected either to systematic statistical analysis or content analysis, depending on the nature of the enquiry and of the data the sources contain. The findings from the meta-analysis are then presented, conclusions are reached, and the overall contribution to knowledge is assessed.

Some examples of meta-analysis in the field of luxury include Kumar *et al.* (2022; a meta-analysis of conspicuous consumption, involving 59 studies), Bharti, Suneja and Chauhan (2022; on socio-psychological influences on luxury consumption, involving 42 studies) and Eisend, Hartmann and Apaolaza (2017; on the purchasers of counterfeit luxury, involving 98 studies).

BIBLIOGRAPHIC CITATION ANALYSIS

Gurzki and Woisetschläger's study is a *meta-analysis* (see Box 2.1) of all academic literature on luxury published from 1899 to 2015. In order to delineate their investigation, they used the following keywords: 'luxury', 'conspicuous consumption', 'status consumption', 'prestige brand' and 'status brand' (Gurzki and Woisetschläger, 2016, 148). This casts the net reasonably widely, in the sense that it includes both consumption (and, by continuation, consumers) and brands, but it also suggests a leaning towards the socio-behavioural aspect of luxury consumption through the inclusion of conspicuity, status and prestige. In so doing, the authors have set the definitional boundaries of the field of luxury with which their analysis will engage, in the process potentially excluding such important topics as sustainability, democratisation, digitalisation, counterfeiting and so on. It is also relevant to point out that the keywords they used were all in the English language, thereby largely excluding research written in other languages and, possibly, following other epistemologies or doctrines. Other authors who have attempted similar meta-analyses of luxury research have tended to cast their definitional nets more narrowly (e.g., Mason, 1984: conspicuous consumption; Ciornea *et al.*, 2012; Veloutsou, Christodoulides and Guzman, 2021; Aliyev, Urkmez and Wagner, 2019: Rathi *et al.*, 2022: all luxury marketing).

Having operationalised 'luxury' for the purposes of their analytical overview, Gurzki and Woisetschläger engaged in *bibliographic content analysis* (a form of documentary meta-analysis) of all articles published in the field of luxury. The academic literature is the key repository of the body of knowledge contributed by research. Conventionally, we build new research upon the existing body of knowledge through 'literature review' – this is an intellectual process that delves into the *content* of the body of knowledge, to draw together the essence of a particular research field and/or to lay the foundation for further research. Bibliometrics looks quantitatively for patterns, trends and clusters using the *skeletal* elements of publications (authors, networks, citations, institutions, keywords, funding sources, etc.). A form of information science, bibliometric content analysis (BCA) helps us identify the intellectual foundations of a research field, its evolution across time, the most influential works/authors/institutions, and emerging trends and topics. BCA essentially uses quantities – most particularly the frequency of citations – to proxy for the quality and contribution of academic research. Large electronic databases and public domain software have made BCA readily accessible to most academics and students.

Gurzki and Woisetschläger used as their data source the ISI's (Institute for Scientific Information) Web of Science,[2] which is a digital database containing information on publications and citations in academic articles across all disciplines (in addition to sets of conference proceedings and some other forms of publications), searchable using keywords or search terms and divisible by date, discipline, keywords, citation frequency and so on. The Web of Science also contains core collections in the sciences, social sciences, and arts and humanities. Most university libraries should offer access to the Web of Science (which was previously known as the Web of Knowledge), as well as similar databases such as Scopus.

Gurzki and Woisetschläger's interrogation of the Web of Science on 14 November 2015 using the keywords mentioned above yielded 1,503 publications dating back as far as 1899. In terms of the disciplinary orientation of publications on luxury up to 2015, 56.5% of all publications since 1899 lie in the research field of business and economics according to the categorisation system employed by the Web of Science; 30.4% were in business studies; 20.6% were in economics; 13.4% were in social sciences; 11.4% were in psychology; 10.7% were in the field of management; 7.5% were in hospitality; 6% in history; and only 4.8% fell within the field of sociology (Gurzki and Woisetschläger, 2016, 149; there was some double-counting involved). In total, the publications fell within 87 individual research fields.

Reflecting the relative youth of luxury studies as an academic field, 1,315 (87%) of these items had been published since the year 2000. Gurzki and Woisetschläger's analysis focused on these items, which had been written by 2,425 authors and published in 533 different journals (Gurzki and Woisetschläger, 2016, 148). Their analysis aimed to identify the most influential authors and publications across the history of luxury research. This was achieved by recording the articles and authors which were most frequently cited by researchers of luxury. One of the conventions of academic writing is that authors must identify (cite) all the sources they have used in building a platform for their own research, including theories, concepts, empirical evidence, investigative frameworks, methodologies and so on. Across the 1,315 articles examined by Gurzki and Woisetschläger, there was a total of 49,139 citations, many of which will have been multiple citations of the same sources or authors in several publications on luxury. By identifying the most frequently cited authors, works and topics, Gurzki and Woisetschläger were able to recognise the subject areas which predominate in luxury research, and also the most influential authors in this research field.

Interestingly for prospective researchers who are thinking about appropriate keywords to guide their initial literature search, a total of 5,028 author-generated keywords were suggested across the 1,315 articles, which in itself indicates how broad the field of luxury research can be even within the slightly restricted parameters that Gurzki and Woisetschläger used to define 'luxury'. We will return to this point shortly when we present the findings of our own analysis of Web of Science publications data.

The field of luxury research is conventionally traced back to the work of Thorstein Veblen, whose *The Theory of the Leisure Class* (1899) introduced the concept of conspicuous consumption and the acquisition of expensive, rare and visible commodities for social rather than utilitarian purposes. In line with the influence Veblen had on helping us to understand the phenomenon of conspicuous consumption, the social motivations behind ostentation provided the core focus for 'luxury research' up until, and into, the turn of the 21st century. The first meta-analysis that might be considered to lie in the field of luxury, by Roger Mason in 1984, focused entirely on conspicuous consumption (Mason, 1984; see also Kumar *et al.*, 2022, for a more recent meta-analysis of conspicuous consumption).

BOX 2.2

How Well Do You Know Thorstein Veblen?

Thorstein Bunde Veblen (1857–1929) is arguably the author who has had the most significant and enduring influence on the study of luxury. His book *The Theory of the Leisure Class*, published in 1899, is the publication that is most frequently cited by scholars writing on luxury (Gurzki and Woisetschläger, 2016,

150), principally because, in Chapter 4, he introduced[3] the notion of 'conspicuous consumption', which has since become a central pillar of the consumer psychology branch of luxury studies. His name is attached to a key concept in the field of luxury: the Veblen good,[4] an item for which demand rises as price increases (typical of many luxury products and services), contradicting marginal utility theory (or the law of demand) which states that demand falls as price increases beyond the optimum marginal utility of a good to the consumer. Veblen used sociological factors to explain this economic phenomenon, based on his observations of *fin-de-siècle* United States society. People appeared willing to pay more for sumptuous goods in part because of the enhanced status that accrued to their possession and ostentatious display. This 'signalling' served the purpose of advertising their wealth and affirming their membership of the upper echelons of society while differentiating them from the lower classes who, in turn, engaged in 'pecuniary[5] emulation', purchasing expensive goods in an attempt to exude a higher status than their social station ordinarily decreed (Veblen, 1899, 24). Few students of luxury can ignore the contribution of Thorstein Veblen, however contentious, to our understanding of what motivates people to purchase luxury goods.

But did you know that Thorstein Veblen wrote *The Theory of the Leisure Class* as a very uncomplimentary critique of the changes he observed taking place in American society as the effects of industrial capitalism penetrated ever deeper? Indeed, his treatise has even been called "cynical" and "satirical" (Dorfman, 1932; Camic, 2020; Skousen, 2009). His perspective on American society was fundamentally influenced by his background as the sixth child of first-generation Norwegian immigrants. His Lutheran upbringing drummed into him the virtues of hard work and the evils of sloth (Camic, 2020). Wastefulness and ostentation were anathema to his moral beliefs, and yet everywhere he looked – as his career took him from Minnesota to Connecticut to up-state New York to Chicago and then to California – he found what he described as 'pecuniary people' engaged in non-productive and what he considered 'parasitical' activity, being ostentatiously wasteful in order to convey an impression of wealth and success: a "leisured class" living/showing off the accumulated spoils of capitalist production. Veblen positioned himself as a critic of the capitalist system and the behaviours and attitudes it had bred, and indeed he was one of the few American academics at the time to teach about the principles of socialism (Skousen, 2009). Thus 'conspicuous consumption' in Veblen's view was a vice to be disdained, rather than a largely unproblematised cornerstone of luxury aspiration as it tends to be seen today.

In the present context, it is also worth briefly reflecting on Thorstein Veblen's credentials as an academic researcher. For all his brilliance as both an economist and a sociologist, Veblen was often criticised for his approach to the advancement of knowledge. He was accused of sloppy scholarship and using unsupported evidence (Skousen, 2009), and of relying on casual observation rather than systematic research. Soon after his book was published, he was described as "a dilettante that brought Sociology into disrepute among careful and scientific thinkers" (Banta, 2007, ix). Certainly, he was not a researcher who placed a great deal of importance on referencing: *The Theory of the Leisure Class* does not contain a single reference! Veblen justifies this in his Preface by claiming that all the sources and quotations he has used should be familiar to the fairly well-read reader, and so "the usage of citing sources and authorities has therefore not been observed" (Veblen, 1899, 3–4). Try getting away with that in your dissertation!

Intellectually, Veblen was described by Russell Jacoby (1987, 94) as a "wobbly": a term given to "American anarchists who opposed nearly everything and everyone". From the perspective of research objectivity, or lack of it, he perhaps positioned himself as a "curmudgeonly contrarian" (Banta, 2007, xx) who stood in opposition to public opinion (and neoclassical economics); in other words, his casual observations of American life matched to his ingrained moral compass and ideological leaning provided the ammunition for him to construct a damning critique of the established order and of the way that society was heading in the modern capitalist era. It is difficult to imagine that a 19th-century maverick intellectual, who by all accounts dressed like a tramp (Skousen, 2009), might have anticipated that his treatise on conspicuous consumption would stand the test of time and would provide a cornerstone for understanding the world of luxury in the 21st century.

How do we generate an overview of a 'domain of knowledge' such as luxury? Conventionally, we read as much of the relevant literature as possible and create our own vision or interpretation of the field. But, given that there are at least 1,500 articles (to 2015, plus more than 2,600 between 2016 and 2022 – see below) published in this field since 1899, this represents quite an onerous task. If we are fortunate, some research teams may already have undertaken and published *systematic reviews* of a research field which provide an overview of that field and help to identify key trends and research foci. In the field of luxury, four such overviews exist, in addition to those by Gurzki and Woisetschläger (2016) and Mason (1984). All four had a narrow focus on luxury marketing. Ciornea *et al.* undertook two studies of the luxury sector: the first, published in 2012, covered the period up to 2005, the second covered the period since 2005. However, the latter report does not appear ever to have been published. One strength of this study is that it looked at publications in French, Italian, Romanian and German, as well as English. Aliyev *et al.* (2019) looked at literature published between 2000 and 2016, but, because they undertook qualitative (reading articles) as well as quantitative (the 'skeleton' of the literature) analysis, they were restricted to sources they could access through their institutions, totalling 242 key references and 1,105 co-citations. Veloutsou *et al.* (2021) looked at everything published on luxury marketing (1,151 articles from 427 contributors) before 2019, using the Scopus database (produced by Elsevier in the Netherlands), and their analysis yielded 587 author-generated keywords, although only 89 of these (15%) appeared more than once, and only 33 more than four times, again indicating the breadth of subject matter that falls under the umbrella of 'luxury'.

As we were going to press, one further overview of the literature on luxury was published (Rathi *et al.*, 2022). This, too, was focused on luxury marketing, covering the period 1986–2020 and focused on 893 relevant articles identified from the Scopus database (see below). Similar to the analysis by Gurzki and Woisetschläger (2016), this study used bibliographic citation and content analysis to identify seven key clusters of luxury research from this body of literature: in order of importance, they were conceptualisations (the meaning of luxury) and responsible luxury (e.g., sustainability); luxury consumer behaviour; luxury brand management; luxury social media marketing; conspicuous consumption; customer perceived value; and luxury counterfeiting (Rathi *et al.*, 2022, 246). The thematic differences between the clusters identified by the two pieces of research can largely be attributed to the significant spurt in luxury-focused research in recent years (37.1% of the articles that appeared during the 34-year reference period covered by Rathi *et al.* were published in 2019 and 2020 alone), which explains why themes such as sustainability, social media marketing and counterfeiting are more to the forefront. The article presents a breakdown (*ibid.*, 249) of the principal fields of luxury (e.g., fashion, jewellery, handbags, services such as tourism) that are the focus of research in different regions of the world. The paper finishes (*ibid.*, 253–254) by identifying a series of research questions which might guide future research in the seven thematic clusters, which is something that students researching luxury should find very useful (see also Chapter 4).

Systematic reviews are helpful to the researcher of luxury, but, as we have seen above, these may be limited by subject focus, definitional keywords and methodologies employed by the reviewers, and they may very quickly become out of date. Chaomei Chen (see Chen, 2004, 2016) has developed a public domain software tool, called CiteSpace, which any researcher should be able to use to conduct their own profiling of a domain of knowledge, using their own search terms and visualisation criteria. The software, used in conjunction with literature databases such as the Web of Science and Scopus, allows the researcher to define the parameters of their knowledge domain through the keywords they deploy, trace the evolution of the subject area across time, identify the key academic players in this field of study and its core research or subject clusters, and visualise how these subject clusters and academic contributors are connected to each other (Chen, 2016). The analysis is based on researchers' contributions to the knowledge domain – principally in the form of academic publications – and the weight of their contributions as ascertained by the frequency with which these publications are cited by other researchers in their own publications. The general assumption is that the most frequently cited contributions over time are also the most influential in the knowledge domain.

Gurzki and Woisetschläger used CiteSpace to analyse the 49,139 citations that were identified through their search of the Web of Science using the keywords mentioned above. There were four components to their analysis: citation frequency, which identifies the most influential authors in the field of luxury research (Veblen, 1899, was the most frequently cited publication); co-citation networks and research clusters, where groups of researchers regularly cite one another in their publications; betweenness, which identifies the key publications which 'bridge' the various research clusters and networks that make up the field of luxury research; and citation bursts, where certain subject fields have risen to prominence within the knowledge domain at certain points across time. We will just look at research clusters here as it is the most useful for presenting a visual overview of luxury as a domain of knowledge.

Gurzki and Woisetschläger used CiteSpace to identify 'landmark nodes' (clusters) from the 49,139 citations at their disposal. Figure 2.2 presents the key research or subject clusters that were revealed by their analysis. The identified research clusters included the 'foundations' of luxury research, which viewed luxury consumption as a social practice; 'signalling', where luxury goods are acquired for their status value; the 'economic perspective', which interprets luxury industry and consumption behaviour in relation to income, materialism and so on; an 'intercultural view', which places culture as a determinant of luxury consumption; a focus on 'luxury culture', where luxury goods are carriers of cultural meaning; 'self-concept and brands', where the luxury brand becomes a source of identity; 'brand equity', where the brand is a source of financial value; 'counterfeiting', which also touches on topics such as authenticity and legitimacy; an 'evolutionary view', which presents luxury across time as a signal to others and as a source of value; and 'brand management and strategy', which includes the operational

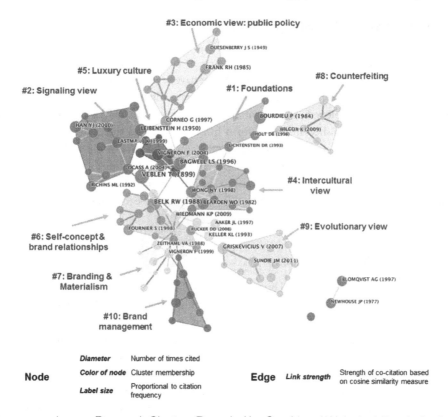

FIGURE 2.2 Luxury Research Clusters Revealed by Gurzki and Woisetschläger's Analysis.

Source: Gurzki and Woisetschläger, 2016, 152.

principles that build luxury value. Just to reiterate, these 'clusters' of luxury research are constructs created by Gurzki and Woisetschläger, but based on patterns that their analysis revealed whereby researchers in cognate sub-fields of luxury regularly cite one another's work. Thus, while researchers of luxury each have their own intellectual identities and motivations for undertaking their research, certain subject fields begin to emerge where their interests and activities overlap or coalesce.

According to Gurzki and Woisetschläger's analysis, the knowledge domain of luxury had (up to 2015) evolved from its initial sociological focus, where luxury consumption was a social activity connected with status, class and culture, to a point where society, culture and psychology came together in terms of the influence of the cultural environment on self-concept, and then shifted to a point where economic studies of luxury came to the fore, with an emphasis on the brand as a symbol of luxury. More recent luxury research has focused on luxury business and the principles of luxury management. As we will see in Chapter 4, there has also more recently been a gradual shift from quantitative to qualitative studies of luxury, and most recently cross-cultural and cross-generational studies have come to the fore, together with an emphasis on sustainability and social responsibility.

BRINGING THE ANALYSIS UP TO DATE

Gurzki and Woisetschläger's analysis was undertaken in 2015, at a time when the luxury sector was on the cusp of thoroughgoing change. As we have seen, their study also placed a rather heavy emphasis on the 'conspicuous consumption' aspect of luxury, given the definitional criteria that the authors employed. We have attempted to bring this analysis up to date, looking at *all* luxury research published in article form from late 2015 to the end of 2022. The following section will present a summary of our findings and a picture of the wider landscape of luxury research that emerges from this analysis. But, parallel to presenting an overview of luxury research today, we will be introducing students to the use of *literature databases* as a starting point not just for their literature search but also for identifying core research clusters that are relevant to their own particular investigation.

Searching the Web of Science

We used the Web of Science – owned by the company Clarivate and one of the most frequently used literature databases in academia – to identify all publications on luxury published between 1 December 2015 and 10 October 2022. Using 'luxury' in the topic field (Figure 2.3) yielded an initial 5,106 results (Figure 2.4). We refined this search in two ways before settling on the final body of knowledge. First, we selected (Figure 2.5) only academic papers (including an early view of not-yet published items) and review articles. Although conference proceedings provide an interesting insight into current research on luxury, they rarely go through the peer review 'quality control' process; the same is true of other 'grey literature' sources. Book reviews do not generally contain original research. Restricting the search to academic articles reduced the yield to 4,241 items (Figure 2.6).

FIGURE 2.3 Initial Web of Science Field Search: Luxury. Data from Web of Science, provided by Clarivate. Web of Science and Clarivate are trademarks of their respective owners and used herein with permission.

FIGURE 2.4 Publications on Luxury, 2016–2022: Initial Results. Data from Web of Science, provided by Clarivate.

FIGURE 2.5 Narrowing the Array of Publications. Data from Web of Science, provided by Clarivate.

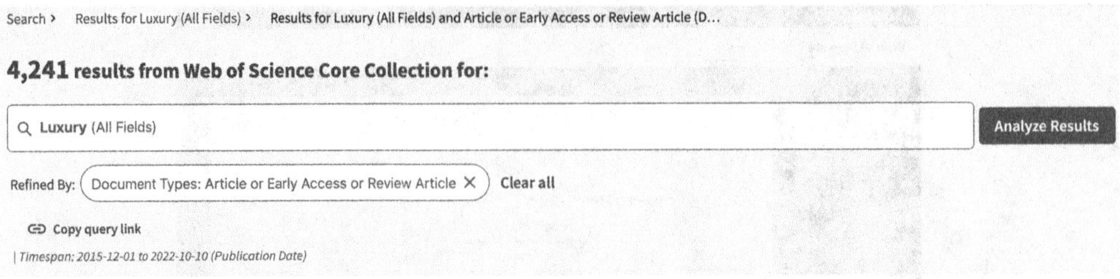

FIGURE 2.6 Search Results after Restricting Document Type. Data from Web of Science, provided by Clarivate.

Second, we further refined the search by limiting the subject fields to ones that we deemed to be relevant to luxury research. This is because the use of the single keyword 'luxury' for the literature search risked including a number of articles that use the word luxury in a way that does not connect with our focus on the luxury industry, luxury consumerism and the essence thereof. The refinement or filtering of subject categories in the Web of Science can be done in three ways. Web of Science "Categories" and "Research Areas" allocate published articles to conventional disciplinary and sub-disciplinary groupings (multidisciplinary articles may straddle more than one category or area), along the lines we have suggested in our simplified model in Figure 2.1. More recently, the Web of Science has also introduced a third refinement or classification tool which is called "Citation Topics Meso". This loosely mirrors the approach adopted by Gurzki and Woisetschläger in their bibliographic citation analysis, where cognate research clusters are identified through groups of papers which coalesce through citation (referring to each other's work). Classification through citation can be thought of as 'live research' because the categories evolve and emerge (through the use of real-time algorithms) as more publications and citations are fed into the system. Figure 2.7 provides a glimpse of the three classification tools mentioned above.

Refining the initial search using 34 out of a possible 98 Web of Science subject categories (the first illustration in Figure 2.7) narrowed the core body of literature down to 3,119 relevant articles (Figure 2.8). It is worth comparing this number with those accessed by Gurzki and Woisetschläger (2016) in their own analysis: a total of 1,503 publications from 1899 to 2015, including 1,315 articles published from 2000 until the date of their literature search on 30 November 2015. Although we are not precisely comparing like with like because of the different keywords and search processes followed, this does reinforce the view that research in the field of luxury continues to flourish, with an average of more than 420 articles on luxury published each year from 2016 to 2022 inclusive.

Using the "Analyze Results" function on the Web of Science, the disciplinary breakdown of these 3,119 papers can be presented as a tree map chart (Figure 2.9) and as percentage values (Figure 2.10). From the latter diagram, we can see that research publications in the field of luxury during the period since Gurzki and Woisetschläger completed their own analysis fall predominantly within the disciplinary fields of business studies (36.197%) and management studies (16.640%). However, because a number of studies fall into more than one category, a more representative disciplinary profile of research articles is provided in Table 2.1, which shows that research with a social science focus is in fact more prevalent that that with a purely business focus. This can partly be attributed to the importance of social and psychological factors in luxury consumption, and partly to the growing interest in the socio-cultural dimensions of luxury around the world. There is a particularly large cluster of publications on luxury hospitality and tourism.

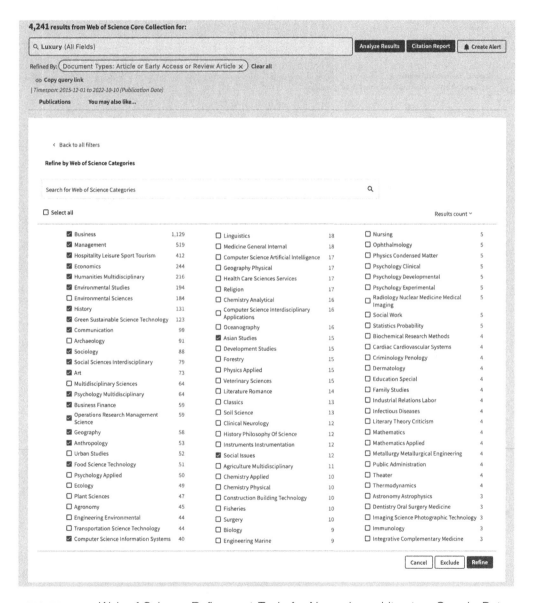

FIGURE 2.7 Web of Science Refinement Tools for Narrowing a Literature Search. Data from Web of Science, provided by Clarivate.

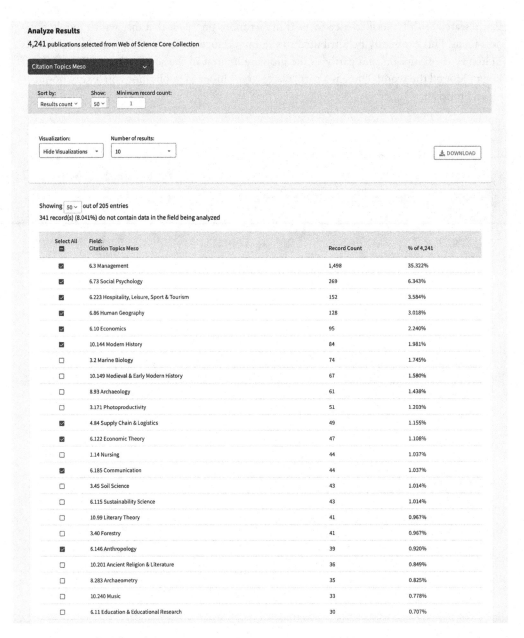

FIGURE 2.7 Continued.

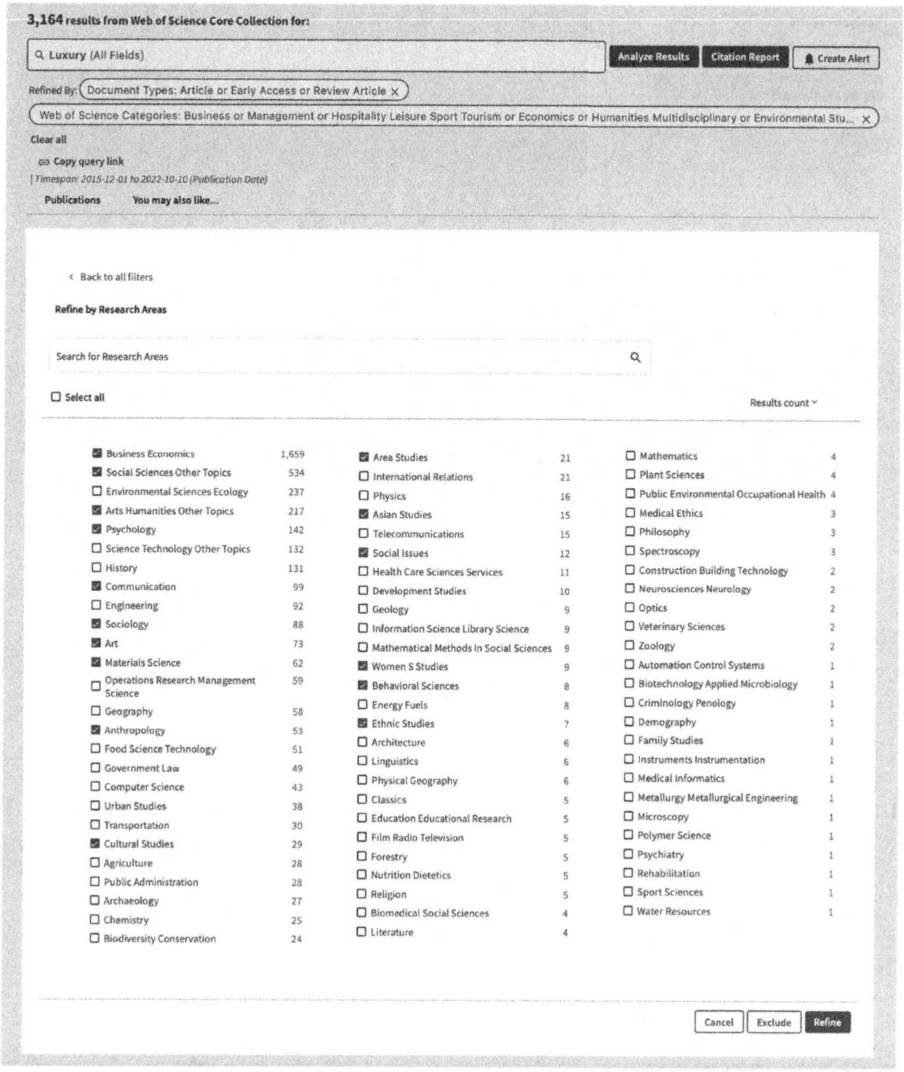

3,164 results from Web of Science Core Collection for:

🔍 Luxury (All Fields)   [Analyze Results] [Citation Report] 🔔 Create Alert

Refined By: (Document Types: Article or Early Access or Review Article ✕)

(Web of Science Categories: Business or Management or Hospitality Leisure Sport Tourism or Economics or Humanities Multidisciplinary or Environmental Stu... ✕)

Clear all

⊂⊃ Copy query link

| Timespan: 2015-12-01 to 2022-10-10 (Publication Date)

Publications   You may also like...

‹ Back to all filters

Refine by Research Areas

Search for Research Areas   🔍

☐ Select all   Results count ⌄

☑ Business Economics	1,659	☑ Area Studies	21	☐ Mathematics	4
☑ Social Sciences Other Topics	534	☐ International Relations	21	☐ Plant Sciences	4
☐ Environmental Sciences Ecology	237	☐ Physics	16	☐ Public Environmental Occupational Health	4
☑ Arts Humanities Other Topics	217	☑ Asian Studies	15	☐ Medical Ethics	3
☑ Psychology	142	☐ Telecommunications	15	☐ Philosophy	3
☐ Science Technology Other Topics	132	☑ Social Issues	12	☐ Spectroscopy	3
☐ History	131	☐ Health Care Sciences Services	11	☐ Construction Building Technology	2
☑ Communication	99	☐ Development Studies	10	☐ Neurosciences Neurology	2
☐ Engineering	92	☐ Geology	9	☐ Optics	2
☑ Sociology	88	☐ Information Science Library Science	9	☐ Veterinary Sciences	2
☑ Art	73	☐ Mathematical Methods In Social Sciences	9	☐ Zoology	2
☑ Materials Science	62	☑ Women S Studies	9	☐ Automation Control Systems	1
☐ Operations Research Management Science	59	☑ Behavioral Sciences	8	☐ Biotechnology Applied Microbiology	1
☐ Geography	58	☐ Energy Fuels	8	☐ Criminology Penology	1
☑ Anthropology	53	☑ Ethnic Studies	7	☐ Demography	1
☐ Food Science Technology	51	☐ Architecture	6	☐ Family Studies	1
☐ Government Law	49	☐ Linguistics	6	☐ Instruments Instrumentation	1
☐ Computer Science	43	☐ Physical Geography	6	☐ Medical Informatics	1
☐ Urban Studies	38	☐ Classics	5	☐ Metallurgy Metallurgical Engineering	1
☐ Transportation	30	☐ Education Educational Research	5	☐ Microscopy	1
☑ Cultural Studies	29	☐ Film Radio Television	5	☐ Polymer Science	1
☐ Agriculture	28	☐ Forestry	5	☐ Psychiatry	1
☐ Public Administration	28	☐ Nutrition Dietetics	5	☐ Rehabilitation	1
☐ Archaeology	27	☐ Religion	5	☐ Sport Sciences	1
☐ Chemistry	25	☐ Biomedical Social Sciences	4	☐ Water Resources	1
☐ Biodiversity Conservation	24	☐ Literature	4		

[Cancel] [Exclude] [Refine]

FIGURE 2.7 Continued.

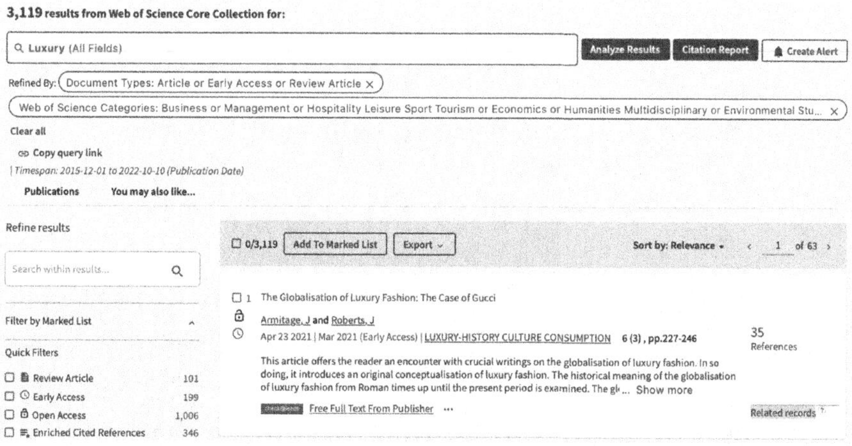

3,119 results from Web of Science Core Collection for:

🔍 Luxury (All Fields)   [Analyze Results] [Citation Report] 🔔 Create Alert

Refined By: (Document Types: Article or Early Access or Review Article ✕)

(Web of Science Categories: Business or Management or Hospitality Leisure Sport Tourism or Economics or Humanities Multidisciplinary or Environmental Stu... ✕)

Clear all

⊂⊃ Copy query link

| Timespan: 2015-12-01 to 2022-10-10 (Publication Date)

Publications   You may also like...

Refine results

Search within results...   🔍

Filter by Marked List   ⌃

Quick Filters

☐ 📄 Review Article   101
☐ 🕐 Early Access   199
☐ 🔓 Open Access   1,006
☐ ≡ Enriched Cited References   346

☐ 0/3,119   [Add To Marked List]   [Export ⌄]   Sort by: Relevance ▾   ‹ 1 of 63 ›

☐ 1   The Globalisation of Luxury Fashion: The Case of Gucci

🔒   Armitage, J and Roberts, J
🕐   Apr 23 2021 | Mar 2021 (Early Access) | LUXURY-HISTORY CULTURE CONSUMPTION 6 (3) , pp.227-246   35 References

This article offers the reader an encounter with crucial writings on the globalisation of luxury fashion. In so doing, it introduces an original conceptualisation of luxury fashion. The historical meaning of the globalisation of luxury fashion from Roman times up until the present period is examined. The gl ... Show more

Check@iusb Free Full Text From Publisher •••   Related records ⁵

FIGURE 2.8 Document Yield after Restricting Thematic Categories. Data from Web of Science, provided by Clarivate.

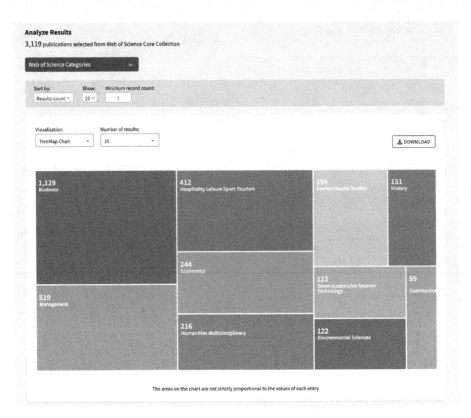

FIGURE 2.9 Disciplinary Tree Map Chart for the Refined Literature Search Using the "Analyze Results" Function. Data from Web of Science, provided by Clarivate.

Select All ☐	Field: Web of Science Categories	Record Count	% of 3,119
☐	Business	1,129	36.197%
☐	Management	519	16.640%
☐	Hospitality Leisure Sport Tourism	412	13.209%
☐	Economics	244	7.823%
☐	Humanities Multidisciplinary	216	6.925%
☐	Environmental Studies	194	6.220%
☐	History	131	4.200%
☐	Green Sustainable Science Technology	123	3.944%
☐	Environmental Sciences	122	3.912%
☐	Communication	99	3.174%
☐	Sociology	88	2.821%
☐	Social Sciences Interdisciplinary	79	2.533%
☐	Art	73	2.340%
☐	Psychology Multidisciplinary	64	2.052%
☐	Business Finance	59	1.892%
☐	Operations Research Management Science	59	1.892%
☐	Geography	58	1.860%
☐	Anthropology	53	1.699%
☐	Food Science Technology	51	1.635%
☐	Psychology Applied	50	1.603%
☐	Computer Science Information Systems	40	1.282%
☐	Urban Studies	38	1.218%
☐	Transportation	30	0.962%
☐	Cultural Studies	29	0.930%

FIGURE 2.10 Disciplinary Distribution of Documents from the Refined Search. Data from Web of Science, provided by Clarivate.

TABLE 2.1 Disciplinary Distribution of Luxury Research Articles Published from December 2015 to October 2022

Branch of Science	Discipline or Sub-discipline	Total	Percentage
Business studies	Business (1,089), business finance (57)	1,146	33.5
Management studies	Management (497), operations research (25)	522	15.3
Social sciences	Social sciences (93), hospitality (401), economics (171), psychology (129), communication (88), sociology (80), law (26), geography (45), anthropology (30), cultural studies (22)	1,178	34.5
Humanities	Humanities (201), history (116), art (68)	385	11.3
Environmental studies	Environmental studies (88), environmental science (28), biodiversity conservation (23)	139	4.1
Science	Food science and technology (25), materials science (23)	48	1.4
Total		3,418	100.0
Total without Multiple Counting		3,119	

Data source: Web of Science (accessed 11 October 2022)

FIGURE 2.11 The Keyword Search Facility in the Scopus Database. Copyright Scopus, Elsevier.

The Web of Science does not offer the facility to search for literature sources using keywords as opposed to disciplinary categories. However, an alternative literature database, Scopus, which is run by the publisher Elsevier, does make this possible, and we believe that this provides a particularly useful tool for students who are looking for a body of literature on a quite narrowly defined research topic. The "Refine Search by Keywords" facility uses keywords that have been suggested by authors at the time of publishing their papers, and as such we might expect these to be more accurate, refined and nuanced than attempting to narrow down a literature search using broad subject categories. For the subject of "luxury", the Scopus database provides upwards of 3,000 keywords, which are searchable in alphabetical order. Figure 2.11 displays some of the 160 keywords that appeared most frequently in all articles on luxury that were published between 2016 and 2022.

TABLE 2.2 Thematic Clustering of Keywords Used in Publications on Luxury, 2016–2022

Keyword Cluster	Individual Keywords
Luxury (681)	Luxury (448), luxury goods (96), luxury products (54), luxury value (21), luxury industry (16), luxury effect (10), affordable luxury (9), luxury retail (9), luxury values (9), new luxury (9)
Luxury brands (538)	Luxury brand(s) (309), luxury branding (71), luxury fashion brand (31), brand loyalty (19), brand personality (19), brand equity (17), brand experience (16), brand image (14), brand love (13), brand attitude (10), brand extension (10), brand communication (9)
Luxury consumption (504)	Luxury consumption (85), consumer behaviour (81), consumption behaviour (78), purchase intention (68), conspicuous consumption (38), status consumption (20), consumption (19), status (18), customer experience (17), customer satisfaction (17), consumer (16), consumer attitudes (16), shopping activity (12), social comparison (10), purchasing (9)
Luxury brand management (299)	Corporate social responsibility (53), retailing (43), sales (37), innovation (32), COVID-19 (23), supply chain management (20), decision-making (18), luxury service(s) (16), brand management (15), service quality (14), costs (10), business model (9), supply chain (9)
Sustainability and responsibility (289)	Sustainability (109), corporate social responsibility (53), sustainable luxury (36), sustainable development (32), animal welfare (18), circular economy (14), sharing economy (9), sustainable consumption (9), sustainable fashion (9)
Socio-psychological aspects (263)	Perception (40), materialism (33), attitude (22), psychology (16), need for uniqueness (15), motivation (14), satisfaction (12), social status (12), emotion (11), experience (11), luxury experience (11), hedonism (10), loyalty (10), willingness to pay (10), ethics (9), identity (9), perceived quality (9), trust (9)
Luxury hospitality (208)	Luxury hotels (122), luxury tourism (38), hotel industry (16), tourist behaviour (12), hospitality (11), hospitality industry (9)
Digital media and technology (192)	Social media (73), e-commerce (32), Instagram (23), social networking (12), communication (11), social media marketing (11), technology (11), digital marketing (10), artificial intelligence (9)
Luxury sectors (166)	Luxury fashion (120), luxury vehicles (21), fashion industry (15), luxury restaurants (10)
Luxury marketing (154)	Luxury marketing (85), advertising (20), luxury market (15), marketing strategy (13), social media marketing (11), digital marketing (10)
Demographics (150)	People (52), millennials (30), adults (15), males (15), females (14), gender (13), Generation Y (11)
Countries (141)	China (62), India (35), Hong Kong (13), emerging markets (11), France (11), Chinese consumers (9)
Counterfeiting (46)	Counterfeits (26), counterfeiting (10), crime (10)
Art and design (38)	Design (15), product design (12), art (11)
Culture (37)	Culture (17), authenticity (11), religiosity (9)

Data source: Scopus database (accessed 11 October 2022)

In Table 2.2, we have further refined this information through a summary analysis of these 160 keywords, clustering them according to discrete fields in the realm of luxury. From this analysis, we can see that research on luxury over the last six years has been spread reasonably evenly across the three principal fields of luxury – brands, consumers and the 'essence' of luxury – with a particularly strong focus on various aspects of luxury brand management. Consumer perceptions, feelings and behaviour, including the socio-psychological motivations that lie behind this, are naturally a quite important focus for academic scholarship in this research field. From a luxury management point of view, a significant number of recent studies approach luxury from a brand perspective and/or focus on particular sectors of the luxury industry. Articles that look at the challenge of sustainability are also quite prevalent and have certainly come much more to the forefront than was evident in Gurzki and Woisetschläger's own analysis in 2016, as have studies that look at various aspects of digitalisation and social media, and at younger consumers of luxury. Marketing per se was a focus for only a relatively small proportion of publications, in contrast to the various meta-analyses that we referred to earlier which had a clear marketing focus, although marketing is presumably also subsumed within other 'categories' such as luxury, brands and management. As we will see below, a number of publications present case studies of particular countries, most particularly China and India, which have moved rapidly towards the forefront of luxury consumption in recent years. Overall, the list of keywords available in Scopus provides an excellent starting point for a student's literature search.

The Web of Science also has the facility to generate a citation report. Essentially, all academic publications will include a list of references (or citations), and, as we saw with the bibliometric content analysis undertaken by Gurzki and Woisetschläger, the more frequently an article is cited by others, the greater its presumed weight or influence in its research field (although it is theoretically possible for an article to be frequently cited as an example of poor research!). The Web of Science citation report lists individual publications by total frequency of citation. Figure 2.12 presents a citation report for the 3,119 articles included in our refined search. There is naturally a time lag between an article's publication and its appearance in citation records, but the data show that these articles had been cited in a further 18,570 articles and 30,182 times by the time we undertook our Web of Science investigation, at an average of 9.68 citations per article on luxury. Having refined their literature search to key research areas and topics using the various Web of Science functions, the student researcher of luxury could usefully start to build their own list of priority readings by consulting the list of articles that appears below the chart (we show just one item in Figure 2.12), which can be ranked by the highest number of citations, which should identify those items that are the most influential in their chosen research field.

Regional Focus

A final facility offered by the Web of Science is the opportunity to identify the country or regional focus of research in the field of luxury, which is particularly opportune given the profound influence of processes such as globalisation and democratisation on the luxury industry in recent decades. Applying the "Countries/Regions" tool to our body of literature yields the

FIGURE 2.12 Citation Report for Documents from the Refined Literature Search. Data from Web of Science, provided by Clarivate.

summary information presented in Figure 2.13. In Table 2.3, we have collated this information to depict the regional focus of luxury research during our reference period from December 2015 to October 2022. It is important to note, however, that the countries/regions analysis facility in the Web of Science relates primarily to the specified country of each author's institutional affiliation and rather less to the spatial focus of their research (although there may often be some overlap). Roughly two-thirds of scholarship on luxury over our reference period has been produced by scholars who are based in Western countries (Europe, North America, Australasia), but a significant proportion of luxury scholarship also emanates from Asia, reflecting the extent to which luxury consumption in particular has expanded in this region on the coat-tails of globalisation and the democratisation of luxury.

This phenomenon is even more striking when we look at the regional make-up of luxury research across time. Table 2.4 illustrates even more strikingly the extent to which scholarship on luxury has grown, proportionally and absolutely, in Asia, from accounting for just 5% of research in the 1990s to around 23% today. On a much smaller scale, a similar trend is emerging in the Middle East and Latin America, although progress appears to be faltering in Africa. Non-Western scholarship on luxury increased from 8.7% of all scholarship in 1992–2002 to

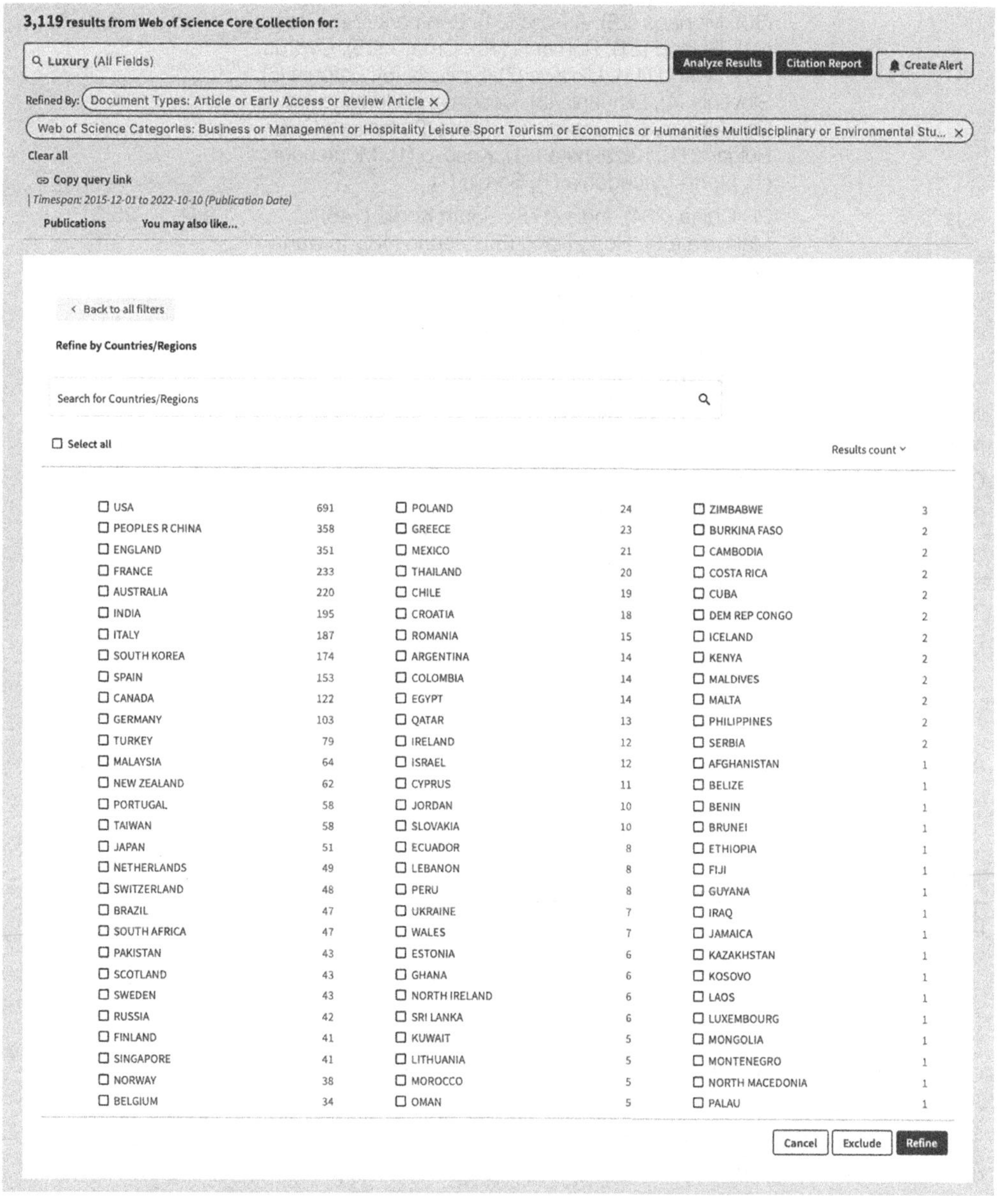

FIGURE 2.13 Country/Regional Focus of Research on Luxury. Data from Web of Science, provided by Clarivate.

TABLE 2.3 Publications on Luxury, from December 2015 to October 2022, by Country and Region (Authors' Affiliations and Thematic Focus)

Region	Country	Total	Percentage
Europe	United Kingdom (341), France (206), Italy (141), Spain (124), Germany (83), Portugal (48), Russian Federation (42), Netherlands (40), Finland (39), Switzerland (39), Sweden (36), Norway (31), Belgium (30), Monaco (28), Austria (24), Denmark (24), Greece (21), Poland (21), Romania (15), Croatia (15), Cyprus (11), Ireland (11), Ukraine (7), Slovakia (6), Estonia (6), Slovenia (4), Lithuania (3), Bosnia and Herzegovina (3), Hungary (2), Georgia (2), Malta (2), Iceland (2), Bulgaria (1), Kazakhstan (1), Kosovo (1), Montenegro (1), North Macedonia (1), Serbia (1)	1,413	38.00
Asia	PR China (284), India (178), South Korea (146), Malaysia (60), Hong Kong (50), Japan (43), Taiwan (40), Pakistan (36), Singapore (32), Vietnam (25), Indonesia (16), Thailand (14), Sri Lanka (5), Bangladesh (3), Philippines (2), Maldives (2), Cambodia (1), Lao PDR (1), Brunei (1), Mongolia (1), Papua New Guinea (1)	941	25.31
North America	USA (613), Canada (101)	714	19.20
Australasia	Australia (194), New Zealand (60), Fiji (1), Palau (1)	256	6.89
Central and South America	Brazil (42), Mexico (16), Chile (14), Colombia (11), Argentina (9), Ecuador (8), Peru (6), Puerto Rico (4), Costa Rica (2), Cuba (2), Dominican Republic (1), Guatemala (1), Jamaica (1), Martinique (1), Belize (1), Guyana (1), Trinidad and Tobago (1), Turks and Caicos (1)	122	3.28
Middle East	Turkey (67), UAE (33), Saudi Arabia (23), Iran (23), Qatar (12), Israel (9), Lebanon (8), Jordan (8), Kuwait (4), Oman (2), Bahrain (1), Iraq (1), Palestine (1), Afghanistan (1)	193	5.19
Africa	South Africa (38), Egypt (12), Ghana (6), Tunisia (5), Morocco (3), Mauritius (2), Nigeria (2), Rwanda (2), DR Congo (2), Tanzania (1), Tonga (1), Zimbabwe (1), Burkina Faso (1), Kenya (1), Swaziland (1), Togo (1)	79	2.13
Total		3,718	100.00

Data source: Web of Science (accessed 11 October 2022).

18.9% in 2002–2012 and to 33.9% in 2012–2022. Although research output in North America continues to expand, it is doing so at a slower rate than other parts of the world, especially the emerging economies.

Because the country/region filter in the Web of Science does not relate to the spatial focus of the scholarship, we also conducted a crude longitudinal appraisal of the regional focus of luxury research over the last three decades. This was achieved by entering 'luxury' in the primary topic field, for each of the last three decades, and then entering selected countries and regions in a secondary topic field; the countries we chose were some of the more dynamic emerging economies and, in parallel, have been the countries where luxury consumption and

TABLE 2.4 Regional Affiliation of Authors of Publications on Luxury, 1995–2002, 2005–2012 and 2015–2022 (1 December to 30 June for Each Period)

Region	7/1992–6/2002	7/2002–6/2012	7/2012–6/2022
Europe	137 (41.3%)	367 (40.4%)	1,968 (39.3%)
Asia	16 (4.8%)	113 (12.4%)	1,155 (23.1%)
North America	143 (43.1%)	308 (33.9%)	1,017 (20.3%)
Australasia	23 (6.9%)	62 (6.8%)	329 (6.6%)
Middle East	5 (1.5%)	18 (2.0%)	247 (4.9%)
Central and South America	4 (1.2%)	15 (1.7%)	167 (3.3%)
Africa	4 (1.2%)	26 (2.9%)	119 (2.4%)
	332	909	5,002

Source: Web of Science database (accessed 21 July 2022)

TABLE 2.5 Country or Regional Focus of Publications on Luxury, by Decade, 1992–2022 (Selected Countries)

Country or Region	2012–2022	2002–2011	1992–2001
China	524	103	11
India	220	41	14
Korea	77	10	1
Japan	76	41	11
Malaysia	58	7	2
Thailand	32	5	2
Indonesia	45	3	2
'Asia'	174	41	11
Russia	55	12	6
Brazil	56	7	3
'South America'	26	8	2
Nigeria	13	6	0
South Africa	52	19	5
'Africa'	125	51	13
UAE/Dubai	32	4	0
Saudi Arabia	17	2	0
Arab	27	4	0
'Middle East'	36	8	6
Total Publications	5,913	1,901	950

Source: Web of Science database (accessed 21 July 2022).

the luxury industry have expanded most rapidly in recent years. The results of this crude analysis are presented in Table 2.5. From relatively modest beginnings in the 1990s, there has been a phenomenal expansion of scholarly interest in several of these emerging economies, especially in the last decade: the intensified focus on China, and to a lesser extent India and other parts of Asia, has been remarkable.

LUXURY PRACTITIONERS' VIEWS ON RESEARCH

In the previous sections, we have explored the 'landscape of luxury research' from an academic perspective using the Web of Science as a data source. Understanding where luxury is placed as a field of academic scholarship is an essential step for any student of luxury, but it is quite reasonable for the same student to ask why so much emphasis is given to scholarly research perspectives on luxury when their main motivation for studying may be to build a platform for a practice-based career in the luxury industry? Our answer would be that the academic and practical worlds of luxury research are not − or, perhaps, need not be − as far apart as the question implies. We will discuss this matter further in Chapter 9, where we argue that the academic research skills that students acquire during the course of their programme of study have an array of potential applications in luxury management.

To round off this introductory discussion, we would like to cast some light on how, and to what extent, research fits into the routine management activities of luxury brands. To achieve this, we undertook some research of our own, with a survey of luxury industry professionals that sought information on how their brands commissioned, undertook and used the results of research as part of their business strategy.

Before we present the findings of the survey, we will start with a few general observations on research involving luxury industry professionals, which students investigating aspects of luxury and hoping to enter the luxury business should be aware of. As we will discuss further in Chapter 9, luxury research, particularly in academic circles, tends to be heavily oriented towards the luxury consumer as the subject of investigation. For example, of 160 academic papers on luxury published in the last six months of 2021, 102 used surveys or interviews as their principal research methodology, but the data for only two of these papers were based on surveys or in-depth interviews with luxury professionals.[6] The remainder largely focused on a consumer perspective. The reason for this is quite straightforward: luxury consumers are omnipresent and are generally accessible as research participants; luxury professionals tend not to divulge information that they or their brand managers consider potentially to be commercially sensitive. Insightful and in-depth information from a brand and practitioner perspective is, in relative terms, severely lacking in luxury research.

Our experience in building the survey is illustrative of the challenges that researchers face in this regard. LinkedIn was selected as the platform for the circulation of the research survey − this, in itself, was fairly unusual as few academic researchers make use of this platform as a source of primary data (Douha, 2020; Mirabeau, Mingerat and Grange, 2013). The use of LinkedIn seemed optimal for several reasons. First, although it is classified as a social media platform, LinkedIn is in fact the world's largest professional network, with nearly 830 million members.[7] Second, LinkedIn has also become "a key destination for luxury brands to communicate their messaging to [their] highly engaged audience", as stated by Tatiana Dupond, the global head of luxury at LinkedIn, in an interview with the Luxury Society in 2021.[8] Third, LinkedIn offers a relatively democratised professional space where members can follow and connect with not only the C-level executives of large luxury conglomerates but also a myriad of business practitioners and entrepreneurs from small and medium luxury enterprises. Finally, we wished to obtain opinions and inputs from a wide array of luxury sectors, not just fashion, and LinkedIn was an ideal platform for this.

In reality, the process to acquire survey data via LinkedIn was not as smooth as originally envisaged. The survey questionnaire was created on Google Forms, with ten questions, and took less than five minutes for participants to complete; we anticipated that busy professionals would not be willing to spend time on a lengthy and convoluted questionnaire. Prior to the launch of the survey, the researchers received ethical approval from their host university (see Chapter 5). One of the co-authors, Kelly Meng, used her own (non-Premium) LinkedIn account to circulate the questionnaire on 28 June 2022, with the hope of receiving at least 250–300 completed forms over the following 35 days. This initial estimate was based on the fact that Kelly's LinkedIn page was visible to more than 5,400 professional first-degree connections worldwide at the time, and she was also part of several LinkedIn groups focused on the luxury industry (e.g., Luxury and Lifestyle Professionals), where Kelly could share the survey on the group pages to potentially reach 200,000–300,000 group members. However, the reality was rather disappointing: only a dozen responses had been received after one week! The outcome was not symptomatic of any particular shortcomings in the research process; it simply reflected the luxury industry's reluctance to share brand-sensitive information with the wider public.

To overcome this issue, Kelly decided to distribute the survey using the messaging option within the LinkedIn platform: this allows members to message other members if they are connected on LinkedIn. Instead of sending 5,400 messages to all her LinkedIn contacts, Kelly decided to filter her contact list by using a single keyword, 'luxury', to identify survey participants who are 'self-labelled' as being associated with the luxury industry. This left just over 1,000 contacts to be messaged with the survey questionnaire. From 11 to 25 July 2022, Kelly sent out an average of 80–100 messages every day to invite her LinkedIn contacts to participate in the survey. This new approach helped to boost the response rate, and, by the time we closed the survey on 3 August 2022, we had managed to gather 81 responses in total. This may still appear to be quite small, but, in reality, it is quite an achievement! Statistically, the response rate was around 8%, and so the findings should be considered indicative rather than necessarily representative (see Chapter 5 for a fuller discussion of representativeness).

Of the luxury industry professionals who contributed to our survey, 65% indicated that they had been involved in the luxury industry for more than 10 years (see Figure 2.14), and 26% for more than 20 years, and so we were fortunate to gain a panel of experts with a great deal of industry experience.

Table 2.6 presents a summary profile of the survey participants by the luxury sector they work in and shows that the survey managed to cover practitioners from a reasonably broad cross-section of luxury industry segments. Forty-one participants worked for luxury brands that specialised in a single segment of the luxury market, principally in fashion (including apparel and small leather goods) and jewellery (including timepieces), as shown in the top data row in Table 2.6. Eight participants fell outside these five principal sectors (including consultancy, training and strategic planning; retail; automotive; audio; events; concierge; window display). However, a great many luxury brands straddle two or more sectors, and this is reflected in the survey results: 18 participants indicated that they operated in two of these luxury sectors; 7 in three sectors; 1 in four sectors; and 2 participants even operated in all five sectors. The second data row of Table 2.6 shows the luxury sector representation of these multi-sector operators. The final row shows the total representation of each luxury sector among our 81 survey participants.

How many years have you worked in the luxury industry?

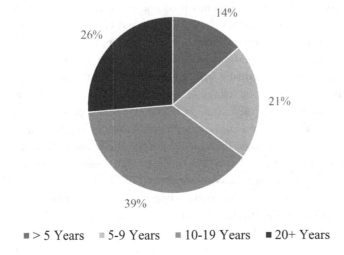

<table>
<tr><td>■ > 5 Years</td><td>■ 5-9 Years</td><td>■ 10-19 Years</td><td>■ 20+ Years</td></tr>
</table>

FIGURE 2.14 Survey Participants' Experience in the Luxury Industry.

TABLE 2.6 Luxury Sectors in Which the Surveyed Luxury Professionals Operate

Luxury Sector in Which You Operate (Single Sector)					
Fashion	Beauty	Jewellery	Hospitality	Food and Drink	Other
20	0	14	5	2	8

Luxury Sector in Which You Operate (Multiple Sectors)					
Fashion	Beauty	Jewellery	Hospitality	Food and Drink	Other
26	12	23	6	4	3
46	12	37	11	6	11

Data source: authors' survey, August 2022

We now move on to present some of our findings on the importance of research to the luxury brands that were covered in this survey. We defined research as the process of seeking or obtaining information or data which have value to the operations of the participants' luxury business. We asked our research participants to indicate the relative importance of research to their company's operations. Figure 2.15 shows that it is clearly important: half of the industry professionals surveyed said that research is "highly important" to their business or brand, and a further 40% indicated that research is "important" but not, in their judgement, vital.

While one-third of the surveyed firms undertook all of their research in-house (i.e., using their own research personnel and facilities), almost 60% of firms relied, to a greater or lesser extent, on external consultants for research data and analysis (see Figure 2.16). Just under 10% of firms made no use of primary research, instead relying entirely on secondary research information (see Chapter 5).

To what extent do you believe research is critical to your
company's success?

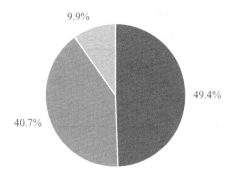

- Highly important: the business is highly reliant on research information
- Important: research information is useful to have but not essential for our operation
- Of limited importance: research is only very occasionally used in our operations

FIGURE 2.15 The Relative Importance of Research to Luxury Brands.

How does your organisation usually undertake research?

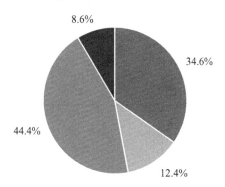

- In-house
- External consultants
- Combination of in-house and external consultants
- Use secondary research information only

FIGURE 2.16 Surveyed Brands' Principal Means of Undertaking Research.

Unsurprisingly, there is a close connection between the importance of research to a luxury brand and whether or not the brand has an in-house research capability, as can be clearly seen from Table 2.7.

Table 2.8 highlights some of the reasons why the surveyed luxury brands relied on external consultants to conduct the primary research they needed for their routine operations.[9] Clearly,

TABLE 2.7 Association between the Importance of Research to a Luxury Brand and the Operation of an In-House Research Facility

How Important Is Research to Your Luxury Brand?	Does Your Brand Possess an In-House Research Facility?		
	No (%)	Yes (%)	Total (%)
Highly important (%)	37.5	62.5	100
Important (%)	60.6	39.4	100
Limited importance (%)	87.5	12.5	100
Total (%)	51.8	48.2	100

Data source: authors' survey, August 2022.

TABLE 2.8 Luxury Firms' Reasons for Using External Research Consultants

Reason for Using External Research Consultants	Single Response	Multiple Responses	Total Responses
Limited in-house research capacity	11	15	26
Consultants have more specialist research expertise	12	20	32
Consultants use specialised research methods	10	15	25
Consultants maintain good connections within the luxury industry	6	9	15
Not applicable	18	18	18
Total responses	81	81	81

Data source: authors' survey, August 2022.

a lack of specialist expertise and familiarity with specialised research methods in-house is an important factor in firms' reliance on external research agencies, although one firm did indicate that using external consultants was a useful way of maintaining a balance between internal and external perspectives. The fact that more than half of all surveyed luxury brands had no means or expertise for conducting research in-house suggests that there is considerable scope to increase research capacity within the luxury industry, and postgraduate research training in the field of luxury management may potentially make a valuable contribution in this regard. We will return to this important point in our concluding discussion in Chapter 9.

Table 2.9 reinforces the importance that the surveyed luxury brands attach to market research. Almost half of the brands undertook research at least four times each year, and three-quarters of all firms engaged in primary research at least annually. As we will discuss further in Chapter 9, the frequency and feasibility of research tend to vary across different sectors of the luxury industry and are also influenced by the size of the enterprise. The larger brands clearly have a greater capacity to support a dedicated research team than many of the niche brands.

TABLE 2.9 Luxury Firms' Frequency of Undertaking Market Research

Frequency of Undertaking Market Research	Number of Responses	Percentage of Responses
Weekly	10	12.4
Monthly	11	13.6
Quarterly	24	19.6
Annually	24	29.6
When needed	4	4.9
Every 2–3 years	2	2.5
No response	6	7.4
Total	81	100.0

Data source: authors' survey, August 2022

Also, some luxury sectors – particularly fashion and apparel – launch new products up to four times each year in a highly dynamic market setting, which renders market research far more challenging than for sectors which change their product offerings much less frequently, such as luxury automobiles. As one interviewee indicated:

> in fashion [regular market research] is impossible because we have too many seasons and they change too fast. So, the research we undertake in fashion tends to be quite broad and related to the market: a consumer market survey, not an in-depth survey of products.

Table 2.10 shows that the undertaking or commissioning of market research by luxury brands is not a trivial matter, with approximately one-third of research projects taking at least four months. Equally, one-third of brands indicated that each research activity could generally be completed within a month. The duration of research projects can also vary considerably across the different luxury sectors. We were given an example where a perfume brand owned by a luxury conglomerate took one year to conduct a thorough programme of research, including nearly 100 in-depth interviews with key stakeholders, before it could finalise a business strategy to define its next decade's development direction, with sustainability as a key focus.

Figure 2.17 summarises some of the main reasons why luxury brands conduct market research (participants were allowed to give multiple responses). A shift in marketing strategy, the introduction of a new product or service, or the adaptation of an existing product were all usually preceded by a market research exercise. Similarly, entering a new market or introducing a product to a new market also required the brand to conduct market research to ensure that its strategy was consistent with the new market setting.

Finally, we asked our survey participants to identify the principal research methods that they tended to adopt when conducting research investigations (research methods are discussed further in Chapter 6). The findings are summarised in Table 2.11. Approximately one-quarter collected only secondary data for quantitative research analysis; 17.4% used questionnaires to obtain primary data, also for quantitative analysis; 28.4% used interviews or focus groups to

TABLE 2.10 Average Duration of a Market Research Project

Average Duration of a Market Research Project	Number of Responses	Percentage of Responses
Less than 1 month	25	30.9
1–3 months	31	38.3
4–6 months	14	17.3
7–12 months	6	7.4
More than 1 year	4	4.9
No response	1	1.2
Total	81	100.0

Data source: authors' survey, August 2022.

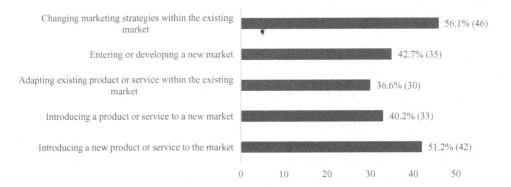

FIGURE 2.17 Main Reasons for Conducting Market Research.

TABLE 2.11 Methods That Luxury Brands Typically Adopt for Market Research

What Research Methods Do You Principally Use?	Single Response	Multiple Responses	Total Responses	Percentage of Total Responses
Gather secondary data for quantitative analysis	9	27	36	23.2
Collect primary data for quantitative analysis	5	22	27	17.4
One-to-one interviews	2	24	26	16.8
Focus groups	3	15	18	11.6
Mix of quantitative and qualitative methods	18	30	48	31.0
Total	37	118	147	100.0

Data source: authors' survey, August 2022.

obtain qualitative primary data. Qualitative methods were often deployed by luxury brands when insightful, 'drill-down' data were required. In addition, approximately one-third of survey respondents used a combination of quantitative and qualitative methods, including those indicated above. The most interesting finding from this final table is that more than three-fifths of all participant firms used qualitative methods in at least part of their research activities. This contrasts with an overwhelming focus on quantitative methods by academic researchers of luxury. This divergence of research approaches will be discussed further in Chapter 5 and in the concluding discussion in Chapter 9.

SUMMARY AND CONCLUSION

This chapter has explored the landscape of luxury research, principally from an academic perspective but also starting a conversation about how research on luxury dovetails with the needs and interests of the industry itself. Two key take-aways from this introductory discussion are the diverse array of themes and issues that lie under the umbrella notion of 'luxury' and the explosion of research interest in the field of luxury that has taken place over the last decade or so. Both can be attributed in part to the way that the industry has metamorphosed in recent years, both substantively and geographically, and the challenges this has given rise to. There is much to understand.

The chapter has also introduced two important research methods: meta-analysis, which facilitates a holistic overview of this field of study, and literature search, which is a fundamental starting point in the process of building a research investigation and grounding it within the existing body of knowledge. We now move to explore the process of framing and defining a research project.

NOTES

1   Although be mindful that journal articles often use phrases such as 'luxury or necessity?', which would yield many largely irrelevant titles in a literature search.
2   The Web of Science is now owned by Clarivate Analytics PLC.
3   See Goodman and Cohen, 2004.
4   Also referred to as the Veblen effect and the Veblen curve.
5   Concerning or involving money.
6   Based on analysis of information obtained from the Web of Science database (accessed 6 January 2022).
7   https://about.linkedin.com/ (accessed 24 September 2022).
8   www.luxurysociety.com/en/articles/2021/09/linkedin-global-head-of-luxury-audiences-are-looking-for-more-storytelling-from-brands (accessed 24 August 2022).
9   Several survey participants gave multiple explanations for their use of external research consultants. The single-response answers are presented separately from the multiple responses in Table 2.8, and these are added together in the final column.

CHAPTER 3

Identifying a Research Topic

In the previous chapter, we have identified some of the principal fields of research that have occupied the minds of academics and practitioners over recent decades. Luxury is a constantly evolving and expanding field of study, both in terms of the industry's own dynamics and in relation to the social, cultural and economic contexts within which it operates. Thus, for the student of luxury in particular, there should be no shortage of issues, themes, processes, challenges and outcomes that could provide the focal point for their individual research project.

WHERE TO START?

There are several factors that may influence the starting point and direction a student follows in identifying a topic for in-depth research. In our experience, students who join programmes of study on luxury management choose to do so for several interrelated reasons. The allure of luxury appeals to them to an extent that following a course of study in this field provides a means of pursuing a personal interest while enhancing their educational and intellectual development. They may already have entered the luxury sector in a professional capacity or may hope to do so upon graduation. They may have a background or interest in cognate fields such as art, design, fashion, social media or marketing which they hope to nurture and later apply creatively within the specific context of luxury. Typically, students will already have a particular interest in a segment of the luxury industry (such as fashion), and there may even be themes and issues (e.g., sustainability, celebrity, digitalisation, brand extensions, etc.) that they are especially inquisitive about. Their interest in and approach to luxury may be influenced by their disciplinary background, their nationality, even their demography, and by their personal exposure to particular issues, processes or contexts. Then, during the course of their programme of study, new fields and angles will emerge, deeper and broader knowledge will be acquired, inquisitiveness and criticality will be stimulated, intellectual processes will be sharpened, and a clearer picture will form, both of the luxury industry and of the student's future place within it. These entry points, and others, may have a significant bearing on the topic and approach the student initially settles on for their research investigation.

The research journey starts with an honest reflection on what your interests and motivations are, where you are aiming and how you need to develop in order to achieve your objectives. Have a think about the answers you would give to the questions in Box 3.1.

DOI: 10.4324/9781003295372-3

BOX 3.1

To the Student of Luxury

Who are you: how do you self-identify in relation to the field of luxury?
What has been your journey within the realm of luxury so far?
What aspects of luxury are you particularly interested in?
How much, and what, do you feel you already know about luxury?
What are the gaps in your knowledge?
What would be an interesting topic to get more deeply into, both in terms of
    your own personal development and as a contribution to knowledge about
    the luxury industry?
Where in the field of luxury do you hope to go?
What do you need to know and what skills do you need to develop in order to
    take your luxury journey forward?

IDENTIFYING A THEMATIC FOCUS

The research topic must, quite obviously, have a connection with luxury in some shape or form, but, for an industry that in 2021 made up only 1.4% of the global economy,[1] the luxury industry is remarkably complex in both character and the range of issues it gives rise to. A student will typically start by identifying a broad thematic focus for their dissertation research, which must then be narrowed down and operationalised before the investigation can commence. This narrowing-down process will be discussed in detail in Chapter 4. In the paragraphs that follow, we will outline some of the broad themes that students might consider as a starting point for their research and some of the criteria which might apply to their topic selection.

Table 3.1 identifies and exemplifies a far-from-exhaustive range of themes with which a contemporary Master's-level research investigation might be expected to engage. We will return to some of these themes in the following chapters as we go through the process of narrowing them down towards a clear research focus and the operationalisation of key concepts.

An obvious place to start when looking for a cutting-edge theme for a research project is a contemporary *problem* or *challenge*. In addition to the immense human suffering the COVID-19 pandemic and its aftermath wrought around the world, it also sent shockwaves across the global economy from which the luxury sector was far from immune. How luxury brands have adjusted to and bounced back from new post-pandemic economic and social realities provides fertile ground for research on very many aspects of luxury business, marketing and consumption. At the time of writing, the Russia–Ukraine conflict is the epicentre of further global disruption, and the consequent isolation of Russia from conventional markets, in addition to sanctions imposed on Russian oligarchs and wealthy individuals, has removed an important market for luxury goods, the implications of which for luxury brands are worthy of fuller exploration.

TABLE 3.1 Identifying a Thematic Focus for the Research

Thematic Focus	Examples
Problems	Post-COVID-19 recovery challenges for the luxury sector Implications for luxury of the Russia–Ukraine conflict Intellectual property protection for luxury brands
Processes	The technification of luxury (VR, AR, AI, etc.) The 'democratisation' of luxury The digitalisation of luxury
Transitions	Luxury electric/hybrid vehicles Omnichannel luxury retailing/shopping
Contemporary challenges	Luxury and sustainability, circularity; corporate social responsibility The diluted meaning of 'luxury'
Debates	Consume less/consume more luxury Online versus offline retailing/shopping
Controversies	Managing overstock and protecting luxury price thresholds Luxury brands' failed localisation strategies Cultural appropriation in luxury design
Tensions	Heritage and modernity: old luxury meets new luxury Accessible luxury, masstige brands and price competition Digital marketing and brand integrity
Trends	Post-consumerism meets luxury; the luxury sharing economy; hyper-personalisation; social media marketing of luxury brands; celebrities and influencers in luxury marketing; conglomerates, mergers and acquisitions in the luxury sector; etc.
A changing world	Emerging luxury markets Domestic luxury brands Diversification of luxury markets
Demographics	Gen Y and Gen Z luxury consumers; HENRYs (high earners, not rich yet); luxury and gender
Ethics	Inequality and luxury ethicality Brand values
Solutions?	Blockchain confronts counterfeit luxury TRIPS (WTO Agreement on Trade-Related Aspects of Intellectual Property Rights) and luxury IP Country of origin
New forms of luxury	Experiential luxury Luxury and the metaverse
History	Historical re-evaluation of key 'moments' in luxury
Brand management	Critical success factors for luxury brands; service quality; personnel; supply chain management; customer relationship management; store atmospherics; brand storytelling; etc.
Sectors	Personal goods, travel, watches and jewellery, perfume and cosmetics, health and well-being, home and interior design, automobiles, etc.
Consumers	Determinants of and influences on luxury consumer behaviour
Permutations	Disciplinary focus, regional/country cases, brands, social groups, etc.

Sustainability is also a very pressing global issue to which luxury brands and conglomerates are in many instances taking a leading role in responding, and this too is a theme that provides immense potential for in-depth investigation, not least from a consumer perspective. *Debates* surrounding sustainability (and *ethicality*) may also provide an intellectually stimulating point of entry to an investigation of luxury's ecological and social claims, including whether consumers or brands are in the driving seat of changes in both imaging and practice, and whether more luxury rather than less may be a good thing for the planet (see, for example, Sun, Bellezza and Paharia, 2021).

The first two decades of the 21st century have been a period of immense and profound change for the luxury sector. The *process* of change, its drivers, manifestations and implications raise many questions not just about the changing character of luxury business but also about the very essence of luxury itself. Three fundamental shifts in this regard are the so-called 'democratisation' of luxury, where the sector has expanded rapidly beyond its traditional spatial, demographic and social heartlands; the prominent position of social media in almost all aspects of luxury branding, marketing and consumer engagement; and the increased use of 'virtual' technologies and digitalisation in luxury brands' interfacing with consumers and markets. Closely associated with the last category are the *transition* to omnichannel retailing and shopping and the associated *debates* about the relative virtues of online and offline modalities for luxury brands' relationships with customers and devotees. Although luxury brands invest heavily in building brand value, reputation and equity, occasionally they get things wrong, and a forensic exploration of *controversies* and public relations disasters – such a Burberry destroying stock worth £28.6 million in 2017 and £90 million over a five-year period to protect brand value (Zazzara, Rapetti and Tyler, 2020),[2] or Dolce and Gabbana's serious miscalculation in its attempt to 'localise' its brand in the Chinese market (Atwal, Bryson and Kaiser, 2021) – provides a rich storyline upon which to design an in-depth research enquiry.

Table 3.1 lists a number of current *trends* in the luxury industry, any one of which (and a great many besides) could provide the core theme around which to build a primary research investigation. These include trends in society which have implications for luxury consumption, such as philosophical shifts towards post-consumerism and post-materialism, or the growing advocacy of a circular economy, or the predilection for experiential forms of luxury, or the influence of e-word of mouth on the popularity of certain luxury brands. Celebrity culture and the role of influencers and key opinion leaders in building luxury brand imaging and fanhood are currently a very popular focus for dissertation research, not least because of the ready accessibility of qualitative research data, which we will discuss further in Chapter 5. These trends also lead to *tensions*, such as where old luxury (heritage brands) meets new luxury and new branding modalities, and where the boundaries between luxury and non-luxury become increasingly blurred (e.g., 'masstige' and 'accessible luxury').

The *world* within which the luxury sector operates has changed considerably in the last 20 years, with a significant shift in its geographical centre of gravity away from its traditional production and consumption heartlands in Western Europe and the USA increasingly to all corners of the globe (most particularly East and now South Asia, but in future likely to include Africa and Latin America). This global shift offers immense possibilities to conduct research based on regional, national or even sub-national case studies of *emerging markets* and their relationships with luxury, as well as their own attempts to nurture domestic luxury brands. To geographical diversity can be added a wide array of further elements that provide almost infinite *permutations* for thematic investigations, such as demography, gender, social and cultural groups, luxury sector, individual brands and a myriad of aspects of brand management, luxury collaborations with various cultural industries, and even the disciplinary and philosophical approach that the researcher adopts as their point of entry to their research enquiry.

Although there will clearly be no shortage of research themes available to stimulate the curiosity of any student of luxury, certain criteria and considerations need to be reflected on at an early stage in deciding how to develop the topical theme into a research framework. We will outline some of these in the following paragraphs. The relative importance attached to each of these elements, and the weight given to them in a final evaluation, will vary from institution to institution and programme to programme, so the following discussion should be read as indicative rather than prescriptive.

CRITERIA AND CONSIDERATIONS IN SELECTING A RESEARCH TOPIC

A balance needs to be found between an *academic* and a *practical* orientation for the research investigation. It is understandable that a student with a past and/or prospective future involvement in the luxury industry may wish to acquire a myriad of practical skills in various fields of luxury management in order to increase their marketability upon graduation, and an argument can be made that an overly academic programme of study dilutes the practical gains a student can make (this will be further discussed in Chapter 9). But a Master's programme in luxury management aims to nurture thinkers as well as doers, and people who can see the wider picture as well as those capable of handling the fine details. Thus, while a dissertation research project may be oriented towards an issue that is of practical significance in the luxury industry today, this must, by convention, be wrapped up in academic debates and intellectual discourses of the kind that the months of coursework leading up to the dissertation will have exposed the student to. Any dissertation for a university-level programme of study must therefore have a sound academic platform rooted in the theories, concepts, debates and intellectual processes which are archived in a growing luxury management literature and wider cognate disciplinary literatures. In choosing a research topic, therefore, the student needs to consider whether their proposal has a sufficiently robust academic platform upon which to build and an adequate foundation in the existing body of knowledge to provide the material necessary to build this platform. A student is unlikely to be able to make this appraisal unless they already have a good grounding in the relevant body of literature.

A research-based dissertation should also be seen as an original investigation which formulates questions that can be answered through the interrogation of primary information obtained by the researcher themself. Thus, while the finished document may contain descriptive information, such as that which provides background context to the primary investigation, the main body of the thesis should centre on the intellectual development, explanation, execution, interpretation and exposition of an enquiry that has been orchestrated and completed by the researcher. A research dissertation should be able to answer investigative questions such as 'why?'

and 'how?', as well as the descriptive question 'what?'. The scope for, and appropriate balance between, *investigative* and *descriptive* elements need to be factored into the selection of a research topic, the design and structure of the dissertation, and the mapping of a route towards its successful completion.

In selecting a research topic, consideration also needs to be given to the balance between *depth* and *breadth*. There is no perfect formula in this regard. A study can be so broad and all-encompassing as to have no point of focus, whereas an investigation may be so narrow and specific that it risks losing connectivity to wider processes, debates and contexts. For example, a dissertation that explores the sustainability credentials of the luxury industry, while interesting and useful, may be rather too broad and diffuse to allow a primary research focus to be clearly identified and would most likely involve a wide survey of secondary sources rather than a researcher-designed primary investigation; nonetheless, luxury and sustainability provide an excellent general framework for a more focused investigation, as we will see in the following chapter. Thus, a dissertation that examined Generation Z consumer attitudes and responses to brands' sustainability narratives, set within this wider sustainable luxury debate, would offer a great deal of scope for a focused investigation framed by theoretical and conceptual structures gleaned from the luxury and/or sustainability literatures. The latter research focus would more likely match the ideal 'wine glass' shape for a dissertation research investigation (see Figure 3.1) that tapers down from broad to narrow, and from general to specific.

Originality is another consideration. Although, in the context of a Master's-level dissertation, it is unreasonable to expect the degree of originality and *insight* that is a specified requirement for a doctoral thesis, there is little value – intellectual, practical or in terms of grading the final report – in effectively repeating a study that has already been done. Thus, in selecting a

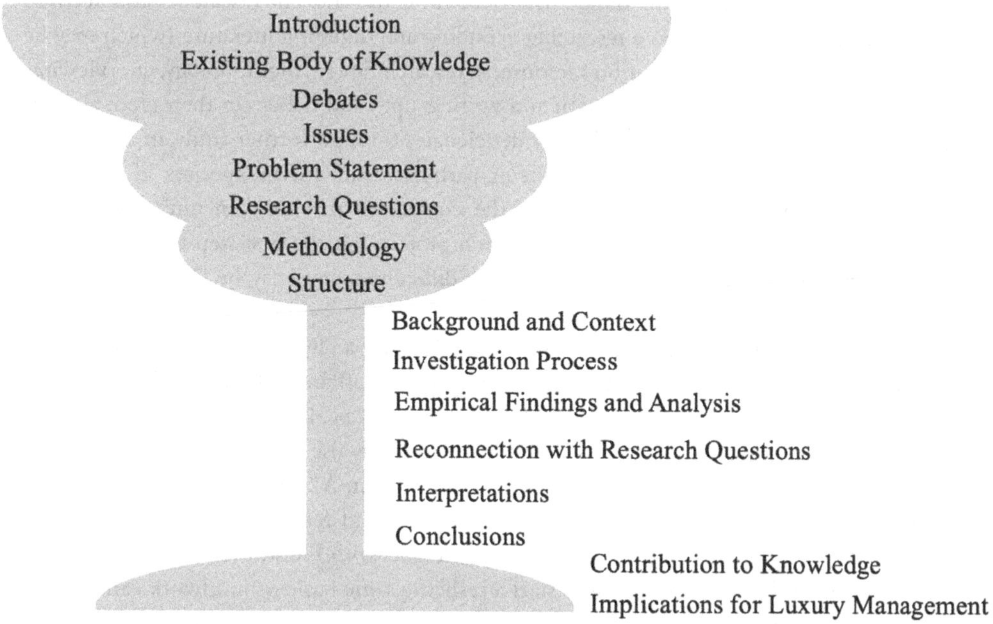

Introduction
Existing Body of Knowledge
Debates
Issues
Problem Statement
Research Questions
Methodology
Structure

Background and Context

Investigation Process

Empirical Findings and Analysis

Reconnection with Research Questions

Interpretations

Conclusions

Contribution to Knowledge

Implications for Luxury Management

FIGURE 3.1 A Suggested Shape and Structure for a Master's Research Project.

research topic, it is incumbent on the student to ensure that they are sufficiently familiar with the existing body of knowledge, both academic and practical, that they are able to see where they may be duplicating extant work, and where they can both see and justify a niche area or angle that would satisfy any originality requirement. Working on a topic that is fresh, timely and near the 'cutting edge' of current developments in the field of luxury, as we discussed in the previous section, is one way to help ensure that a research proposal does not overlap with something that has already been done, although this may possibly be traded off against a limited literature in an emerging field of study. Taking an existing body of research and applying it to a different context (e.g., an emerging market, a particular demographic, a manifestation of 'new luxury') is another way to avoid duplication or repetition.

Crucial considerations at the outset of a piece of research are its *viability* and *manageability* within the constraints faced by the researcher in terms of time, resources, word limits, accessibility to data and their own personal *capabilities* as a researcher. In an ideal world, we would select a topic, read up on the subject, design an investigation and methodology, gather, analyse and interpret data, draw conclusions and make recommendations within a tightly constructed dissertation that satisfies all assessment requirements. In the real world, life is not quite so straightforward. The data we require may not be readily accessible – for instance, past experience has shown that brands are generally much more reluctant than consumers to talk to student researchers – and thus the best-laid plans can sometimes be stymied when assumptions about data availability prove not to be valid. The time taken to organise, execute, process and analyse a survey, or to arrange and conduct interviews or focus groups, may be greater than first envisaged, putting pressure on completion deadlines. Ideally, we might wish to have a sample size that runs into the thousands, in order that we can satisfy the need for representativeness that allows us to make wider inferences from our research findings, but cost and other constraints may determine that samples in the hundreds may be more realistic. The researcher also needs to reflect on their own *capabilities* as a researcher – finding and digesting literature (which may be further constrained by their institution's resources), research design, methodology, interviewing, data processing and analysis, interpretation and writing-up – and either cut their cloth accordingly or be prepared to compensate for any deficiencies through further study, in the process becoming a better researcher. It is often difficult, particularly for the inexperienced researcher, to have a clear vision and understanding of the constraints that may encumber their path towards the successful completion of their research project, but the first step to being able to overcome these constraints is to be mindful of the difficulties they may be likely to face. This book aims to flag many of these constraints.

Students should also build into their research planning a clear but cognate *Plan B* (that is, not an entirely different project but one that moves off in a slightly different direction from the original research idea) in case their initial *Plan A* proves to be unviable. For instance, an investigation into how and why luxury brands use celebrities and KOLs (key opinion leaders) to position their brands in, say, China (Plan A) could quite readily shift to an exploration of how Chinese luxury consumers view and respond to brands which use KOLs to access the Chinese market (Plan B), should access to brand managers for data and insight prove difficult, without having to start afresh: the same basic groundwork can be used as a foundation for both projects.

In line with most university-level postgraduate work, students are expected to adopt a *critical* approach to their research. In simple terms, this means not just collating information and re-presenting it, but orchestrating, interrogating and questioning sources and the perspectives they present. To use an analogy, it means being a *mahout* rather than simply sitting atop an elephant. Thus, in addition to formulating questions to guide an investigation and answering these using data and analysis, the student should seek to weave an argument into their narrative, which they steer while presenting and weighing different viewpoints from the literature and from interpreting their own research. Academic writing is often centred on debates, arguments and perspectives, and it is certainly the case in luxury studies that there is rarely a consensus viewpoint on everything. Thus, to some, luxury products are a pinnacle of creative achievement, whereas, to others, they manifest some of the worst traits of human nature, such as snobbery, desire and indulgence. Making luxury more 'democratic', and thus inclusive, runs counter to a cornerstone of luxury, exclusivity. Engaging in arguments and debates does not necessarily mean that the student has to commit to one side or another, but it is important that they be able to demonstrate familiarity and engagement with critical debates within the luxury sphere and to steer a discussion accordingly. Criticality adds a deeper intellectual layer to the discussion and investigation.

A fundamental requirement of research is that it should be *reliable, trustworthy* and *replicable*, and that it follows established academic *conventions*. In theory, another researcher should be able to come up with more or less the same findings were they to follow the same set of processes and procedures. This is one of the reasons why it is conventional to include a quite extensive statement about methodology in any completed document, whether a dissertation or a published piece of work, so that the reader can ascertain how the research project was conducted, should they wish to follow a similar path in their own research. It also allows the reader (and peer reviewer in the case of published research) to make a judgement about the competence of the researcher and the validity and plausibility of their findings and interpretations.

Another very important convention is the formal attribution of information sources. Figure 3.1 – and much of the foregoing discussion – suggests that any piece of research should be built upon foundations set in the existing body of knowledge, which the researcher may seek to help advance through their own empirical investigation. The existing body of knowledge – that is, *what* we know (accumulated wisdom) and also *how* we know (the intellectual tools to digest information and build an argument) – is conventionally found in books, articles and other information sources that are deemed reliable and authoritative by the institutions and practices of academic 'quality control', which principally involves various processes of peer review.[3] This quality control process, although not without flaws, helps to assure the users of research that the findings and interpretations found within a piece of academic writing are authoritative and trustworthy, although not beyond critical evaluation. When using the existing body of knowledge to lay the foundation for one's own research, it is conventional – indeed, essential – that all sources are fully referenced, both at the appropriate point in any discussion where the source has informed a particular point, and in a comprehensive reference list at the end of the article. Failure to follow this convention to the letter risks the heinous accusation of *plagiarism*, which is passing off someone else's work as the writer's own. This can be deliberate and malicious or, more frequently, it may be unwitting, born of either poor writing practice[4] or a lack of familiarity with formal academic conventions. We will return to this important point when we discuss the writing-up of the thesis in Chapter 8.

Wherever practicable, the researcher should seek to *contextualise* their investigation. This applies particularly where the discussion will focus on, or make use of, case studies, but is a principle that also has a wider resonance. 'Context' can be defined as "the circumstances that provide the setting for something and that enable it to be understood".[5] Luxury brands, luxury consumers, luxury markets and even the huge luxury conglomerates all function within a contextual environment. Indeed, part of the beauty of luxury is its long history and rich heritage, its close association with place, and the centrality of its people − designers, producers, promoters, consumers, followers − each and every one of whom has an identity, a story, a background, a place in society and a view of the world. In our perspective, one of the saddest tendencies in the research process is what is called *reductionism*: taking something complex and boiling it down to its fundamental constituents. In the process, nuance, diversity and contextual intricacy are lost. A sample of 500 people becomes a case study of luxury consumption in England, Japan, Brazil, Russia, Nigeria, when it is nothing of the kind. The focus is on the data, not the people or the places. To compensate, the researcher should leave space in their discussion to set their study within the context from which it was drawn: not just a country or a place, but a culture or counterculture, a generational sub-group, a brand story or a social movement.

Closely linked to this is the question of *representativeness*. It is inevitable that the researcher will have to work with a relatively small sample drawn from a much larger population, but they might wish to make inferences from the sample that can apply to the wider group or segment. Care has to be taken to ensure that the researcher's data allow them to make wider inferences, such as by selecting cases from a suitably created sampling frame and process (which we will discuss further in Chapter 5). Otherwise, the researcher should exercise considerable caution in extrapolating from a sample to the wider population. So, a dissertation sample even of 1,000 people can never form the basis for a representative case study of, say, China, or even Luxembourg for that matter. The safest way to overcome this problem is not to make claims that extend beyond the capability of the data and analysis to support them, and also for the researcher to demonstrate to the reader that they are mindful of the challenges of representativeness. Unless and until the student researcher is able to develop a very sophisticated sampling procedure and has unrestricted access to a representative cross-section of participants, it is probably best for the researcher to think in terms of 'indicative' rather than 'representative'. This particularly applies in the case of qualitative research, which will also be discussed further in Chapter 5.

Another tendency the researcher should be mindful of is a categorical proclivity towards *generalisation* or *homogenisation*. In choosing a topic for investigation, the student researcher will quite sensibly focus on a particular segment of consumers (Generation Z, millennials, HENRYs, the 'new rich', etc.), or particular national contexts, or certain business sectors, rather than seeking to explore the luxury industry as a whole. While such focal groups may indeed have a great deal in common, they are also likely to evince a great deal of diversity, variation and heterogeneity. So, any study that works from the basis that, say, "all Gen Z consumers are the same" or that all luxury consumers of 'street' collaboration lines are advocates of this particular subculture is likely to overlook a great deal of intra-category nuance, in the process simplifying a world that is quite fascinating for its complexity.

In building a research investigation that has a solid foundation in the theories and concepts that form part of the existing body of knowledge, the researcher will almost inevitably have to handle some quite complex and abstract ideas. It is important to recognise at an early stage that concepts might provide an excellent foundation for intellectualising a piece of research, but they are extremely challenging to build a research investigation around. Abstract or intangible concepts such as 'culture', 'lifestyle', 'sustainability', 'streetification', [6] 'globalisation', 'democratisation', 'tradition' – even 'luxury' itself – require *operationalisation* (discussed further in Chapter 7) before they can provide a workable basis for building an enquiry. The student researcher should try to avoid the tendency to 'hide' behind abstract concepts and unquestioned generalisations. It is extremely poor practice, and ultimately self-defeating, for the researcher to include abstract concepts in, say, a survey and leave it to the respondent to wrestle with their meaning.

Comparative studies – for instance, between countries, cultures, brands or groups of consumers – can be interesting, illuminating and insightful if well handled, but the student researcher needs to ensure that there are adequate grounds for comparison, otherwise they risk ending up doing two parallel studies, which may dilute the potential investigative power and depth of a single case study. So, are you comparing like with like? Are differences observed between two groups the direct result of the characteristics that distinguish them from one another, or could they be explained by other, spurious factors, such as a lack of conceptual equivalence (the same ideas apply differently in two settings) or differences in the data sources for the two groups? If we were to compare the handbag purchase motivations of consumers of 'old luxury' and 'new luxury' brands, would it be the brands that provide the principal basis of distinction, or could the age of the respective groups of consumers be the key determining factor? In any case, could we draw a sufficiently clear line of demarcation between the two groups to make any comparison meaningful? If we were to compare attitudes towards conspicuity in Thailand and Malaysia, would differences be attributable to national, ethnic, religious, generational or social factors, and how would the researcher handle the heterogeneity that is evident in both settings?

Cross-cultural comparative studies require deep contextual understanding on the part of the researcher and explication for the benefit of the reader.

Finally, *researching the future* is something best avoided by the student researcher. There is no doubt that creating a clear picture of how a trend, process or phenomenon will evolve across time is of immense potential value to practitioners in the luxury industry, but the methodological tools for doing this are either poorly developed or are far too complex to be considered practicable for a Master's dissertation and 'safe' when it comes to its evaluation. It is possible to make projections based on extrapolations from the present and the past, but so many unanticipated factors might potentially intervene – especially in an industry and a world that are changing so quickly – that would question the precision, and thus the utility, of future prognoses. We would recommend that any engagement with future trajectories be limited to the concluding discussion of the dissertation rather than being its centrepiece.

SUMMARY AND CONCLUSION

The paragraphs in this chapter have outlined some of the matters the student should take into consideration when formulating their research ideas and framework. It is important for the researcher to be mindful of these things at an early stage in the research process so they can be built into the research design and planning. We also believe that it is good practice for the student researcher to be able to demonstrate their mindfulness of these matters to their readers and assessors. Hopefully, the student's motivation in tackling the research dissertation is not simply to pass a segment of their course, but to present the dissertation as the pinnacle of their postgraduate learning process and a showcase for the skills they have developed, and possibly even a document to show potential employers in the luxury industry to demonstrate their competence and value as a researcher.

NOTES

1 Global GDP in 2021 was US$94.935 trillion, or €79.534 trillion at the average exchange rate for 2021 of US$1 = €0.8458 (Statista, 2022: www.statista.com/statistics/268750/global-gross-domestic-product-gdp/, accessed 22 August 2022). The total value of the luxury sector in 2021 was €1.14 trillion (D'Arpizio *et al.*, 2021: www.bain.com/insights/from-surging-recovery-to-elegant-advance-the-evolving-future-of-luxury/, accessed 22 August 2022).

2 https://ssrn.com/abstract=3593785 (accessed 22 September 2022).

3 For example, judging a person's competence to fill an academic position; evaluating the academic and practical merits of applications for research funding; evaluating books and articles submitted for publication; and evaluating the quality of research-based academic departments and institutions.

4 For instance, note-writing without proper attribution: the notes then become the basis for writing-up, and plagiarism seeps unnoticed into the final document.

5 *Oxford English Dictionary*, www.oed.com (accessed 22 September 2022).

6 Where luxury brands have linked up with streetwear brands in order to appeal to younger consumers who dig 'street' counterculture.

CHAPTER 4

Research Approach and Research Design

On the face of it, research is a fairly straightforward process: there is an issue that is deemed worthy of investigation; a platform for a research enquiry is laid based on the existing body of knowledge; a research investigation is designed based on specified research questions; a methodology is chosen that is suitable for this particular investigation; data are collected, processed, analysed and interpreted; the findings are presented, along with interpretation and argument; the contribution to knowledge is shown; and the researcher reflects on any shortcomings or limitations and makes suggestions for further research building on what they have achieved in their own investigation. This might work as a basic formula for research, but there are further layers that the student needs to reflect on in determining how they wish to approach their investigation and why. Research should be not just a mechanical process of steps and procedures but also a reflection on where the researcher stands in relation to the enterprise of knowledge generation, and even their values and worldview. There are contrasting, and often polarised, philosophical standpoints on the advancement of knowledge which the student should understand and reflect on before committing to a particular angle of approach.

PHILOSOPHICAL APPROACH

We have already touched on the existing body of knowledge and how it is both built and safeguarded. But what is knowledge in a philosophical sense? *Epistemology* is the philosophy of knowledge, the ways of knowing and learning about the world (Ritchie *et al.*, 2013, 6). The term epistemology is derived from two Greek words: *episteme* (or the Ancient Greek *epistamai*), which can be translated as knowledge, a system of understanding, acquaintance with – or, what we know, how we know, and how we come to know; and *logos*, which means human rationality, argument and reasoned discourse. *Episteme* is conventionally contrasted with *doxa* (derived from the Ancient Greek verb *dokein*: to seem, to appear, to think), a noun meaning popular opinion or a common belief. The juxtaposition of *episteme* and *doxa* draws a distinction between, essentially, what we feel (a hunch) and what we know (a fact), and this points towards a very important distinction in the field of research: that between supposition and certainty. For knowledge to be accepted as truth or fact, we need to eliminate all ambiguity, uncertainty, subjectivity and preconception; in other words, statements such as 'it seems', 'it appears' and 'I think' are simply not strong enough to convince the reader that your findings and propositions are valid.

DOI: 10.4324/9781003295372-4

Authoritative research comes from adherence to the accepted principles of best practice, which involve, inter alia, systematic rigour, reasoned and balanced argument, critical self-reflection, and techniques to underpin confidence in the validity of research results.

When a researcher investigates a phenomenon or process, it is essential that their enquiry and findings should fit and represent *reality*, not an imagined or subjective distortion of reality. In other words, research should be accurate, honest and unambiguous. But this immediately begs questions about the nature, and even the true existence, of reality. There are essentially two contrasting views of what is called *ontology*: the study of being, or the nature of reality. The *realist* view is that there is an absolute, objective reality which exists independently of human constructs and conceptions; the challenge of research is to achieve the closest possible approximation to reality, notwithstanding the biases, subjectivities and path dependencies that we may bring to our interpretations of the world. The *idealist* perspective argues that there is no reality beyond that which we create in our conceptions, beliefs and understanding of the world. Our subjective reality *is* reality. Thus, research that seeks to objectify the subjective risks trying to create an artificial and simplified order out of a reality of chaos, diversity, complexity, contingency and contextuality.

This binary of perspectives – realism and idealism – dovetails with several other polarised positions which lie at the heart of research as an enterprise in knowledge advancement. We can already sense from the discussion of ontology that there is, on the one hand, an approach to knowledge generation that is clinical, precise, objective, scientific and categorical, and, on the other, one that is fluid, flexible, imaginative, contingent and humanistic. This division can best be summarised by the opposition of positivism and interpretivism. *Positivism* is derived from the true meaning of positive, which is expressing certainty, absolute, formally laid down, dealing only with facts. In terms of the investigation of the social world, of which luxury is a part, it concerns the application of scientific and empiricist reasoning and method developed originally in the natural sciences. *Interpretivism* places a greater emphasis on meanings than facts. It argues that the reality that surrounds us is socially constructed, not objective and detached, and, because it is influenced by the beliefs, reasoning and experience of all social actors, there is no singular, universal, objectifiable reality but instead multiple, contingent realities, each with different meanings to different people. Human life is best observed from within, in all its complex detail, rather than from a panopticon looking down from above, which may tend to reduce this complexity to generalised patterns. Research itself is a socially constructed activity where the past informs the present, and established views of the world influence new ideas and perspectives. Closely connected with this polarisation of standpoints is another fundamental binary in the approach to research, between *quantitative* and *qualitative* methods, which we will explore in more detail in Chapter 5.

So, where does luxury fit into this structure of knowledge? Figure 2.1 showed us that luxury studies links most closely with cognate disciplines in the social sciences and the humanities. These are disciplines that, by and large, rely on arguments and propositions informed by rational and reasoned discourse, rather than by laws and truths. The knowledge these disciplines generate is constantly evolving, either building incrementally upon long-established foundations of understanding, or starting afresh in new directions, or challenging established discourse and presenting alternative theories and propositions, a process known as 'rethinking'. The last reinforces the danger of seeing knowledge as synonymous with truth. The work of Michel Foucault (Foucault,

1970, 1972) was influential in emphasising how established knowledge is the result of processes which are substantially underlain by the power differentials that characterise the modern world. Rather than a single, universal epistemology, there are in reality multiple epistemologies existing in different places at the same time. Through the functioning of the 'power–knowledge system', certain epistemologies and accepted 'truths' tend to predominate, while alternative voices and perspectives tend not to be heard or accepted as authoritative. *Postcolonialism* was an attempt to give voice to these alternative epistemologies, such as non-Western views liberated from the hitherto unquestioned dominance of Western discourse and the power structures which underpinned it. Luxury is certainly not immune from such criticism: although the heartland of luxury and luxury discourse in the modern era has tended to be centred on the West (Western Europe in particular), the so-called 'democratisation of luxury' is drawing many other parts of the world inexorably into its sphere of influence, which makes it incumbent on luxury researchers to look for, listen to and understand multiple localised ways of understanding its functioning and diverse people's relationships with it, and in more languages than just English.[1]

Another weakness of luxury studies is that most of the theories that are used as the basis for research and discourse are borrowed from cognate disciplines. Table 4.1 presents a short overview and explanation of some of the theories that have been used as a platform for research on luxury over the last decade or so; these are drawn variously from sociology, psychology, cultural studies, management and marketing. Even the theory of conspicuous consumption, which provides a bedrock for the concept of luxury, is rooted in social psychology.

TABLE 4.1 Some Theoretical Formulations Used in Luxury Research

Theory	Brief Explanation
Social adaptation theory	The passive and active processes whereby the individual adapts to their physical, material, social and spiritual environment, most particularly to the existing norms of society
Self-determination theory	A theory of self-motivation, where a person's self-determined values are influenced by a combination of intrinsic (internal to the person) and extrinsic (external) motivations
Grounded theory	Theory that is rooted in real-world empirical observation. It is based on inductive reasoning, where concepts and theories emerge from (often qualitative, rich, nuanced) data
Balance theory	Attitudes (psychological motivation), and subsequent behaviour, are formed based on how an individual perceives something (e.g., a luxury good) and how others perceive this thing; a triadic relationship between a person, another person and an object which must be harmonised for action to follow
Theory of planned behaviour	How a person's behavioural decisions are influenced by their intentions, attitudes, motivations and norms. The stronger the intentions, the more likely the person is to expend the effort to perform a particular behaviour (such as luxury consumption)
Three-factor theory	The asymmetric influences on customer satisfaction with service provision, which are categorised as satisfier (excitement factors), dissatisfier (necessary factors) and a hybrid (performance factors)

(Continued)

TABLE 4.1 (Continued)

Theory	Brief Explanation
Production of culture theory	Posits that smaller firms have a greater propensity to produce innovative cultural products than larger companies and conglomerates, which more typically innovate by incorporating smaller firms and subsuming their creative talent. The luxury industry is a relevant test case for this theory
Functional theories of attitudes	How a person's attitudes, feelings and beliefs guide their behaviour in relation to gratification (including consumption decisions), living in society (including gaining status) and maintaining values (including materialism)
Consumer perceived risk theory	How consumers learn through past consumption experiences (their own and others') and use this to ascertain the risks associated with future consumption behaviour (e.g., suspicion, conservatism, reassurance-seeking). Relevant to how luxury brands can work to minimise consumers' risk-aversity
Self-affirmation theory	Is concerned with the psychology of self-esteem, and particularly how people respond when their self-esteem is threatened. It is based on the premise that people wish to maintain a favourable self-perception. Luxury consumption behaviour may be linked to a person's actual or projected self-perception
Narrative theory	How stories function to help people understand the world around them, sometimes in contrast to scientific ways of understanding, and how people make sense of, and react to, the stories they receive (e.g., luxury storytelling)
Signalling theory	How firms (or luxury brands) convey signals about their quality to outside observers (e.g., luxury consumers) in a situation of information asymmetries, and how receivers interpret and act upon these signals
Role theory	People occupy a variety of roles in daily life and behave predictably according to normative expectations associated with these roles. Consumer behaviour is one application of role theory to luxury studies
Theory of innovation diffusion	Is concerned with how a product or idea gains acceptance and spreads within a population or social group, typically asymmetrically. Early adopters through to laggards are posited to exhibit different characteristics. Luxury brands must understand clearly the characteristics of their target markets
Theory of conspicuous consumption	People purchase expensive goods as a public display of wealth and status. One of the cornerstone theories of luxury consumption, first posited by Thorstein Veblen in 1899
Anti-laws of marketing theory	One of a limited number of frameworks to have been developed specifically for the luxury industry, it argues that, were luxury brands to follow conventional marketing processes, they would quickly cease to be defined as luxury. A luxury strategy was proposed involving 24 anti-laws of marketing which are key to preserving the essence of luxury
The French luxury model	Relates to the way that luxury conglomerates, supported by large financial groups, have changed the organisational character of the luxury industry in the era of globalisation, but at the same time have seemingly (debatably) overcome the theoretical contradiction between mass production and luxury

One inevitable consequence of this theoretical borrowing is that luxury studies has tended to be a hostage to the approaches that these disciplines adopt when undertaking research. There are two largely oppositional (but sometimes complementary) approaches that researchers can adopt when building an investigation into their chosen issue or problem: deductive and inductive (see Table 4.2 and Box 4.1). A *deductive approach to research* has as its starting point a theory, idea, proposition or an assumption, usually expressed as a hypothesis or series of hypotheses, the validity of which is tested with empirical data which are analysed using scientific methods (positivism), and on the basis of this the original idea is either accepted or rejected. Theory therefore precedes and is the starting point of an investigation. An *inductive approach to research* has the formulation of new theories and concepts as its ultimate objective, based on empirical observations of phenomena or processes in everyday life. Conclusions are thus drawn from facts and observations (interpretivism) and are expressed as probabilities rather than certainties. Conclusions tend to be strong (convincing) or weak (unconvincing) rather than right or wrong. Inductive reasoning may provide a useful starting point for a research investigation, providing a platform for more systematic deductive research. As such, the two approaches should be seen as complementary paths towards theory-building (see Box 4.2) rather than strictly oppositional.

TABLE 4.2 Some Key Characteristics of the Deductive and Inductive Approaches to Research

Deductive Approach	Inductive Approach
Theory precedes investigation	Theory emerges from investigation
Top–down	Bottom–up
From broad generalisation to specific observations	From specific observations to broad generalisation
Typically associated with scientific method	Enquiry through rational evaluation
Hypotheses precede analysis	Propositions emerge as the investigation proceeds
Proof through analytical rigour	Proof through reasoning
Focus on causality	Focus on association
Predominantly quantitative	Predominantly qualitative
Rigid	Flexible
Focus on explaining 'what?'	Focus on explaining 'how?' and 'why?'

BOX 4.1

Inductive and Deductive Reasoning and the White Swan

This is an adaptation of a classic discussion of inductive and deductive reasoning which has its roots in Sir Francis Bacon's philosophical work of 1620, *Novum Organum* (New Logic; Bacon, 1902; see also Taleb, 2010).

An amateur ornithologist in the UK takes an interest in swans. They regularly encounter resident mute swans, which all have white plumage. Occasionally, during the winter migration season, they may also see whooper, Bewick and whistling swans which fly in from the northern tundra and are also white-plumaged. Over many years of close observation, they reach the inductive conclusion that all swans are white. They have used empirical observation spread over a significant period of time to reach this conclusion; theory is thus derived from observation. There are approximately 800,000 white swans in the world, but there are also some 500,000 black swans, which are native to Australasia and tend only to be found in very small numbers in other parts of the world, where they have been introduced as ornamental species. There are also proportionally very few white swans in Australia. So, an amateur ornithologist in Australia using inductive reasoning based on observation may well conclude that all swans are black. Neither theory is correct, but the inductive reasoning behind each is logical and – until evidence to the contrary presents itself – plausible. A UK ornithologist using deductive methods, in contrast, may start with the theory that all swans are white, but, being of an inquisitive disposition, then set out to test this proposition, using the simple hypothesis 'all swans are white'. A systematic investigation then ensues to gather data to test this hypothesis. If their data gathering takes them across the globe or they stumble on a non-native black swan, they are likely to find an evidential basis for rejecting their hypothesis. But, if they are restricted in the data gathering they can manage, they may well reach the same conclusion as the inductive ornithologist. The weakness in both cases lies not so much in the approach per se as in the scope of their research. Good research trumps poor research, whether inductive or deductive.

BOX 4.2

Induction and Deduction: A Hypothetical Example from the Field of Luxury

Let's take a hypothetical example from the field of luxury. A researcher perceives from frequent observation that Generation Z consumers are particularly drawn to social media channels and posts by luxury brands that make heavy use of K-pop stars. They decide to use netnography (internet-based ethnography) as a qualitative technique to look more deeply into the ways that the net-savvy younger generation is drawn to social media content that links K-pop stars with luxury brands. After collating and evaluating a substantial amount of social media content, they publish their principal finding, based on an inductive approach to research that moves towards theory from observation, that net-savvy Gen Z consumers are at the forefront of the confluence of pop culture and luxury today, and why they think this is the case. But, in the course of their investigation, the question arises as to what process is driving this phenomenon: is it luxury brands mobilising K-pop stars to position their products? Is the K-pop industry itself – and its commercial orientation – driving a process that others are keen to capitalise on? Or are the social media-saturated lives of Gen Z creating the conditions that both K-pop and luxury brands are keen to respond to? The researcher develops a series of hypotheses to enable them to test this directionality and uses a systematic survey to obtain data to allow these hypotheses to be tested empirically and scientifically. They thus start with a theoretical standpoint and either accept or support this through data analysis: deductive method. The whole process could just as easily have been conducted in reverse: a systematic investigation of Gen Z interaction with luxury brands and pop culture, followed by some case study research which adds depth, detail, nuance and context to the slightly depersonalised quantitative analysis.

LUXURY STUDIES: INDUCTIVE OR DEDUCTIVE?

Because luxury research draws most of its theoretical formulations from other disciplines, it is also something of a hostage to fortune in terms of the approaches to research that tend to dominate in these disciplines. Positivism and deductivism have historically been very influential in the fields of management studies, business studies, psychology and other branches of the social sciences, as the following quotation alludes: "a persistent assumption in IB [international business] research (and management disciplines more broadly) is that scientific knowledge is and should be context-free" (Welch *et al.*, 2022, 5). It is therefore not surprising that the hypothetico-deductive approach (forming and testing hypotheses in order to validate theories) is predominant in these fields (Woiceshyn and Daellenbach, 2018, 184) and tends to be reinforced by the institutions and gatekeepers that make up these disciplines. Openness towards alternative approaches to research tends to be somewhat constrained, although we can detect, in recent years, a growing number of inductivist and qualitative research studies in several of these disciplines (Turner *et al.*, 2021, 1), and this is beginning to filter into the field of luxury research, as we will see below.

Using data from the Web of Science, we looked at the 200 most recently published articles (in 2021) with 'luxury' in the title field in order to evaluate the methodological approach they adopted. This involved reading through and collating (in an Excel file) information from the methodology sections and other relevant parts of all publications. Forty were eliminated from the evaluation because their use of 'luxury' lay outside the conventional understanding of the concept from a luxury industry point of view. Of the 160 valid cases, 9 made no statement about methodology, and a further 16 were theoretical, conceptual or practical papers which made no use of a formal methodology or data (see Table 4.3). Of the remaining 135 articles on luxury, 102 (75.6%) adopted what might be broadly viewed as a deductive approach. Just over half (n = 73, 54.1%) used hypotheses to frame their investigation, and all (100%) applied quantitative methods to interrogate their data in order to test these hypotheses or answer research

TABLE 4.3 Philosophical and Methodological Approaches Adopted in the 160 Most Recent Publications on Luxury

Approach	Number
Hypothesis-testing	73 (54.1%)
Modelling	59 (43.7%)
Quantitative	102 (75.6%)
Quantitative, including mixed methods	113 (83.7%)
Mixed quantitative and qualitative	11 (8.2%)
Qualitative	22 (16.3%)
Qualitative, including mixed methods	33 (24.4%)
Valid cases	135 (100.0%)
Conceptual, theoretical or practical (invalid)	16
Unstated (invalid)	9
Total	160

Source: Web of Science database, July 2022.

questions. Twenty-two studies (16.3%) adopted an inductive and qualitative approach to their investigation. Included in these figures were 11 studies (8.2%) that adopted a mixed methods (quantitative and qualitative) approach. Thus, 83.7% adopted, fully or in part, a deductive and quantitative approach to their investigation. These figures are consistent with the findings of a similar but much smaller survey of management research articles by Pat Bazeley in 2008, who found that 60% of 35 articles adopted a purely deductive and quantitative approach, a further 22.8% employed a mixture of quantitative and qualitative methods, and only 17.1% might be considered purely qualitative studies (Bazeley, 2008, 135). These findings tend to reinforce the view that luxury research, by virtue of its intellectual association with certain academic disciplines, adopts a predominantly deductive approach to investigation. These data present a snapshot of luxury research at a moment in time (2021) and thus give no indication as to trends in the adoption of deductive and inductive research approaches in luxury studies across time.

SO, WHICH APPROACH SHOULD I ADOPT?

In planning an investigation, the student should ultimately decide which approach is most suitable for and compatible with the topic and objectives of their research, rather than enter the project oblivious to the choices available or blinkered by convention and predetermination. The foregoing discussion has tended to present the choices (deductive/inductive, realist/idealist, positivist/interpretivist, quantitative/qualitative) as oppositional and polarised, which is often how they are seen and treated in real life, but, in many ways, they are complementary and, indeed, should be viewed as continua rather than binaries. Both have their weaknesses and strengths, many of which are a product of perspective and positioning rather than inherent deficiencies. Good research makes use of the best intellectual and practical tools available and starts with an informed understanding of options and possibilities.

For a student undertaking dissertation research on a topic in the field of luxury, the choice of approach may be constrained by the conventions of the discipline on which they will focus for their investigation, or may in fact be specified by their supervisor or in the rubric for their project. Given a free choice, a student must bear in mind some of the considerations which were outlined in Chapter 3, most particularly 'do-ability' and capability: for instance, there is no value in adopting a hypothetico-deductive approach if the student is unlikely to obtain a strong, representative body of data and is not familiar with model-building and complex statistical analysis. As the student researcher in the field of luxury may typically be expected to explore a topical issue or problem in the broad sphere of luxury management, the choice of approach may boil down to whether their investigation should aim to distil reality into a series of variables that can be interrogated through quantitative analysis, or their study would gain from offering rich insight into how people individually and collectively engage with aspects of luxury. In ideal circumstances, the investigation could perhaps include a combination of both approaches. The choice may be influenced as much by the nature of the topic as by the personality of the researcher.

RESEARCH DESIGN

In Chapter 3, we discussed the various processes that might lead a student to selecting the topic for their research investigation. The next step is to develop that theme for the purposes of designing a research enquiry. Themes such as 'celebrity endorsement in luxury', 'the localisation of global luxury brands' or 'the use of social media in building luxury brand identity' do not have an obvious starting point or structure for an ensuing investigation. In the remainder of this chapter, we will introduce a number of devices to help the student with research design. We start by exploring how we can build an investigative structure around a theme or issue.

JOINED-UP THINKING

Much of research design is an intellectual rather than a mechanical process: it requires thinking deeply about the core elements of a chosen theme, how these elements can be organised into an investigative structure, and how terms are defined and operationalised. It is useful to start by constructing a mental map of the research topic as a way of identifying and logically arranging its various thematic components. This is best explained by way of some examples.

Our research theme here is *sustainable luxury*, one of the most pressing issues facing the industry and something that most brands have been taking very seriously over the last decade or so. A study as broadly defined as luxury and sustainability has no obvious point of focus, and without this the investigation would most likely end up as a broad survey of the current situation, probably using secondary sources such as literature- and web-based information about individual brands and luxury conglomerates. This would, of course, be interesting and useful, but it would be unlikely to satisfy any institutional stipulation that the investigation should be based on primary (i.e., self-generated) data derived from an enquiry that the student has designed themself. So, we need to determine an investigative focus and structure.

The first stage is to identify a number of keywords that relate to the chosen theme. There is no off-the-shelf formula for this intellectual stage of the research, and it is highly likely that mental maps constructed on the topic of sustainable luxury may differ widely. If the student already has an idea about which aspect of sustainable luxury they wish to concentrate on, this will help to streamline the list of keywords and the mental map that they will construct. This part of the process will be strongly influenced by the student's reading on, knowledge of, and intellectual capacity for processing, this knowledge. If you struggle at this point, it is possibly because you do not yet have the requisite knowledge about the subject in hand – in which case, read more – or you have not yet trained your mind to think abstractly about important contemporary issues. The exercise in Box 4.3 may help those who find it difficult to identify a cognate array of keywords around a chosen research topic.

BOX 4.3

Developing a 'Keyword Tree' for the Concept of Sustainable Luxury

If you are struggling to think of keywords that map out your chosen research theme, apply your imagination in creative ways to help the process. In this example, we looked to the literature for guidance with the aim of constructing a 'keyword tree'. The dendritic shape of most trees (and river systems) leads outwards (or, for rivers, inwards) from a core or trunk to the outer branches, which are all directly or indirectly connected to the main stem. In the same way, the individual components of a 'keyword tree' all connect, intellectually, to a central theme, either directly or indirectly. The keyword tree consists of a cognate array of keywords that are arranged in a logical and connected order, from which it should be possible to detect potential investigative storylines.

A search of the Web of Science using the phrase "sustainable luxury" yielded a total of 52 academic articles published between 2012 and 2022. Reading the literature review sections of these articles would be invaluable and, eventually, essential in building up students' understanding of the key components of this debate, but we used a shortcut to help set the process in motion. We copied the abstracts from all 52 papers (these are freely available in the Web of Science database) into a single Word file. We then used word count software (we used NVivo, but there are many websites which provide free software for this purpose; see Chapter 7) to identify which words were most frequently used by the authors of these papers. Sifting relevant from irrelevant words requires some knowledge of the subject and a little patience. Having narrowed the words down to the most important and relevant, we then produced a word cloud (shown on the right-hand side of Figure 4.1) which contains the material from which we then (manually) constructed our keyword tree. This, too, is an intellectual process

FIGURE 4.1 Keyword Tree and Word Cloud, Sustainable Luxury. Data from Web of Science, provided by Clarivate.

which requires not only a sound knowledge of the subject but also the ability to visualise how the keywords might be arranged in a logical structure that flows from the extremities (concepts or processes that are only indirectly connected to sustainable luxury) to the core stem. We have built into this arrangement 'brand' and 'consumer' halves of the tree. This can be a useful starting point to building 'mental maps', which is discussed below. The exercise is not fail-safe: several themes that are relevant to sustainable luxury, such as the circular economy, were not included in the abstracts but might have emerged from the literature review sections. This exercise is not a substitute for reading and understanding!

Data source: Web of Science database, October 2022

In contrast to the exercise outlined in Box 4.3, the keywords contained in Figure 4.2 were put together by one of the authors based upon their extensive academic involvement in sustainable development from a geography and development studies background. So, sustainable luxury does not exist in a vacuum: both its intellectual background and practical application are rooted in wider processes and movements that are taking place in the world and into which the luxury industry is fundamentally integrated. Thus, we start with the capitalist economic system – which arguably underlies the ecological and social pressures we are presently seeking to combat – and the process of economic globalisation – which has drawn all parts of the world into its sphere of influence, to a greater or lesser degree. A fundamental ingredient of both processes is mass consumption, and a highly influential factor in the environmental consequences

Joined-Up Thinking: Sustainable Luxury

KEYWORDS

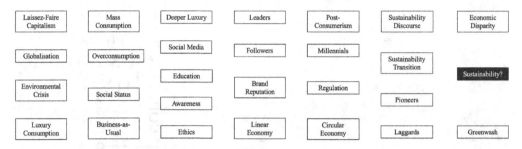

FIGURE 4.2 Sustainable Luxury: Keywords.

of global capitalist development is overconsumption. This is, of course, a subject of much debate and is something the researcher will no doubt already have explored in their literature-based engagement with the challenge of sustainability. We see it as an important ingredient and, therefore, include it in our *conceptual model*. In practice, the researcher is likely to refine their list of keywords, and their arrangement in the model may go through several iterations.

Luxury consumption, driven in part by considerations of social status, contributes to environmental damage and the depletion of the world's natural resources, perhaps symbolically more than substantively because, by definition, it centres on non-essential consumption, even though its proportional footprint is in fact quite small. Inequality can also never be very far from any discussion of luxury consumption. Debates about the extent of the sustainability crisis include advocates of a business-as-usual evolutionary approach and those who put the planet before profit, including advocates of 'deeper luxury'. Regardless, we are undeniably in the midst of a quite thoroughgoing sustainability transition. A prerequisite for sustainability action and the ethics that underpin this is awareness, to which education and social media make a valuable contribution. In the process of change there will be leaders and followers: those who chart a path and those who eventually join the journey, for whatever reasons and with varying degrees of conviction and commitment. Change *is* happening, with sustainability discourse now widespread and with the circular economy beginning to take over from the linear model of produce, consume, dispose, repeat. Post-consumerism even raises its head as a movement that challenges many of the assumptions of the modern economy, with, debatably, the younger generations at the forefront of this attitudinal, even moral, shift. Luxury brands, concerned about their reputations, have signed up to the principles of sustainability, some leading the way, others joining the movement rather late in the day; some because they see it as the right thing to do, others because the regulators are forcing their arm. But fundamental to all the above is what 'sustainability' actually means, and whether – especially if we adopt a more radical or idealist stance – much of the action – and the publicity that often accompanies brands' sustainability efforts – constitutes a greening or a greenwashing of luxury.

This is just one of many storylines for sustainable luxury and at least provides a starting point for an arrangement of conceptual elements, as shown in the schema in Figure 4.3. The organisation of the constituent elements is fundamentally an intellectual or logical process

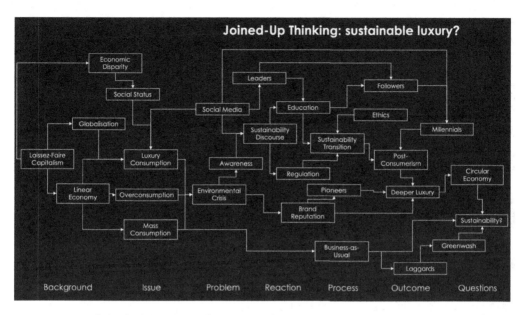

FIGURE 4.3 Sustainable Luxury: Conceptual Diagram.

which places the keywords at, debatably, the relevant stage of an evolutionary process. We have identified the sustainability *issue* and *problem*, and some of the *background* factors that lie behind it. We highlight the point at which actors *react* to the problem and the ensuing *processes* and actors that underpin the shift in the direction of sustainability, leading to some of the *outcomes* that we can see today, albeit with *questions* remaining about its utility, given the nature of the environmental crisis facing the world.

One may ask whether it is necessary to include so many elements if the research focus is on, say, the link between the younger generations and post-consumerism, or whether it is luxury consumers or luxury brands who are driving the sustainability agenda. We would argue that a wider conceptual diagram serves two purposes: it helps to identify some of the elements that need to be engaged with leading up to the research focus – for example, in the literature review – and it aids the identification of research questions and outlines the context within which they are placed.

IDENTIFYING A RESEARCH FOCUS

Identifying a research theme or topic is an essential starting point for an investigation but is insufficient, in itself, as a guide to the researcher. In the present example, the theme 'sustainable luxury' is simply too broad and fluid to allow identification of a clear starting point, and the conceptual model is too all-inclusive to allow specification of a point of focus. Figure 4.3 contains 28 elements and multiple linkages between them, both arranged in a logical (but not incontrovertible) order. Each and every box and connection could provide a subject for closer examination. Figure 4.4 takes the conceptual model and suggests six elements that might provide a focus for a research investigation at the 'business end' of the model.

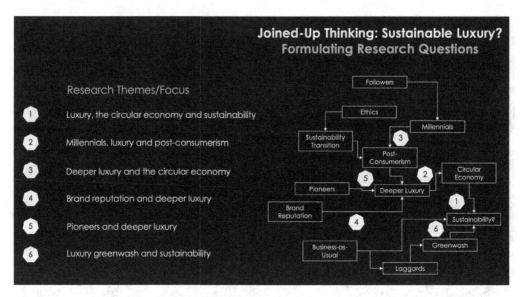

FIGURE 4.4 Identifying a Research Focus.

FORMULATING RESEARCH QUESTIONS

Research questions are an essential organisational device for any research investigation. They help define its boundaries, parameters and limits, give it clear direction and purpose, and provide a crucial reference point for evaluating whether the enquiry has achieved its objectives. The research question should ask something that we do not already know in order to satisfy the requirements of originality and usefulness. Research questions also help to identify the approach the research might adopt and the methods it might deploy.

Where do research questions come from? This, too, is fundamentally an intellectual process informed by the student's wider grasp and understanding of the topic and the context within which it is placed, which re-emphasises the value of the conceptual diagram discussed above. This is the point at which the student takes control of the research and imprints their personality on the investigation. Research questions should be clear and unambiguous (i.e., not containing multiple questions or vague phraseology) and should quite obviously be answerable (or testable if framed as hypotheses), and the outcomes should be achievable within the constraints of the time, resources and capabilities available to the researcher. Figure 4.5 suggests a series of research questions which operationalise the six focal themes that were identified in Figure 4.4.

Research questions might be:

- *Descriptive*: for example, what are the characteristics of the luxury market in China's first-tier cities? This might lead to new knowledge, but it lacks an investigative focus.
- *Explorative*: for example, do luxury brand extensions affect how consumers feel about these brands? "Feel" in this question would need further clarification. What is the impact of KOLs on luxury brand equity? We might prefer to ask about the impact on sales, but the requisite data may be hard to come by.

Joined-Up Thinking: sustainable luxury?
Deriving research themes from the mental map

Research Themes/Focus

1. Is the growth of the circular economy a meaningful contributor to sustainable luxury?
2. What is the connection between 'deeper luxury' and the growth of the circular economy?
3. What is the contribution of younger luxury consumers to progress towards sustainable luxury?
4. To what extent is concern about brand reputation a factor in progress towards sustainable luxury?
5. What actors/processes are making the most significant contribution to sustainable luxury?
6. Is action deep/profound enough to constitute sustainable luxury?

FIGURE 4.5 Formulating Research Questions from the Thematic Focus.

- *Evaluative*: for example, how effective have luxury brand collaborations with streetwear brands been in appealing to Generation Z consumers?
- *Explanatory*: for example, how can we explain failures in some luxury brands' localisation strategies?
- *Predictive*: for example, will the use of blockchain prove to be an effective way of preventing infringements of luxury brands' IP (intellectual property), such as through counterfeiting? Predictive investigations may be very valuable from the perspective of luxury brand management, but any research investigation that looks into the future is fraught with difficulties.
- *Comparative*: for example, what are the key differences in consumer behaviour between fine wine consumers in Britain, the Netherlands, Germany, France and Italy? As well as paying more attention to what is meant by "consumer behaviour", it is imperative that such studies should be centred on a legitimate basis for comparison and should also include informative contextual material.
- *Experimental*: for example, do millennials/Gen Z feel differently about themselves when given the chance to wear luxury apparel/carry luxury accessories? This could be evaluated by means of a lab-based experiment.

A NESTED HIERARCHY OF RESEARCH QUESTIONS

A very useful device for framing a research investigation is to use *multiple research questions*, hierarchically layered – what we call a "nested hierarchy of research questions" (see Figure 4.6). We start with a principal or *primary research question* (PRQ), such as those outlined above, but we break this question into subordinate but essentially cognate *secondary research questions*

(SRQs; and even *tertiary research questions*: TRQs). The rationale behind this approach is that the main research question, intended as a point of focus for the research, may still be a little too broad to be useful for helping to frame the investigation that will follow. There may well be angles and sub-elements that lie behind the PRQ which are also worthy of investigation (as we will demonstrate below), perhaps individually, but, because they are cognate to the principal question, they all join up thematically and intellectually. The formulation of SRQs (and TRQs) allows the investigation to be broken down into focused components, which might be explored in different ways, using secondary and primary sources, for instance, or quantitative and qualitative techniques.

A further, very important advantage of the nested hierarchy approach is that it aids analysis and organisation of the writing-up of the research. Ultimately, the aim of the research is to provide an informed answer to the main research question. Completing the analysis of the SRQs provides the building blocks of an overall answer to this question. Viewed schematically, the nested hierarchy forms a pyramid, with the main research purpose at its pinnacle and the investigation spread out and disassembled below (solid lines and arrows in Figure 4.6); at the analysis and writing-up stage, the pyramid is inverted, and all paths lead back towards the main research question (broken lines and arrows in Figure 4.6).

A third advantage of this method is that it helps to specify the boundaries or parameters of the investigation: everything inside the pyramid is a point of focus for the enquiry; nothing outside the pyramid is relevant to the research. Figure 4.7 is an alternative way of representing the nested hierarchy; it emphasises the cognate character of the individual elements and the clear boundaries that surround the research investigation.

The PRQ guides our thinking and assists with project organisation. It helps map out the broad scope of the investigation. The PRQ should not be so broad as to become unmanageable or so narrow as to be too restrictive. As we discussed in Chapter 2, the level of profundity of the

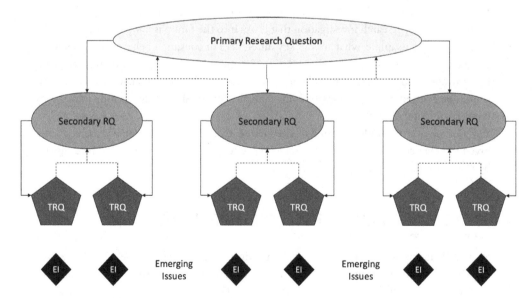

FIGURE 4.6 A Nested Hierarchy of Research Questions.

PRQ: Principal Research Question

SRQ: Secondary Research Question

TRQ: Tertiary Research Question

**A Nested Hierarchy
of Research
Questions**

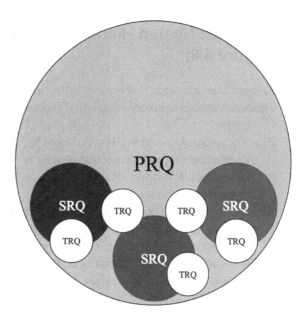

FIGURE 4.7 The Nested Hierarchy of Research Questions and the Boundaries of the Research.

PRQ will be determined in part by the level of the enquiry – industry data collecting, Master's dissertation, PhD thesis, academic research – and in part by the resources, time and expertise available to the researcher. The PRQ is a key source of orientation and discipline. Formulating a suitable and effective research question is a crucial early step that provides a point of focus and structure, and a basis for *efficiency* in an investigation. It helps to link the researcher's literature review to the kinds of data that will need to be collected. It plays a pivotal role in the research, because decisions about research design and methods must be made in order to yield answers to the PRQ. Research questions should be clear, concise, intelligible, researchable; neither too abstract nor too ambitious. Ultimately, they should relate to and chart a path towards advancing the existing body of knowledge.

The SRQs and TRQs help break the PRQ down into component elements, direct the empirical investigation and help further to *specify* the investigation or study. They are subordinate to, but fundamentally connected with, the PRQ: if this is not the case, they may lead to multiple, parallel investigations rather than a single integrated piece of research.

The PRQ and SRQs are not predetermined: they are something that the researcher takes control of, and that gives the research the investigator's DNA. There may be a range of possibilities to select from (as was also the case with the conceptual model that we introduced earlier: Figures 4.3 and 4.4), the choice of which may be informed by the researcher's preferences, interests, needs and capabilities, but may be restricted by any institutional requirements or disciplinary constraints. The RQs should be pitched appropriately between breadth/generality and depth/focus, with a leaning towards the latter. The SRQs should quite obviously be more focused than the PRQ and must obviously be cognate with the thematic focus of the PRQ. Box 4.4 is an operational example of the nested hierarchy of research questions.

BOX 4.4

Example: Nested Hierarchy of Research Questions (Figure 4.8)

Research area: counterfeiting and luxury intellectual property protection.
Research problem: luxury intellectual property protection is an unwinnable battle.
Primary research question: "Is it possible to have an effective international intellectual property protection regime [e.g., TRIPS: Trade-Related Aspects of Intellectual Property Rights] for luxury goods when national legal systems and provisions are so variable?"
Secondary research questions: "What factors influence variations in the enforcement of IP protection legislation at the national level?" "How is international IP protection legislation communicated at the national and sub-national levels?" "What bottom–up mechanisms exist to ensure that the international IP protection regime is relevant to and workable in national and local situations?"
Tertiary research areas: how deeply rooted are the principles of IP protection within local societies? How does "Realpolitik" influence the degree of commitment to enforcement of national legislation? Who is responsible for IP protection messaging at the national and sub-national levels? What do local people feel about IP protection legislation? Is the notion of IP protection sufficiently "localised"? What channels exist for incorporating a localised perspective into the framing of IP protection measures?
Emerging issues: assumptions of variation, access to grassroots insight, operationalising "Realpolitik" and localisation, identifying the tension between words and deeds, information on the extent of counterfeiting, gaining access to key stakeholders.

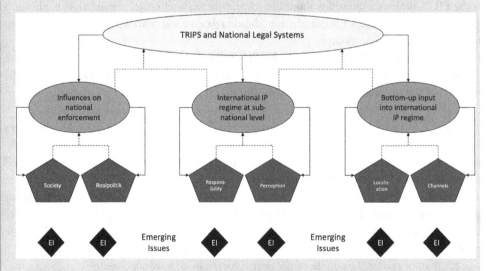

FIGURE 4.8 Nested Hierarchy of Research Questions for International IP Protection.

EMERGING ISSUES

When formulating research questions – be that a single question or a hierarchical assembly of questions – it is useful to reflect at an early stage on some of the challenges that the researcher is likely to encounter when building a framework for their investigation. These are indicated as "emerging issues" in Figure 4.6 and are resonant with the discussion of *operationalisation* in the previous chapter. Abstract ideas need to be concretised in order to provide a workable platform on which to build a research investigation.

In the example in Box 4.4, we must first consider whether the proposed investigation is based upon an assumed premise that may not stand up to closer scrutiny: that the enforcement of legislation that is intended to protect luxury intellectual property is quite variable across the world. Furthermore, if this premise holds – which seems likely – the researcher would also need to be confident that such variability may be explained by contextual factors such as knowledge, awareness, concern, culture and politics, and by underlying external/internal and top–down/bottom–up tensions. Clearly, an investigation that extended to the entire global system would be unmanageable in the time available, and thus the empirical focus would have to be narrowed to a small number of settings, possibly explored comparatively, or a single country case study. That choice would have to be based upon the setting's consonance with the investigative framework being developed and may also be guided by data availability and the likelihood of the researcher being able to access the actors and stakeholders who have the knowledge and insight needed to address the research questions. The researcher would also have to ensure that their investigation had a specific focus on luxury IP, otherwise it might end up as a more generic evaluation of IP protection enforcement. Counterfeiting and fake luxury are a central area of concern here, but both are quite sensitive topics and notoriously difficult (and potentially dangerous) to unearth. Accordingly, the researcher might wish to focus on the formulation and enforcement of IP protection legislation explicitly and leave counterfeiting as an implicit component of the enquiry.

The engagement with and resolution of "emerging issues" are referred to as *specification*, which is a crucial stage in the research process and a precursor to the design of an appropriate methodology. Part of the process of specification is the *operationalisation* of key concepts and ideas, which may often be too vague or abstract to provide a tangible basis for further investigation. In the example above, concepts such as "Realpolitik" and "localisation" require breaking down into constituent elements.

A study by Shukla, Rosendo-Rios and Khalifa (2022) gives us a recent illustration of how the broad concept 'democratisation of luxury' might be operationalised. This frequently used umbrella term in fact incorporates a wide range of processes that are presently manifest in, and have a profound impact upon, the luxury industry. These include the forces of globalisation, the growing number of affluent and middle-class consumers in developing countries, and the associated emergence of new markets for luxury goods around the world. This 'global shift' has also precipitated social change, including the increased social and economic role of women, delayed marriage, smaller families, more leisure time, and so on. Meanwhile, advances in technology and social media have been 'shrinking' the world while spreading consumerist values more widely. Many luxury brands, especially the larger conglomerates, have shifted production facilities to low-cost, labour-rich locations in developing regions and, at the same time, have developed strategies to capitalise on geographically and socially expanding markets. Hitherto localised luxury brands have globalised and have readily embraced both mass production and mass consumption, with a growing prevalence of 'masstige' brands and downward brand extensions which, to some observers, have quite fundamentally transformed the character and essence of 'luxury': its distinctiveness, exclusivity and the self-differentiation of luxury brands (Shukla et al., 2022, 784–785). All of these processes, and more, are subsumed within the single, simple phrase 'democratisation of luxury', which quite evidently provides only a very abstract basis for building a research investigation. Any one of the above-mentioned trends could provide a topic for deeper investigation, with 'democratisation' providing the broad, literature-based theoretical context within which it is placed. It is also worth pointing out that a study by Collier and Levitsky in 1997 identified more than 550 definitions of the word 'democracy', which Shukla et al. (2022, 792) boiled down to 44 aspects that were relevant to the context of luxury, before settling on just 8 as the basis for their own investigation.[2]

SUMMARY AND CONCLUSION

This chapter has focused on some of the intellectual processes that are involved in building an investigative research framework, using examples from the field of luxury. We have once again emphasised the importance of keywords in helping to define the 'skeleton' of a research investigation, to be fleshed out in due course by the 'meat' of empirical data gathering, analysis and interpretation. Having organised the key components of the research topic into a logical structure which identifies a clear focal point for the research, a layered series of research questions is then formulated to guide and shape the subsequent investigation. It is at this point that the researcher needs to give careful attention to identifying and specifying the epistemological and methodological approach(es) that best suits the character, objectives and possibilities of their research enquiry. The remaining chapters of this book will introduce the student to different aspects of research methodology to help inform their choice of approach and technique.

NOTES

1 In the last 10 years, 91.2% of all luxury publications appearing on the Web of Science were in English; of the 8.2% written in other languages, only 0.2% were Asian or African languages (Web of Science database, accessed 22 September 2022).
2 These were: differentiation, distinctiveness, exclusivity, mass ownership, mass production, rarity, regular and uniqueness.

CHAPTER 5

Data for Luxury Research

Obtaining data is a crucial stage of any piece of primary research, whether it be a scientific study of the ecological footprint of luxury fashion brands, which may rely on generating and statistically analysing copious volumes of numerical data, or a qualitative study of luxury customers' sensory reaction to in-store atmospherics, which may document shoppers' feelings, emotions and aesthetic appreciation expressed principally in words. Just as the nature of research varies considerably, as we discussed in Chapter 3, so too the word 'data' (and its singular form, 'datum') covers a diverse array of forms and characteristics. The aim of this chapter is to introduce the student of luxury to the nature of data, some principal sources of data as an input for luxury research and analysis, the challenge of representativeness, as well as legal and ethical considerations when obtaining and using data.

THE NATURE OF DATA

In undertaking research, we set out to inform our understanding of the research topic and to find ways of answering our research questions. To help us achieve our objectives we make use of information and data – words which are often used interchangeably. But there is an important technical distinction to be drawn between the two. *Data* are raw and unstructured elements – facts, figures, values, measurements, observations, records – which have limited intrinsic meaning until processed or interpreted: imagine a spreadsheet full of numbers which may seem meaningless unless given labels and organised by data processing. *Information* has meaning and may be a source of knowledge; it informs. In a research project, information may be both an input into and output from our investigation: the existing body of knowledge consists of information which is of value to us and is derived from past research and other forms of intellectual endeavour, including the gathering and processing of data. It provides the platform upon which we can build our own enquiry, which aims to advance knowledge and understanding in its chosen field, typically through an original exercise in data gathering and processing. In simple terms, we use existing information to build an investigation, which helps us build a framework for obtaining and analysing data, from which we derive fresh information which is hopefully of interest and value to those who access and use it.

DOI: 10.4324/9781003295372-5

PRINCIPAL FORMS OF DATA

Data which have some value for research can generally be derived from two distinct types of sources: secondary and primary. *Secondary data* have been created by a party other than the researcher. These may consist of pure data (such as sales figures, costs, prices, footfall, market dynamics) or publicly available information which the researcher can convert into data for the purposes of their investigation, such as blogposts, comments, likes and shares on social media. *Primary data* are collected by the researcher themselves from first-hand sources, such as by using methods that we will explore in detail in Chapter 6. An advantage of using primary data for research is that the researcher is in control of the methodology and can set the data parameters, whereas, with secondary data, these will have been determined by another party and may have to be converted for the specific purposes of the researcher. Primary data can also be collected in real time, whereas there may be a time lag with data from secondary sources.

Fundamentally, data can be divided into two forms: numerical and non-numerical. *Numerical data*, obviously, take the form of numbers which derive from phenomena that are measurable or quantifiable (e.g., sales, materials costs, carbon footprint). *Non-numerical data* take any form that does not consist of numbers, are derived from observation not measurement, and may be categorical (e.g., gender, education level, yes/no, preferred luxury brands), descriptive (e.g., words/text that convey some meaning, such as emotions or satisfaction, or even poetry) and many other forms which we might not conventionally think of as data (e.g., music, art, photographs, advertisements, video). Numerical data are amenable to analysis using arithmetic or statistical tools, whereas other techniques must be applied when processing and interpreting non-numerical data.

A significant weakness in luxury research (and many other kinds of research) is the tendency for investigations to consist of a 'snapshot' – a view of a particular phenomenon or process at a single moment in time. This is inevitable given the conventional sequencing of a research project – problem identification, question formulation, methodology design, data gathering and processing, analysis, interpretation and presentation of findings – all usually to a finite and often tight delivery timetable and deadline. A student wishing to look at trends across time will find it extremely challenging: their own research will have to fit into a single time window, and so self-generated *time-series* or *longitudinal data* will be very difficult to obtain; they will therefore have to rely on time-series data generated by secondary sources, which may also be difficult to access, or they will have to rely on recall and reconstruction by present-day research participants, which is often a flawed process.

In an ideal world, longitudinal data would consist of findings from the same cohort of people or segment of the luxury industry who have been asked exactly the same questions across a significantly meaningful period of time – say 20 years. One could then trace, with accuracy and certainty, the evolution in performance, behaviour or attitude across time. Such research may have started as a snapshot but evolved into a time series. The imaginative researcher can find ways of reconstructing the past. For example, most estate agents these days provide quite detailed information, often freely available in the public domain, on house prices over time, so that a researcher interested in luxury housing price trends, linked to spatial or locational factors, could use these data as a reasonably reliable basis for a time-series investigation (Walters and Carr, 2015). Similarly, using media reports across time, it should be possible to reconstruct the evolution of opinions on certain aspects of luxury.

Research that looks at a particular issue *longitudinally* (across time) is extremely rare in luxury: a search of the Web of Science database using 'luxury' in the title field and 'longitudinal' in all fields yielded just eight studies since 1900, all in fact undertaken since 2008. One additional study used the phrase 'time-series' rather than longitudinal. The word 'longitudinal' appeared in two further studies – both pointing to the need for more time-series research in the field of luxury![1]

QUANTITATIVE AND QUALITATIVE DATA

In Chapter 4, we introduced the distinction between quantitative and qualitative approaches to research. Although not strictly synonymous, we will broadly characterise numerical data as quantitative and non-numerical data as qualitative. The root of *quantitative* is having quantity; thus, quantitative data typically represent aspects of the world in the form of numbers. But, look out of the window and you will see very few aspects of social life with numbers attached to them! The challenge – and potential weakness – of quantitative methods is the need, therefore, to convert aspects of the social world into numerical form, rendering its intricate fluidities measurable. The conversion process (measurement, categorisation) is potentially fraught with pitfalls, but numerical data also offer many advantages: for example, ease of use and precision at the analysis stage, consistency, replicability, non-ambiguity. Measurement requires the identification of indicators which will represent a concept or its component elements. This requires flair, imagination, understanding, accuracy and authenticity. There is an inevitable trade-off between the potential benefits of quantitative analysis and its shortcomings.

Rendering the social world measurable – converting observed phenomena into a numerical form – requires human judgement and, inevitably, a degree of generalisation or simplification (the social world is often more complex than research can sometimes handle; see Box 5.1). The perceived degree of precision from using quantitative or scientific methods in social research can be misleading: categories and measurements are not natural but are created, based on judgements and interpretations. This leaves much scope for error and inaccuracy. So, although the (e.g., statistical) techniques that are used to analyse numerical data may be rigorous and scientific, the data themselves may be suspect. It is thus expedient for the researcher of luxury to reflect on the validity and accuracy of the numerical data they are using rather than simply assuming that, by using numbers and sophisticated statistical analysis, their research can be deemed to be sufficiently scientific.

BOX 5.1

Converting Personality Traits into Numbers

The luxury research literature is replete with studies which explore the influence of various social and psychological factors on different aspects of luxury consumption. Taking just one example at random from the recent literature: in April 2021, Christian Navia and colleagues published an article exploring the influence of various personality traits on middle-aged female fashion consumers' inclination to participate in 'collaborative consumption' – the shared use of luxury fashion products through renting, swapping or using second-hand markets (Navia, Khire and Lyver, 2021). The personality traits they were interested in were: the need for uniqueness; fashion leadership; and materialism. We will just focus on the need for uniqueness here. This is quite a complex socio-psychological phenomenon and has been defined by Tien and colleagues as "an individual's pursuit of differentness relative to others that is achieved through the acquisition, utilization, and disposition of consumer goods for the purpose of developing and enhancing one's personal and social identity" (Tien, Bearden and Hunter, 2001, 50). These are thus personalised actions, driven by a psychological need and influenced by a perceived place in society and the potential for consumer goods to signal or reinforce that place, all linked to identity and social positioning. To boil all these elements down into an array of numbers and a single variable for the purposes of quantitative analysis is quite a challenge.

As is very typical of much quantitative research in the field of luxury, the authors created what is called a 'latent variable' (discussed further in Chapter 7) for 'need for uniqueness' based on research participants' responses to three statements (Navia et al., 2021, 518).[2] These responses were recorded on a five-point Likert scale (see Chapter 6) that ranged from "strongly disagree" to "strongly agree". The operationalisation of 'need for uniqueness' was guided by a previous study (Lang and Armstrong, 2018; they used a six-point Likert scale that avoided a neutral option) which had used similar indicators in a broadly similar research investigation.

On the face of it, reducing a highly complex socio-psychological phenomenon to three simplified elements (two of which are actually quite similar), which range in scores from 1 to 5, in order to have numerical values that can be used for statistical analysis is boiling real life down to its barest bones, but this is a very common practice in quantitative research. However, if one traces the operationalisation of 'need for uniqueness' back to its intellectual origins, we find that both studies (Navia et al., 2021; Lang and Armstrong, 2018) drew their framework from a remarkably detailed and thoroughgoing operationalisation exercise undertaken by Tien et al. in 2001, which in fact explored 31 factors (ways of identifying need for uniqueness in order to build a latent variable),[3] divided into three groups[4] and all verified using sophisticated statistical techniques to identify those which most powerfully indicated need for uniqueness (Tien et al., 2001, 55–56). This study has become the benchmark for subsequent research involving this variable.

Reducing complex social phenomena to a series of numbers and a single variable is established practice in quantitative research, including much of the research on luxury, and is typically the end-result of extensive exercises in validation that have provided the key identifiers which have subsequently been used by a wide array of researchers. It is not our place to judge the validity of such a practice, not least because it is so widespread, but we feel it is incumbent on the researcher of luxury to reflect on the nature, origins and general representativeness of the numerical data they are using, rather than adopting them unquestioningly.

The foundational element of *qualitative* is qualities (features), which tend to be represented by words rather than numbers. The advantage of qualitative work is that it theoretically delivers a closer, more nuanced and flexible approximation to 'reality' than can be achieved through the reduction of social life to numbers. Qualitative research can be highly fluid or rigidly structured and systematic, depending partly on preference and partly on need. As a result, there may be a greater or lesser tendency to build the research around predetermined categories and structures. Predetermining categories means that the structure of the research, the data and the analysis are influenced by the researcher rather than by the subjects of the research: there may be more subjectivity, and thus more scope for human bias or misjudgement to distort the 'true' character of the data. The less formally structured the research is according to predetermined categories, the more structure should emerge at the interpretation and analysis stages (inductivism). While the inductive approach 'allows the data to speak for themselves', the more fluid, varied and unstructured the qualitative data are, the greater is the difficulty of handling them, which is one of the biggest challenges of the qualitative approach. Fluid data rarely deliver consistent, precise or unambiguous results and are very difficult to standardise when compared with quantitative methods. But qualitative epistemology in any case challenges the need for data standardisation as a basic requirement of research. The researcher's desire for generalised clarity and workability is in tension with the particularism (the quality of being individual) that typifies social reality.

Qualitative research is an aid to the acquisition of knowledge through the experiencing of the social world, but the representation of that experience as knowledge constitutes a significant challenge. The words we use become 'a researcher-constructed text', and so the researcher using qualitative data needs to exercise self-awareness, critical reflectivity, care, skill, imagination, humility and democracy.

Qualitative research thus involves a trade-off between accuracy/representativeness and ease/efficiency. The same might also be said of quantitative research. And, at the end of the day, it is also quite difficult to remove the thumbprint of the researcher from both qualitative and quantitative research.

In Table 5.1, we have attempted to summarise the key characteristics of quantitative and qualitative data and the principal differences between them. The table also incorporates some of the epistemological principles that were introduced in Chapter 4. The table deliberately presents an oppositional character for the quantitative and the qualitative in order to emphasise their key defining features, but the reality for all of these elements is that they tend to be placed at points on a *continuum* between these two extremes, rather than being strictly dichotomous.

SOURCES OF DATA

Data for research and analysis can either be *primary* – gathered by the researcher themself from first-hand sources, also referred to as *self-generated data* – or *secondary* – data that have been created by an individual or institution other than the researcher, or through a procedure that has not been directly controlled by the researcher. To this we might add an in-between category of *primary data gathered from secondary sources*, where the researcher is not directly involved in the

TABLE 5.1 The Key Characteristics and Differences of Quantitative and Qualitative Data

	Quantitative	Qualitative
Character	Numbers	Words, audio, video, images, etc.
Focus	Behaviour	Meaning
Viewpoint	Viewpoint of the researcher	Viewpoint of the subject
Proximity	Researcher is distant	Researcher is close
Scale	Macro	Micro
Flow	Static	Process
Setting	Artificial settings	Natural settings
Theory	Theory tested in the research	Theory emerges from the research
Structure	Structured	Unstructured
Engagement	Detached	Engaged
Emphasis	Generalisation	Contextualisation
Data	Hard, rigid, reliable data	Fluid, rich, deep data
Representativeness	Typically a probability-based sample – broadly representative	Usually a non-probability-based sample – narrowly representative
Generalisation	Generalisable	Non-generalisable
Answers	Answers how many? When? Where?	Answers why? How?
Epistemology	Deductive; tests hypotheses	Inductive; formative
Data handling	Data handling more efficient, but lacks contextual detail, insight	Rich data, but time-consuming to analyse
Design	Design decided in advance	Design emerges as study unfolds
Instrument	The tools are the instrument; the researcher is less paramount	The researcher is the instrument

generation of the data but makes use of publicly or commercially available information for the purposes of their own primary analysis.

The following discussion will focus on the latter sub-category, as the self-generation of primary data will be the principal thematic focus of Chapter 6. Before we start exploring some of the sources of data for luxury research, it is worth reflecting on the meaning of 'self-generated' – the key differentiator between primary and secondary data – as the distinction between these categories has become slightly more blurred across time. Back in the day, surveys (the principal means of obtaining primary data) had to be conducted face to face or by post. Face-to-face interviewing tended to be somewhat localised, whereas postal questionnaires made a wider geographical span logistically more straightforward, and less costly than extensive travel. The advent of electronic mail speeded up the postal survey process, allowing more people to be reached in more locations more quickly, and it may have precipitated a reduction in face-to-face contact and, with it, less direct control over the data extraction process. With greater use of the internet, online surveys (in combination with electronic mail) became more commonplace, potentially reaching most corners of the globe almost instantly. Zoom, Microsoft Teams, Google Meet, Skype and other video-conferencing platforms allowed the retention of a face-to-face option in the data gathering process. More recently, there has been a proliferation of online commercial firms offering various survey and other data gathering services to researchers; although the latter retain responsibility for, and control over, the design of the research tools they use, and may sometimes suggest a body of participants to be targeted for their research, they often have several components of the data generation (and analysis) process undertaken for them by the commercial providers, including building research panels for data generation (referred to as *crowdsourcing*). Although any facility that helps increase speed and convenience in data collection is surely welcome, a question mark hangs over the extent to which the wide availability and use of both commercially available services and free public-domain software (freeware, shareware) for data gathering, together with the remoteness and impersonality of online media, diminish the depth and breadth of the learning experience of the student seeking to generate data for luxury research, and their first-hand familiarity with their research participants.

SECONDARY DATA

A distinction should be drawn between secondary literature, secondary sources, secondary information and secondary data. *Secondary literature* conventionally refers to published sources which do not use primary data or research, but instead review or collate information from a variety of sources, including previous primary research, which may be presented in the form of a review article, meta-analysis or state-of-the-art overview of a particular research field. The bibliographic citation analysis of luxury research by Gurzki and Woisetschläger (2016) that was discussed in Chapter 2 is an example of research based on secondary literature. For the student researcher of luxury, *secondary sources* would include output that is produced and presented outside the conventional structures of academic publishing, most particularly the rigorous process of *peer review*, which helps to assure the quality (academic rigour, degree of originality, appropriate methodology, validity of argument and findings) of published work. Secondary sources – which may include conference proceedings, in-house reports by luxury brands or industry commentators, weblogs and vlogs – can be informative and rich sources of insight into current trends in the luxury market, but would generally be seen by an examiner to constitute an insufficiently authoritative basis upon which to build a scholarly argument. For this reason, secondary sources are sometimes referred to as '*grey literature*'.

At the beginning of this chapter, we drew a distinction between unprocessed *data* and meaningful *information*. As such, *secondary information* would consist of material that has been produced by someone other than the researcher but may be of value as background material for their own research. A great many organisations (e.g., Statista,[5] Bain and Company,[6] McKinsey,[7] Deloitte,[8] Euromonitor International[9]) produce regular reports on the current state of the luxury market and its component elements, and the information they contain helps keep the researcher of luxury up to date with current trends and developments. Bain and Company, for instance, has been producing a luxury goods worldwide market study every year since 2000, which is based on longitudinal data collected by its luxury goods worldwide market observatory database covering 280 or so luxury companies and brands. Its latest report from this series, "From Surging Recovery to Elegant Advance: The Evolving Future of Luxury", was produced in December 2021 (D'Arpizio *et al.*, 2021). This is an example of a company that generates its own data which are digested and presented as secondary information to a public readership and, in a more detailed form, to its corporate clients. Such luxury industry reports can be valuable to the student researcher in helping to inform a background discussion of an aspect of luxury on which their investigation focuses: for example, placing an academic literature-based theoretical discussion in a real-world context, prior to explaining the basis of their own primary investigation (see Chapter 8). Such secondary information would not generally be considered to be authoritative enough in academic terms to provide the intellectual foundation for the research investigation as a whole.

A number of commercial organisations also produce primary data which can be made available to clients on a commercial basis or, more typically, digested for them to help them gain insight into their market segment. For the student researcher of luxury, these would be considered to be *secondary data* as they have not been gathered by the researcher themself. Companies such as Statista and Fortune Business Insights[10] produce luxury market outlooks which are available to corporate clients, but these would generally be inaccessible to the student researcher because of their considerable cost, and in any case the data would be targeted at business users and would not typically be suitable or a workable substitute for self-generated primary data (this is discussed further in Chapter 9). Secondary data generated by luxury brands themselves for their own business purposes (referred to as *internal secondary data*; e.g., sales reports, annual accounts, marketing budgets, human resource management figures, client databases) are very unlikely to be made available to student researchers of luxury because of commercial sensitivity and competitiveness concerns. However, data on the economic or environmental performance of luxury brands can be found with a certain amount of detective work. For example, luxury companies that are publicly listed (i.e., their shares are traded on a public stock exchange) are obliged to make regular statutory filings such as income statements, revenue, balance sheets, assets, liabilities and so on, which can help the researcher to build a picture of economic performance across time. Companies such as the Burberry Group, Aston Martin Lagonda and Watches of Switzerland regularly post their financial results on the London Stock Exchange website (londonstockexchange.com). Similarly, luxury brands are becoming increasingly transparent about their ecological footprint and regularly publish data on progress towards sustainability. For instance, the LVMH group published data on energy and water consumption, CO_2 emissions and waste for all its business groups in its *2020 Social and Environmental Responsibility Report* (LVMH, 2021, 128–135).

PRIMARY DATA GATHERED FROM SECONDARY SOURCES

One of the great advantages of the internet for the student researcher is that, with the right institutional support, almost everything they need to complete their investigation is available, bang up to date and almost instantly, at their fingertips. Reflect for a moment on their counterpart little more than three decades ago who had to rely on card catalogues in libraries, reference and data deliveries that took days or weeks rather than milliseconds, and analysis relying on a huge stack of computer cards (not to mention writing dissertations on typewriters!). The internet is also a ready and vast potential source of both qualitative and quantitative data for anyone researching the luxury industry. In July 2022, there were 5.03 billion internet users globally, accounting for 63.1% of the total population, including 4.7 billion active social media users (59% of the global population, or 75.5% of the population aged 13 and over).[11] Table 5.2 and Figure 5.1 show the scale of social media use over the last decade or so.

The communications traffic on social media offers an immense potential resource for researchers, but how does one go about extracting data from the various platforms? The simple answer for most student researchers will probably be manual extraction: cutting and pasting the material that they need into a Word or Excel file, which can be tedious and time-consuming and also runs the risk of falling foul of legal and ethical considerations, which will be discussed shortly. Students who are able to write computer code may be able to construct their own *web-scraping* tools to automate this task, and there are several YouTube videos to help the beginner with this.[13] There are some open-source web-scraping tools, such as provided by Selenium, BeautifulSoup and Scrapy (which use the Python programming language) and Puppeteer (which uses the Node.js development platform), but these still require a certain familiarity with coding. Alternatively, scraped social media content can be obtained by commercial web data companies who will extract the required web content and deliver ready-to-use data sets to clients, including demographic profiles of the data content. Personal information such as email addresses can be extracted from some social media platforms (LinkedIn, for example, although these are not always validated), which might be used to contact participants for follow-up interviews, but, for other platforms (Facebook, for instance), personal details are excluded under data protection principles (see below).

TABLE 5.2 Active Monthly Users of Social Media by Platform, January 2022

Social Media Platform	Year Platform First Introduced	Active Monthly Users in January 2022 (millions)
Facebook	2004	2,910
YouTube	2005	2,562
WhatsApp	2009	2,000
Instagram	2010	1,478
Weixin/WeChat	2011	1,263
TikTok	2016	1,000
Douyin	2016	600
QQ	2009	574
Sina Weibo	2009	573
Kuaishou	2012	573
Snapchat	2011	557
Telegram	2013	550
Pinterest	2016	444
Twitter	2006	436
Reddit	2005	430
Quora	2009	300

Source: user data from statista.com[12] and internet search.

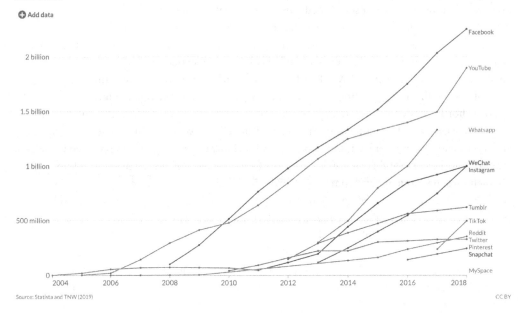

Number of people using social media platforms, 2004 to 2018

Estimates correspond to monthly active users (MAUs). Facebook, for example, measures MAUs as users that have logged in during the past 30 days. See source for more details.

FIGURE 5.1 Trends in Social Media Use from 2004 to 2018, by Principal Social Media Platforms.

Source: Our World in Data, 2020 (https://ourworldindata.org/rise-in-social-media (accessed 31 August 2022).

SOCIAL MEDIA AND LUXURY

Social media and the internet more generally have become integral to the way that the essence of luxury is communicated around the world, most particularly since the COVID-19 pandemic significantly shifted the balance between offline and online modalities. Each set of social media communications involving the principal actors or stakeholders in the field of luxury – social networks, brand websites, review sites, forums, blogs, video- and photo-sharing and so on – is potentially a set of data for the researcher.

Figure 5.2 presents a highly simplified schema of the communication web between luxury brands and the wider public and highlights some of the interfaces that could potentially provide the focus for deeper research investigation. The focus here, in research terms, is on process, influence and impact (how?, why? and to what effect?), rather than a descriptive overview of each element (what?), although most lines of communication inevitably start with or centre on brand stories, values and identities (A). The principal line of communication runs between the brands and the wider public (B). Messages and signals flow in both directions. But, in the schema, we try to disaggregate the 'general population' into sets of actors, which include the actual customers of luxury brands (C), but also avid fans and followers (D), brand ambassadors and a newly emerging category of key opinion consumers (KOCs), as well as members of the wider public, who may not be active purchasers of luxury goods but are drawn into the alluring

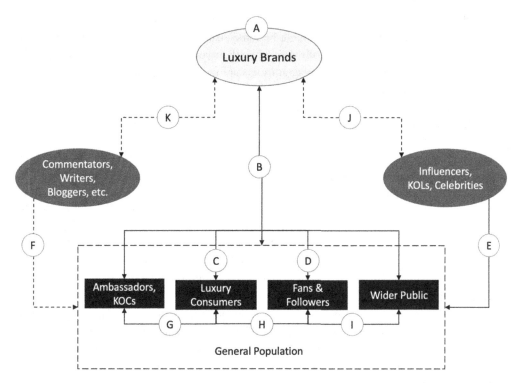

FIGURE 5.2 Simplified Schema of the Social Media Web of Communication between Luxury Brands and the Wider Population.

narratives that surround luxury. A very important secondary channel of social media communication concerns how the various advocates of luxury communicate with each another (e.g., G, H and I). We have funnelled the myriad of third-party actors (i.e., not specifically brands or consumers) into two further categories: the influencers, key opinion leaders (KOLs) and celebrities, who can play a powerful role in directly swaying the public's engagement with certain luxury brands (E); and the various commentators on luxury who may simultaneously inform and even critique the directions that luxury takes, indirectly influencing consumer sentiment (F). The nature, strength and directionality of the relationship between luxury brands and these two sets of actors (J and K) are also facets that researchers may help to unravel.

Let us take a look at a few examples out of the millions that are available to us. For brand stories (A) we could explore the official social media accounts of a luxury brand such as Cartier, comparing the approaches the brand adopts to communicating with its followers on, say, Instagram and LinkedIn.[14] At the time of writing, Cartier had 12.3 million followers on Instagram and 865,000 followers on LinkedIn, but the constituencies of the two social media platforms are quite different. Accordingly, the way the brand presents itself, and thus communicates with its followers, varies across these and other platforms as well, as does the nature of followers' reactions to the brand's posts. While the storyline may be similar, the way it is presented, and also the frequency of postings, may be quite different. Both sets of posts have art and culture as their thematic focus, but, for LinkedIn followers, who are mainly luxury industry professionals, both the content and the comments might be somewhat deeper than the lighter touch offered to Instagram users, who are principally defined by their youth – it is the favourite platform for Millennials and Gen Z (70.1% of Instagram users are under the age of 35).[15] Research might focus on a comparative *content analysis* of the brand's posts on different social media platforms (discussed further in Chapter 7).

An investigation into luxury brands' direct communication with consumers (C) might look at how Gucci[16] uses short videos on TikTok to present its brand stories and products to its 2.2 million followers on this platform. Analysis could focus on the content of these videos and both the overt and subliminal messaging they contain, set against the principal demographics of Tik-Tok users. One might also look at the comments that followers post in reaction to these short videos: in general, where the clips feature celebrities, the comments will tend to focus on the personality rather than the product, whereas other more market-oriented posts will solicit reactions to the brand and its featured products. As such, the researcher might use this as an example of brands reaching consumers indirectly via fans, followers, ambassadors and influencers (D, E, H and G). A content analysis of followers' comments could help to reveal how brands engage with actual and potential consumers via third-party actors.

A great case for exploring the way that influencers help to raise the profile of certain luxury brands (E) would be an investigation of the Italian luxury house Bottega Veneta. In 2021, the brand seemingly bucked the trend by closing all its official social media accounts, including Facebook, Twitter and Instagram, in essence relying on its story to sell the brand instead of the brand having to work hard to sell its story. A consequence of this bold move was to create space for an immense number of influencers and KOLs to create their own social media content to showcase the brand (and themselves!) to a very wide audience. Examples include the influencer Rose Huntington-Whiteley, whose Instagram account (@rosiehw) has more than 16 million followers and who frequently sports Bottega Veneta fashion items; and Leaf Greener, who has 320,000 followers on Instagram (@leaf_greener) and 33,700 on Weibo (叶子LeafGreener) and who is a very active Bottega Veneta fan.[17] We can assume there is no official connection between the brand and the influencers as this is not declared in their posts, as is now required by law. This influencer communication traffic provides a very rich seam of data for any researcher wishing to explore the modalities and impact of influencer-marketing in the luxury industry.

A final example relates to the role played by commentators of various kinds in raising the profile and adding depth to narratives about luxury (F). These might include the regular webinars and reports produced by Positive Luxury on sustainability in the luxury sector;[18] vlogs on luxury posted to YouTube or LUXE.TV; blogs, such as on luxury cars, yachts and aviation by Robb Report,[19] luxury fashion and beauty by Caviar and Cashmere curated by Caitlyn Chase,[20] and luxury lifestyles in *Upscale Living Magazine*;[21] or podcasts, such as on the luxury segment of the tourism and hospitality market by Luxury Travel Insider, created by Sarah Groen (see Box 5.2).[22] This internet content provides the researcher with a rich variety of qualitative material on almost every aspect of luxury, which can provide the basis for content analysis of trends, perspectives, issues, controversies and anything to do with the fundamental essence of luxury.

BOX 5.2

Turning Words into Data

Taking one of the most recent (at time of writing) podcasts (23 August 2022) featured on Luxury Travel Insider, [23] we can explore some of the essential elements of the experiential aspect of luxury travel. The podcast is a conversation between the curator of Luxury Travel Insider, Sarah Groen, and the proprietor of Passalacqua on the shore of Lake Como in Italy, Valentina de Santis. The conversation takes us through the history, character, features, setting and essence of the luxurious and fabulously appointed villa-cum-hotel and offers Valentina the opportunity to showcase her family's unique property to potential clients as well as an interested wider public, while adding to Sarah's impressive portfolio of luxury travel podcasts.[24]

To the researcher, the 8,600 words contained in the transcript (we created and cleaned up the transcript ourselves) of the conversation provide many examples of the ways in which a proprietor seeks to create and deliver an exceptional luxury experience for their clients, and, as such, the material (perhaps allied to a dozen or so similar podcasts or articles) will help them to identify some of the factors that might help to define and operationalise the notion of 'experiential luxury travel'.[25] The podcast is replete with references to locality – local identity, history and culture – suffused with a rich flavour of 'Italianness' and authenticity. The conversation also draws extensively on the senses and on an aesthetic appreciation of landscape, nature, homeliness, cuisine, art and design. A flavour of this can be gleaned from the word cloud in Figure 5.3.

FIGURE 5.3 Podcast Word Cloud. Copyright QSR International.

As a precursor to a more rigorous interrogation of this podcast to pull out the key experiential elements associated with luxury travel today, the transcript has been thematically 'coded' using the NVivo software application, as shown in the screenshot in Figure 5.4, thereby turning the words into data. A fuller content analysis might include several more podcasts or articles on a similar theme – for example, where locality is an important feature of the tourism product – balanced by a parallel content analysis of clients' reviews and reactions.

FIGURE 5.4 Preliminary Content Analysis of the Podcast Using NVivo. Copyright QSR International.

On the surface, the internet in general, and social media in particular, may represent a 'gold mine' of free and easily accessible data to the researcher of luxury. The archive of what Robert Kozinets (2020, 16) calls 'online traces' is massive and fundamentally borderless. But, from a research perspective, there are also a number of shortcomings that the student researcher should be aware of and reflect on, even if these do not directly impinge on their own investigation. The sheer volume of data may be a bane as well as a boon: it is largely unstructured and may contain an immense amount of 'noise' that must be filtered out to yield meaningful data. Material extracted from the internet is 'found' by the researcher rather than being created according to precise research questions and a clear research design. The data may be decontextualised and quite shallow, and the researcher may be distant from the cyber communities they are interested in – an onlooker rather than an immersed participant. Research may be biased towards public internet content: private sites may only be accessible to members, will be password protected and, as such, may not be revealed as frequently by internet search engines. To gain access to these sites, the researcher may join with the specific intention of extracting data, which may not be to the members' liking and may contravene site-specific prohibitions. Permission may need to be sought from the site's administrators, and the members may need to be informed of the purposes of the research and the use to which the findings will be put. It is also very difficult to validate findings and interpretations when using data derived from social media.

There are also legal and ethical issues associated with the use of data from the internet, as well as questions of representativeness. We will look at these in a little more detail below.

DATA, THE LAW AND RESEARCH ETHICS

When obtaining and handling secondary data from the internet, as well as when collecting primary research data, there are some important legal and ethical considerations that the researcher must be aware of and comply with. The ethical principles of research are universal (although not always adhered to universally), but legal provisions for the protection of personal data vary from country to country. It is incumbent on the researcher to familiarise themselves with the regulations that apply to their particular research context, but beyond this it is important to be aware of the core principles of data protection and to follow best practice, regardless of minimum legal stipulations.

The core legal principle, as enshrined in the General Data Protection Regulation (GDPR) of the European Union, is that every citizen has a moral and legal right to the protection of data that relate to them (in other words, personal data), including a right to access data that have been collected concerning them and the right to have these data rectified if found to be inaccurate.[26] The legislation governs the extraction, processing (use), storage, accuracy, access to and disposal of personal data; the researcher, as an extractor, user and holder of personal data, is thus fundamentally bound by the provisions and stipulations of data protection legislation.

Other core principles of the GDPR are *transparency* and *informed consent*. If a researcher wishes to obtain data from, or relating to, what the EU calls an "identified or identifiable person", they have to obtain that person's consent, freely given on the basis of transparent, specific, informed and unambiguous information as to the intended use of their data. Data should only be gathered that are sufficient for a specified and legitimate purpose and should not be processed in a manner that is not compatible with this purpose. If these data are held for any length of time, they must be kept up to date and thus accurate. If the data are not anonymised at source (in other words, only data relating to a person, but not their personal data, are used), these data should be held on to no longer than needed for the purpose for which they were originally obtained and should be kept securely and in a manner (e.g., encryption) which protects against theft and/or unlawful use by another party. The participant has a right to access (and request deletion of) any of their personal data that are being held by an individual or organisation. It is the responsibility of the controller (in this case, the researcher) to ensure compliance with these regulations.

It is worth noting that the principles of the GDPR apply to the use of web-scraping to obtain data from, say, social media. It is currently not illegal to obtain publicly accessible data in this way, although some websites may attempt to limit this practice by specifically prohibiting web-scraping in their published terms and conditions in order to protect specified data that may be in the public domain (e.g., price data which may be used by price comparison websites). But, in essence, the process of web-scraping is the same as that used by search engines or web browsers, which are not only legal but also fundamental to the way the internet operates. Should web-scraping (automatic or manual) also obtain personal data, including any data which may make it possible to identify an individual (e.g., name, address, date of birth, employment information), then the recipient or processor of these data will be subject to the provisions of the GDPR. It is worth noting that anonymous and even robotised web-scraping has no provision per se for obtaining the informed consent of a person(s). There are also legal restrictions on the recipient's use of material that is protected under copyright legislation (e.g., images, published work, etc.).

A simple way to avoid transgression of these legal principles when extracting secondary data from social media or the internet is to avoid collecting personal data. However, analysis of these data may require their disaggregation by demographic, economic or geographical criteria, which will require a certain amount of personal information to be obtained and stored, and thus the research will be subject to the principles of the GDPR. These provisions are intended to protect the rights of individual citizens but are not intended as an obstruction to legitimate research:

> the GDPR permits the collection of public data for research purposes by legitimate research actors who are processing data for purposes that are in the public interest ... as long as the researcher acts in keeping with the recognized standards for scientific research.
>
> (Kozinets, 2020, 198)

Because of the centrality of the GDPR, and its national variants, to data handling, it is very important that the research project of any student of luxury should include familiarising themselves with the principles of the GDPR and putting them into practice, not least to ensure that these provide the baseline for any investigations they may carry out in future, including as practitioners in the luxury industry. As well as complying with the GDPR's provisions on handling, updating, sharing and disposing of data, it is crucial that the researcher should obtain the informed written consent of all participants in their research. To do this, they should produce a *consent form* on which the nature and purpose of the investigation are stated clearly to the research participant, along with why they have been selected, what the researcher needs from them, what risks the participant may potentially face in contributing to the research, how their data will be used and stored, and what will happen to their data after the research is completed. The participant should be informed as to whether or not their data will be anonymised, and they should be informed of their right to withdraw participation at any stage during the research, or to refuse participation, and for their data to be deleted if they so request. The signed consent form should be retained for any future reference and updated if circumstances change. If the research is to be conducted verbally rather than 'on paper', or remotely via the internet, a means should be found of indicating that informed consent has been given by the participant. An example of the consent form that we used in our background survey of the use of research in the luxury industry is shown in Box 5.3, together with a participant information sheet (Box 5.4).

BOX 5.3

Example of a Consent Form

Informed Consent Form for a Research Interview

(Background Research for the Textbook *Research Methods in Luxury Management*)

Please tick the appropriate boxes	Yes	No
Participating in the Study:		
I have read and understood the project information sheet given to me on 01–07–2022. I have been able to ask questions about the study and have received answers to my satisfaction.	☐	☐
I voluntarily consent to participate in this study, and understand that I can refuse to answer questions and can withdraw from the study at any time without having to give a reason. I understand that if I do withdraw, my anonymised data cannot be withdrawn from the study after 30-11-2022.	☐	☐
I understand that my participation in the study will involve a face-to-face (online) interview, and discussing how luxury practitioners use research in their routine activities. I understand the interview will last approximately 30–45 minutes and will be audio recorded unless I request otherwise.	☐	☐
Use of the Information from the Study		
I understand that the information I provide may be used for the writing of a book chapter for the textbook *Research Methods for Luxury Management*, to be published in 2023.	☐	☐
I understand that any personal information collected that can identify me, such as my name or where I live, will not be shared beyond the study team. Unless I give my permission below to use my name, any information included in the publications will be strictly anonymised.	☐	☐
I agree that my information can be quoted in research outputs.	☐	☐
I agree that my real name can be used for quotations.	☐	☐
Data Storage, Future Use and Reuse of the Information by Others		
I understand that no data collected from this research will be used for any commercial purpose or circulated to a third party outside this University. The data will be used for the sole purpose of research for the writing of the textbook by 31 December 2022, and any related academic research publication thereafter.	☐	☐

Signatures

_____   _____   _____

Name of participant [IN CAPITALS]   Signature   Date

I have accurately read out the information sheet to the potential participant, and to the best of my ability have ensured that the participant understands what they are freely consenting to.

_____   _____   _____

Name of participant [IN CAPITALS]   Signature   Date

Study Contact Details for Further Information: ....

BOX 5.4

Example of a Participant Information Sheet

Dear _____,

We would like to invite you to participate in our research project. In order to help you comprehend the purpose of the research and what it entails before deciding whether or not to participate, we have prepared the following information sheet. Please take a little time to familiarise yourself with this document.

The Purpose of the Research Project

We are co-authoring a new textbook, entitled *Research Methods in Luxury Management* (to be published by Routledge, London), which aims to be the definitive reference source for students and practitioners who take a research interest in the luxury industry. It is expected that readers of the book will develop a much deeper understanding of the luxury sector itself, the knowledge and data that are required to improve management within the industry, the core principles of undertaking sound, reliable, representative and contextualised research on luxury in order to engage a wide range of needs and challenges, and familiarity with various cutting-edge issues facing the luxury industry and its place in a rapidly changing world.

The small research project we are asking you to contribute to aims principally to obtain data for part of Chapter 2, which asks how luxury industry practitioners commission, engage in and use research in their routine activities. This information will be obtained by means of a brief questionnaire. The survey findings will be followed up with one-to-one interviews of selected respondents in order to obtain more in-depth information to supplement that from the questionnaire, which will be presented in Chapter 9.

Why You Have Been Invited to Participate

Either: you have been invited to participate in the current interview because, during the questionnaire survey, you indicated your willingness to participate further in the current research. Your insight and feedback on the current research subject will be highly appreciated.

Or: given your expertise within the luxury industry, I would like to invite you to participate in a short interview to explore how you commission and use research in managing your luxury brand. Your insight and feedback on the current research subject will be highly appreciated.

Assurances to Participants about Voluntary Participation and Right to Withdraw

Whether or not you participate is entirely up to you. You will be handed this information sheet to keep for future reference and will be requested to indicate that you have given permission for the interview to proceed.

You are free to leave the study whenever you want, without having to give a reason. You will be asked what you want to happen to the data you have provided up to that point, though, if you opt to leave the study. Please take note that anonymized data cannot be removed from the study after 30 November 2022.

Explanation of the Research Activity

The main purpose of this study is to investigate how luxury industry practitioners commission, engage and use research in their routine activities. This will consist of a face-to-face (online) interview, lasting approximately 30–45 minutes, at a time to suit your convenience, in which I would hope to explore your views and gain insightful knowledge on the above topic. An outline of the interview will be sent to you in advance of our meeting. The interview is to be audio recorded for the purpose of note-taking. The recordings will be transcribed after the interview, but will be erased no more than one year after their completion. If you are unwilling to be recorded, please let the researcher know, and only written notes will be taken by the researcher during the interview.

The Potential Benefits of the Research Project

This study will inform future teaching and practice on luxury industry research, and will therefore be of potential value to future luxury industry professionals.

Potential Risks or Disadvantages from Participating in the Research

There are no anticipated disadvantages or discomforts from participating in this study. You can decide which questions you wish to respond to and you are free to leave the interview at any point.

Assurance on Data Protection and Confidentiality

We shall rigorously maintain the confidentiality of all the information we gather about you for the research. You will not be able to be individually recognised in any follow-up studies or publications.

All data collected by the research project will be kept confidential in accordance with the Data Protection Act (enclosed), and your contribution will be anonymised throughout. The interview recordings (upon participants' consent) will be stored in an encrypted file on the University's OneDrive. The recording files will be permanently destroyed once the transcription is completed. The anonymised transcripts will also be stored on an encrypted University server and will only be accessible by the researcher. All other data (including the survey, interview transcripts and notes) will be erased one year after the completion of the book writing. For hard copy data, these will be digitally filed immediately after the data are recorded. The data will then also be stored in an encrypted file on the University's OneDrive. Any paper files will be shredded afterwards.

No data collected from this research will be used for any commercial purpose or circulated to a third party outside the University. The data will be used for the sole purpose of research for the textbook writing, and for related academic research, by 31 December 2023.

In cases where the participant is willing to be identified by name and brand and used as such in the textbook, this will be discussed with the researcher beforehand. This will only happen if the participant's permission is obtained before the interview starts.

Limits to Confidentiality

Confidentiality will be respected subject to legal constraints and professional guidelines. Please note that assurances on confidentiality will be strictly adhered to unless evidence of wrongdoing or potential harm is uncovered. In such cases the University may be obliged to contact relevant statutory bodies or agencies.

What Will the Research Results Be Used For?

This research is being undertaken for the purpose of writing a textbook, *Research Methods in Luxury Management*. Upon publication of the book, a summary of the survey results will be published online (via LinkedIn) which all participants can access. As an interview participant, you will also receive an author discount voucher for the book.

Information about Funders or Collaboration Partners of the Research Project

The research is not funded by any organisation. It will take place under the aegis of our University department and has been approved by both the departmental and University ethics committees.

Contact Information for Complaints and Concerns

Please contact Dr. Kelly Meng (researcher) first if you have any questions or concerns about the study in general or your involvement in the research project. You can also get in touch with the Chair of the University's Research Ethics and Integrity Committee if you feel that your complaint has not been addressed properly [details].

We appreciate you taking the time to read this information sheet and considering your participation in this research study.

Appended: summary of GDPR provisions for academic research.

Beyond protecting citizens' rights and being transparent, honest and trustworthy in one's research approach, two further ethical principles apply to the process of obtaining data: (a) *do no harm*, and (b) *do some good*. Harm can result when the process of collecting data becomes intrusive to research participants or deals with sensitive topics which may make the participant feel uncomfortable or lose face. Particular care and safeguarding measures must be taken where the research involves young or vulnerable people, and the researcher should always reflect on the power dynamics which may be found in the relationship between the researcher and research participants, which may subconsciously compromise the principle of free will. The privacy, safety and dignity of the research participant must always take priority over the data needs of the researcher. It is the responsibility of the researcher to evaluate and communicate the possible risks to the participant from being involved in the research, and a proper risk assessment should provide the basis for seeking informed consent. It is worth re-emphasising that extracting data from social media rarely provides a mechanism or opportunity for obtaining participants' informed consent, and so the researcher should endeavour to use these data with due reference to the principles of the GDPR and the wider ethics of research.

Researchers should also be aware that research can be likened to an extractive industry, where the main drive is to find and extract data from whatever source in order to satisfy the researcher's needs and agenda. There is limited scope in the directionality of the research process for the investigator to give something back, to do some good. We may all convince ourselves that our research serves the noble purpose of knowledge creation, but, as we will see in the discussion in Chapter 9, there may sometimes be a mismatch between what is done and what is needed, or how it is used. Accordingly, people are being inconvenienced to provide data for the researcher (less so with online data extraction, it should be said), but are getting very little in return. An example of reciprocity in this regard might be where a researcher joins an online community for the purposes of obtaining data and insight – let's say, a luxury watch forum such as WatchUSeek,[27] which has 500,000 members and 20 million posts; there are no overt prohibitions about using conversations as a source of data – but is transparent about their objectives with both the moderators and members and shares a summary of their findings with the community when their research is completed.

DATA REPRESENTATIVENESS AND SAMPLING

In this chapter so far, we have looked at the nature of data and have drawn a distinction between extant data (that which already exists in the public or private domains and which the researcher 'harvests' for their investigative purposes) and self-generated data (which the researcher obtains using some of the research methods that will be introduced in Chapter 6). The luxury industry is multifaceted, but research in this field will generally involve obtaining data from a source (or sources) that is best placed to cast light over, and offer insight into, the chosen topic, issue or problem. Having identified the source(s), a means of extracting data has to be built (methodology) while remaining mindful of challenges of scale (do-ability) and accessibility. For example, if we are interested in how luxury consumers form a bond of attachment to Hermès bags, we should theoretically need to find a way of contacting all Hermès consumers, and even latent consumers, to explore the socio-psychology of brand attachment, individually and collectively. If we are an employee within the brand who is tasked with this research, presumably with access to a complete client list from all parts of the world, together with others who have expressed an interest in the brand in the recent past, we would in essence have the means of contacting this entire population to ask questions that are pertinent to our research. This would be quite some undertaking, in time, effort and expense. Could more or less the same results be achieved by talking to a smaller fraction of this total population? This question can be answered in the affirmative if we ensure that the fraction (n) is sufficiently representative of the population as a whole (N) – a key consideration in any survey. This can be achieved through sampling.

The best analogy to give here is an opinion poll taken around the time of a general election: generally speaking, polling companies are able to predict outcomes that closely match actual outcomes on the basis of a sample that measures in the thousands from a voting population in the millions. The principle is that, if you know the demographic and other characteristics of the population as a whole, and can replicate this profile in a much smaller *sample*, you will usually end up with results that mirror the population as a whole.

So, the Hermès executive who wishes to understand how customers engage with the brand and its products does not need to contact every actual and prospective customer: a representative sample will suffice. How do we ascertain and assure *representativeness*? A key requirement is the elimination of bias from the sampling process. In other words, the researcher should not distort the selection of participants in the sample by introducing subjective elements such as choosing locations that are convenient to access. The purest way to achieve a representative sample is through *random sampling*: for instance, using a random number generator to determine who should be included in the survey, which in theory should eliminate human bias. This is referred to as *probability sampling*: each and every unit of the target population should have an equal probability of being selected for the survey.

An alternative approach, especially when the researcher is in possession of a strong sampling frame (that is, they have a complete list of customers and their profiles which tells them their demographic characteristics: age, gender, education, location, economic status and, perhaps, past purchasing behaviour), is to use *quota sampling*, where participants are selected in a way that ensures that the sample matches the known profile of the population. Quota sampling is a form of *non-probability sampling*: the researcher is intervening to steer the sampling process in a particular direction. This is also referred to as *stratified sampling* and *stratified random sampling*. Despite the fact that the researcher thus distorts the selection process, the quota sample may often be a more accurate reflection of the profile of the population than the random sample, as randomness may not reconstruct a mirror profile of the target population. Random numbers do not 'know' the profile of the population, whereas the researcher does, and can ensure it is replicated through the sampling process (in the belief that profile variables influence outcomes). Quota sampling can be undertaken through random sampling, using random processes to identify participants until a particular quota – for example, for age, gender and so on – has been reached.

Without a sound sampling frame, quota sampling can also be deployed in a different way: the researcher chooses the profile of the sample they want to obtain for their research (gender distribution, age, location, etc.) and selects participants accordingly: a sample of 500 participants divided equally between men and women, representing three age groups, and drawn from five specified locations, which should theoretically yield about 17 participants in each of 15 sub-groups if each is weighted equally. Random selection could be used to populate each of these sub-groups.

Stratified sampling works as follows: you may wish to divide your population into a certain number of groups (strata) to ensure that you have coverage to match your theoretical objectives. Thus, you may decide to divide your consumers by location, with Europe, North America, Asia and Africa as individual strata, or perhaps the USA, the UK, China and Brazil. Provided you have a clear definition of location (current place of residence, nationality, etc.), people included in your survey can only have membership of one stratum. You might then use probability (random) sampling to identify participants to populate your survey. This would be called *stratified random sampling*. You are manipulating the content of your sample to suit the needs and interests of your research. You will still need a sampling frame to achieve this – for example, a list of all consumers who have purchased Hermès bags in the last five years, which will hopefully also contain information on location. The researcher decides on the proportion of the total list (N) that will be an adequate sample (n), say 5%, and random numbers will be used to select participants for the survey, which can then be sent using the email addresses the company has on the same customer list. Let us say there are 100,000 customers on this list, of whom 10,000 come from the four countries of interest, split as follows: USA, 3,000; UK, 2,000; China, 4,000; Brazil, 1,000; a 5% random sample should yield 150, 100, 200 and 50 participants, respectively. This would also be called *proportionate sampling*: the same proportion is applied to each stratum. *Disproportionate sampling* would be if the researcher decided to seek an equal quota (cf., *quota sampling*) for each group, irrespective of their numerical distribution on the list, possibly because they wished to pay particular attention to underrepresented markets – thus, 250 for each country as part of an overall 10% sample. When the researcher distorts the sample away from its normal distribution in the population, it is necessary to keep this in mind when referring findings back to the population as a whole. This is similar to *cluster sampling*, where the target population is divided into clusters or unique groups from which a sample is drawn (e.g., by random sampling).

Purposive sampling is a form of non-probabilistic sampling – no claims are made, or can be made, with regard to wider representativeness, and there is no use of a probabilistic sampling technique such as random selection from a sample frame. Instead, participants are selected on the basis that they are known to be able to contribute information and insight appertaining to the research question. In other words, subjects are selected on purpose and to serve the specific purposes of the research. Purposive sampling is commonly used in qualitative research, where insight, depth and human interest are of more value to the researcher than the ability to make claims that extend beyond the target participants. Other terms are *subjective* or *judgemental sampling* or selection: decisions surrounding inclusion/exclusion are based on the judgement of the researcher rather than any scientific means of eliminating potential bias from participant selection. The objectives of the research must obviously be very clear in the mind of the researcher, who should also have a good familiarity with and understanding of the target population(s) in order to inform their judgement as to who best suits the objectives of their research. It is important that no claims of wider representativeness are made in the presentation of findings. 'Indicative' would be a better word than 'representative'.

Convenience sampling is another form of non-probability sampling where the researcher identifies participants based upon convenience of access rather than any specific concerns about unbiased or cross-sectional representativeness. Thus, a sample may be drawn from a close or accessible vicinity to the researcher, or from workmates, classmates, peers or social media contacts – people who the researcher may feel confident will participate in their study (which itself is a source of bias). People may be approached at random, but this does not substitute for representativeness because bias has already been introduced in the selection of the target cohort. Findings thus only relate to that cohort, and not to the wider population. Quite a lot of academic research on luxury is based on convenience sampling; this is why several experimental studies of socio-psychological responses to luxury brands, advertising and identity are conducted by academics utilising their students as subjects, even though they may not represent the ideal and most relevant or representative luxury consumer group.

A key objective for any researcher is to obtain a sample of sufficient size to allow them to make inferences from their analysis and findings. *Snowball sampling* may frequently be applied in circumstances where it is difficult to find participants owing to the highly specialised character of the research: the researcher may be able to identify 20 people who are known to have the traits or behaviour that is relevant to their research, but this sample size may be too small to give confidence in the validity of their findings. Asking each of the 20 participants to suggest or recommend others who share similar characteristics and who might also be willing to contribute to the study is called snowball sampling. The rationale is that these people's personal connections are fairly likely to have similar interests, behaviour and characteristics to the original participants. Snowball sampling is a non-probability technique that may be applied to probability sampling (randomly selected individuals are then asked to recommend other, similar individuals who might also be willing to take part in the survey or research – the snowball or chain-referral approach), or it may be used as a follow-on technique for purposive or convenience sampling where people who participate in the research are asked to recommend others to add to the researcher's sample of participants. Either way, it is classed as a non-probability technique because, in the first instance, the referring participants are introducing judgemental distortions to the selection process, and, in the latter instance, referrals will simply compound biases already evident in participant selection. This may be a good way of increasing sample size, but caution has to be exercised in interpreting results and making inferences beyond the surveyed sample.

Intercept sampling is a commonly used technique in market research and has the potential to be sufficiently randomised to constitute a probability sampling method. Potential participants are 'intercepted' in real-life situations such as visiting a shopping mall or a specific store, or are stopped in the street, or are intercepted as they depart a luxury cruise or leave a Michelin-star restaurant. Bias can seep into intercept sampling through the subjective judgement of the researcher or their assistants: more friendly looking people may be more likely to be approached, or there may be a subconscious gender bias, and so on. One way to overcome this is to have a rigid set of rules where personal choice is eliminated from participant selection – for example, every fourth person who comes out of a shop, regardless of their appearance. Bias can also be introduced into the sample in the other direction: certain people may go out of their way to avoid the researcher, while others may willingly give freely of their time, determining that one kind of shopper will be overrepresented in the survey and another underrepresented.

In our methodological survey of 160 recent luxury publications, 39 mentioned the sampling technique they had used: 13 used random sampling, 9 used purposive sampling, 6 used snowball sampling, 6 used convenience sampling, 2 used the intercept method, 1 each used judgemental and quota sampling, and 1 researcher relied on their personal network for research participants (Web of Science, 2022).

Sampling Error

The principle behind sampling is to obtain data that mirror an entire population while engaging only a fragment of that population; to speak with confidence about N on the basis of a carefully, scientifically derived sample of n. The closer the sample matches the population, the greater the degree of accuracy we can attribute to the data we are using, and, by continuation, the lower will be the level of error in the data and in any statistical tests they are subjected to. The degree of accuracy (or error) and thus representativeness (or distortion) can be ascertained statistically as the *sampling error*: the standard deviation of the population (N) is divided by the square root of the size of the sample (n) and then multiplied by the Z-score value. Let us dissect these three things.

The *standard deviation* (SD) is a statistical indication of the dispersion of a set of values from the mean or average of these values (see Box 5.5). The wider the scale and scatter of values from the mean, the higher will be the standard deviation value. A low standard deviation value will accrue when values are located in close proximity to the mean. As a rule, the higher the standard deviation (the higher the level of variability within the data set), the greater will be the chance of sampling error. In order to calculate sampling error, it must be possible to ascertain the standard deviation of the population (N).

BOX 5.5

How to Calculate the Standard Deviation and the Coefficient of Variation

Taking as a simple example a total population (N) consisting of 10 clients of a luxury brand: if all clients happened to be aged 35, the mean would be 35, and the standard deviation would be zero (there would be no variation of values from the mean). If the 10 clients were aged 23, 25, 32, 34, 55, 58, 44, 45, 60, 62, the mean (average) age would be 43.8, and the standard deviation would be 13.94, as depicted in Figure 5.5. If the data represented a sample rather than the entire population (in other words, the 10 clients were selected from a client list of 100), the standard deviation would be 14.7, as the formula in the top left corner of Figure 5.5 would instead use (n − 1) rather than N.

$\sigma = \sqrt{\dfrac{\sum(x_i - \mu)^2}{N}}$	Age (Xi)	Age-Mean Age (Xi-μ)	Age-Mean Age Squared (Xi-μ)2		
Key:	23	-20.8	432.64		
Xi = Each Value of Age	25	-18.8	353.44		
μ = Average Age	32	-11.8	139.24		
∑ = Sum of	34	-9.8	96.04		
N = Number of Values	55	11.2	125.44		
σ = Standard Deviation	58	14.2	201.64		
	44	0.2	0.04		
	45	1.2	1.44		
	60	16.2	262.44		
	62	18.2	331.24		
μ (Average Age)	43.8		1943.6	∑(Xi-μ)2	Sum of Squares
N = 10			194.36	∑(Xi-μ)2/N	Sum of Squares/N
σ of N			13.94	√∑(Xi-μ)2/N	Square Root

FIGURE 5.5 Calculating the Standard Deviation. Used with permission from Microsoft.

The extent to which the data are dispersed from the mean can be expressed by a *coefficient of variation* (CoV), which is the ratio of the SD to the mean. The CoV is calculated by dividing the SD by the mean: It can be expressed as a percentage by multiplying the result by 100. A high CoV indicates that the data have a high level of dispersal from the mean. In the example given in Figure 5.5, the SD divided by the mean gives a CoV figure of 0.31829, or a percentage variation of 31.829, which indicates a relatively low level of dispersion around the mean.

In our Web of Science survey of research methods adopted by luxury research professionals who published in 2021, the average sample size for quantitative studies using the survey method was 393.9, with a range of 50–1,224 and an SD of 221.3. The CoV – calculated as 221.3/393.9 × 100 = 56% – shows that there was quite a high level of variation in the sample sizes used by luxury research professionals.

The *sample size* refers to the number of people who are targeted as participants in a research investigation (for example, a survey). Depending on the sampling method used (as discussed above), the sample (n) will represent a fixed proportion (say, 5%) of the total population (N). Generally speaking, the greater the sample size as a proportion of the population, the lower the level of sampling error, although this is conditioned by the degree of variability found within this population.

The *confidence level* refers to the level of confidence the researcher is seeking that the results their analysis yields are attributable to a genuine set of determinants and are not simply a random outcome. Most researchers work to a minimum confidence level of 95% – that is, there is a 5% probability or less that their findings will have resulted from chance rather than genuine determinants. A 95% (or 99%) confidence threshold will typically be applied to evaluate the validity of a statistical test (see Chapter 7), but, in the present context, it is used to indicate the confidence threshold for validating a research sample.

The *Z-score* varies in relation to the confidence level (CL) that the researcher is applying to their investigation. Assuming a normal distribution in the data (a Gaussian or symmetrical bell-shaped curve), the Z-score is calculated by ascertaining the area to the left (AL) of the curve at a given confidence level. The AL of the curve at a 95% confidence level will be 97.5%: the 'outliers' at each end of the curve that lie beyond the 95% confidence range each account for 2.25%; the area to the left of the right-hand margin between confidence and outlier will therefore be 97.5%, or 0.975. A simple way of calculating the AL is to use the formula $(1 + CL)/2$: at a 95% confidence level, this is $(1 + 0.95)/2$ or 0.975. Having identified the AL, the Z-score is ascertained by finding this score on a Z-score table (see Figure 5.6) and adding the values indicated in the left-hand column (1.9 in this example) and the top row (0.06 in this example), giving a Z-score of 1.96 for a 95% confidence level.

Sample Size

How large a sample do I need for my research investigation? The obvious answer is 'the more the merrier'. Certainly, too small a sample size may raise questions about the validity of research findings, with a greater prospect of 'outliers' distorting the profile of the sample vis-à-vis the population as a whole. But an unnecessarily large sample may also be costly to administer and more difficult to manage at the processing and analysis stages and also risks imposing on more people (participants in a survey) to a greater extent than is absolutely necessary. The optimum sample size will in effect be the one that is the smallest feasible when set against the parameters the researcher employs to determine adequate representativeness. There is a formula for achieving this. Ideally, the researcher will have some knowledge of the total population size (N) of their research subject – say, the number of visitors to a luxury spa resort over a specified period of time, for example, 8,000 from January to December 2021. The researcher might be interested in ascertaining the attitudes and expectations of guests in the early post-pandemic period. In order to identify an adequate sample to administer a questionnaire to, the researcher must decide on three criteria. First is the confidence level they wish to apply to their analysis (discussed above). Second is the level of error that they are willing to accept in their data; it is almost inevitable that error will creep into any survey, but only a certain level of error is acceptable for

STANDARD NORMAL DISTRIBUTION: Table Values Represent AREA to the LEFT of the Z score.

Z	.00	.01	.02	.03	.04	.05	.06	.07	.08	.09
0.0	.50000	.50399	.50798	.51197	.51595	.51994	.52392	.52790	.53188	.53586
0.1	.53983	.54380	.54776	.55172	.55567	.55962	.56356	.56749	.57142	.57535
0.2	.57926	.58317	.58706	.59095	.59483	.59871	.60257	.60642	.61026	.61409
0.3	.61791	.62172	.62552	.62930	.63307	.63683	.64058	.64431	.64803	.65173
0.4	.65542	.65910	.66276	.66640	.67003	.67364	.67724	.68082	.68439	.68793
0.5	.69146	.69497	.69847	.70194	.70540	.70884	.71226	.71566	.71904	.72240
0.6	.72575	.72907	.73237	.73565	.73891	.74215	.74537	.74857	.75175	.75490
0.7	.75804	.76115	.76424	.76730	.77035	.77337	.77637	.77935	.78230	.78524
0.8	.78814	.79103	.79389	.79673	.79955	.80234	.80511	.80785	.81057	.81327
0.9	.81594	.81859	.82121	.82381	.82639	.82894	.83147	.83398	.83646	.83891
1.0	.84134	.84375	.84614	.84849	.85083	.85314	.85543	.85769	.85993	.86214
1.1	.86433	.86650	.86864	.87076	.87286	.87493	.87698	.87900	.88100	.88298
1.2	.88493	.88686	.88877	.89065	.89251	.89435	.89617	.89796	.89973	.90147
1.3	.90320	.90490	.90658	.90824	.90988	.91149	.91309	.91466	.91621	.91774
1.4	.91924	.92073	.92220	.92364	.92507	.92647	.92785	.92922	.93056	.93189
1.5	.93319	.93448	.93574	.93699	.93822	.93943	.94062	.94179	.94295	.94408
1.6	.94520	.94630	.94738	.94845	.94950	.95053	.95154	.95254	.95352	.95449
1.7	.95543	.95637	.95728	.95818	.95907	.95994	.96080	.96164	.96246	.96327
1.8	.96407	.96485	.96562	.96638	.96712	.96784	.96856	.96926	.96995	.97062
1.9	.97128	.97193	.97257	.97320	.97381	.97441	.97500	.97558	.97615	.97670
2.0	.97725	.97778	.97831	.97882	.97932	.97982	.98030	.98077	.98124	.98169
2.1	.98214	.98257	.98300	.98341	.98382	.98422	.98461	.98500	.98537	.98574
2.2	.98610	.98645	.98679	.98713	.98745	.98778	.98809	.98840	.98870	.98899
2.3	.98928	.98956	.98983	.99010	.99036	.99061	.99086	.99111	.99134	.99158
2.4	.99180	.99202	.99224	.99245	.99266	.99286	.99305	.99324	.99343	.99361
2.5	.99379	.99396	.99413	.99430	.99446	.99461	.99477	.99492	.99506	.99520
2.6	.99534	.99547	.99560	.99573	.99585	.99598	.99609	.99621	.99632	.99643
2.7	.99653	.99664	.99674	.99683	.99693	.99702	.99711	.99720	.99728	.99736
2.8	.99744	.99752	.99760	.99767	.99774	.99781	.99788	.99795	.99801	.99807
2.9	.99813	.99819	.99825	.99831	.99836	.99841	.99846	.99851	.99856	.99861
3.0	.99865	.99869	.99874	.99878	.99882	.99886	.99889	.99893	.99896	.99900
3.1	.99903	.99906	.99910	.99913	.99916	.99918	.99921	.99924	.99926	.99929
3.2	.99931	.99934	.99936	.99938	.99940	.99942	.99944	.99946	.99948	.99950
3.3	.99952	.99953	.99955	.99957	.99958	.99960	.99961	.99962	.99964	.99965
3.4	.99966	.99968	.99969	.99970	.99971	.99972	.99973	.99974	.99975	.99976
3.5	.99977	.99978	.99978	.99979	.99980	.99981	.99981	.99982	.99983	.99983
3.6	.99984	.99985	.99985	.99986	.99986	.99987	.99987	.99988	.99988	.99989
3.7	.99989	.99990	.99990	.99990	.99991	.99991	.99992	.99992	.99992	.99992
3.8	.99993	.99993	.99993	.99994	.99994	.99994	.99994	.99995	.99995	.99995
3.9	.99995	.99995	.99996	.99996	.99996	.99996	.99996	.99996	.99997	.99997

FIGURE 5.6 Obtaining a Z-Score from a Z-Score Table.

the results to be considered valid. Error is usually measured by comparing the mean of a variable in the sample with that of the population as a whole. Assuming the luxury spa sampling frame (guest list) has information on the age of the guests, for instance, it is relatively straightforward to calculate the mean (average) age of all guests (N) and, subsequently, the mean age of the sampled guests (n). The difference between the means is an indication of likely error in the sampling procedure/sample. We will take ±5% as an acceptable error threshold.

Third, we need an indication of the standard deviation of variables in the population (N) in order to gain a sense of the level of variability of the data. Calculating the standard deviation was demonstrated in Box 5.5 and Figure 5.5. If the distribution of cases is highly variable (widely dispersed from the mean: a high standard deviation), there is a greater chance that the sample will not match closely the distributions in the population as a whole; accordingly, a larger sample may be necessary to compensate for this threat to accuracy. A smaller sample may suffice where cases are quite evenly and closely distributed around the average. Note that the standard deviation is a good indicator of variability for data sets that have a normal distribution but is less reliable for skewed data sets where the distribution curve is biased towards the left or the right.

The desired sample size can be calculated manually. To do this, we need to convert the confidence level into a Z-score (discussed above). As we have seen, for a confidence level of 95%, the Z-score is 1.96; for 99%, it is 2.575. We will use a standard deviation of 0.5 and a margin of error of ±5%. The sample size can then be calculated thus:

$$SS = ((Z\text{-score})^2 \times SD \times (1 - SD))/(\text{margin of error})^2$$
$$SS = ((1.96)^2 \times 0.5 \times (0.5))/(0.05)^2$$
$$SS = (3.8416 \times 0.25)/0.0025$$
$$SS = 0.9604/0.0025$$

This yields a required sample size of 384.

Sample size calculators are freely available on the internet.[28] An example is provided in Figure 5.7. Note that the sample sizes recommended by the two methods are slightly different. This is because there are more 'unknowns' in the web example than the worked example, which may therefore be considered to be the more accurate. Nonetheless, in both instances, the recommended sample size was quite close to the average sample size used by luxury research professionals, as reported in Box 5.5.

Sample Size Calculator

Find Out The Sample Size

This calculator computes the minimum number of necessary samples to meet the desired statistical constraints.

Result

Sample size: 367

This means 367 or more measurements/surveys are needed to have a confidence level of 95% that the real value is within ±5% of the measured/surveyed value.

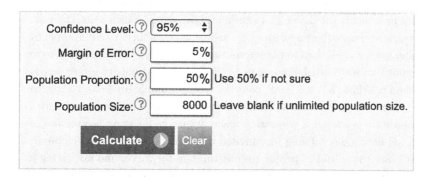

FIGURE 5.7 Sample Size Calculator (https://www.calculator.net/sample-size-calculator.html).

CROWDSOURCING RESEARCH DATA

Before we move on, in Chapter 6, to explore the various methods that can be used to obtain primary data, we want to round off this discussion of sourcing data by looking briefly at the process of *crowdsourcing*, or *online sampling*, which is the practice of obtaining data from a pool of people who make themselves available for this purpose, usually via the internet and typically through a commercial organisation that charges for its services and remunerates panel participants. The researcher is responsible for designing the survey instruments (the commercial body will often provide an array of tools for this purpose) and for specifying the preferred make-up of the target panel (demographic range, nationality, economic status; quota sample criteria, etc.), [29] but the organisation will arrange access to the panellists and will often also preprocess the resultant data prior to delivering them to the researcher. Some of the larger crowdsourcing companies have built panel pools numbering in the hundreds of thousands, spread across the world and encompassing a wide variety of social groups. [30]

There are clear advantages to crowdsourcing for the researcher. Creating one's own panel of participants can be a challenging and time-consuming process, most particularly for the student researcher whose own research network at an early stage in their career may be quite limited. In our experience, difficulty in identifying research participants often leads students to making compromises on their sampling procedures, resulting in a higher reliance on non-probabilistic sampling or even the abandonment of quantitative in favour of qualitative approaches. Having potential access to a panel of the size and diversity that suit the needs of their research investigation, albeit at a not-inconsiderable cost, may seem like an ideal solution to a challenging problem. Crowdsourced panels can often be assembled quickly, and panellists are typically quite experienced at participating in online surveys, incentivised by remuneration, and so results can be delivered in days rather than weeks or longer. In theory, the same panel can be used multiple times across an extensive time period, allowing longitudinal or time-series studies to be attempted.

There are, however, a number of disadvantages to using the crowdsourcing approach that the researcher needs to be mindful of and that may weaken the external validity of their findings. The costs involved may be prohibitive for the ordinary postgraduate student, while those who can afford to pursue the commercial route may gain a significant advantage over those who cannot. Accessing a commercial panel will not mask shortcomings in other areas of the research process, most particularly the design and wording of the survey instruments. The panels may not be as representative of the population as a whole as researchers might assume: by definition, people who are not connected to the internet are excluded, and participants have to be of a certain educational or intellectual standing to be allowed to contribute to survey panels. Some of the panels and panellists are 'overused', contributing to multiple surveys on a regular basis, and so a great volume of research around the world purports to be based on a randomised sample of N (the population as a whole), whereas in reality it may be the same 1–5 million or so participants time and time again. [31] Being incentivised by payments – many can be considered professional panellists – may lead to people rushing through the survey and not giving it the attention the researcher expects and deserves. There are also a growing number of instances where automated programs (bots) have been created to complete surveys and gain payment without actually answering questions properly, leading to high attrition rates in completed

TABLE 5.3 Crowdsourcing Platforms Used by Academic Researchers of Luxury Platform

	Number
Unspecified	10
Amazon Mechanical Turk	12
Academic Prolific	6
Qualtrics	6
Sojump	5
Google Forms	3
Survey Star	1
Survey Monkey	1
Wenjuanxing	1
Cloud Research	1
Toluna	1
Total	47

Source: Web of Science Survey, 2022.

surveys (between 31% and 51%, according to Aguinis, Villamour and Ramani, 2021, 826). Some participants may misrepresent themselves to the crowdsourcing platform, which might raise ethical concerns about the age of some panellists. Most platforms include a tick box to indicate that the participant has given informed consent for the use of their data, but decision-making in this regard may be blurred by financial motivations and so may not be truly meaningful in all instances. Using company-provided data analysis may also allow the student researcher to present research findings without properly understanding the analysis process.

There are a number of ways of overcoming these shortcomings. Crowdsourcing companies are becoming more effective at identifying and excluding surveys completed automatically by bots, and researchers can also more readily identify bot-generated returns through the regular insertion of 'attention questions' (questions designed solely to check the participant's level of attention) and a mixture of closed and open-ended questions (see Chapter 6). Students can help keep costs down by using the crowdsourcing companies' survey design tools and then orchestrating their own surveys without the need to purchase a research panel: they can flag the existence of the survey through social media contacts or forums, and some companies allow them to do this through their own channels.

Crowdsourced research data are becoming increasingly commonplace in research on luxury. Our survey of 160 recent publications in this field using the Web of Science database revealed that at least 47 (29%) had obtained their data via crowdsourcing platforms (see Table 5.3).

SUMMARY AND CONCLUSION

In this chapter, we have introduced students to the nature of data and the principal forms that data take. We have also outlined some of the sources of data that students of luxury are likely to use in their research. We have paid particularly close attention to considerations of data representativeness and to the sampling principles and techniques which can be used to build confidence that the data obtained for research and analysis adequately reflect patterns that are found in wider populations.

Whereas the earlier discussions in this book have cautioned against seeing deductive/inductive, realist/interpretivist and quantitative/qualitative approaches to research as being diametrically opposed, in this chapter we have drawn quite a clear distinction between quantitative and qualitative *data*. This distinction continues in the next two chapters, which introduce an array of data gathering methods and data analysis techniques.

NOTES

1   Web of Science, accessed 27 July 2022.
2   The three statements were: "I often look out for new products or brands that add up to my personal uniqueness", "I dislike brands or products that are purchased by everyone", "I often try to avoid products or brands that are bought by [the] general population" (Navia, Khire and Lyver, 2021, 518).
3   These included: "I often look for one-of-a-kind products so that I create a style that is all my own", "I actively seek to develop my personal uniqueness by buying special products or brands", "I often try to avoid products or brands that I know were bought by the general population" (Tien, Bearden and Hunter, 2001, 55–56).
4   Creative choice counter-conformity, unpopular choice counter-conformity, avoidance of similarity (Tien, Bearden and Hunter, 2001, 55–56).
5   Statista regularly produce statistics-rich reports on the luxury industry, including the *In-Depth Luxury Goods Report, 2021* (www.statista.com).
6   Bain & Company produce an annual *Luxury Report*, based on their Luxury Goods Worldwide Market Study. The 2021 report was entitled "From Surging Recovery to Elegant Advance: The Evolving Future of Luxury" (Claudia D'Arpizio, Federica Levato and Constance Gault, Bain & Company, 2021; www.bain.com).
7   McKinsey and Company produce an annual *State of Fashion* report in conjunction with the Business of Fashion. The 2022 report touches on topics such as post-pandemic 'revenge buying' (www.mckinsey.com).
8   Deloitte annually produces a *Global Powers of Luxury Goods* report. The 2021 report is entitled *Global Powers of Luxury Goods, 2021: Breakthrough Luxury*, Deloitte Touche Tohmatsu Limited (www2.deloitte.com).
9   Euromonitor International's latest luxury report is *World Market for Luxury Goods*, Euromonitor International, February 2022 (www.euromonitor.com).
10   An example is "Luxury Goods Market Size, Share and COVID-19 Impact Analysis, by Product Type (Watches & Jewelry, Perfumes & Cosmetics, Clothing, Bags/Purses, and Others), End-user (Women and Men), Distribution Channel (Offline and Online), and Regional Forecast, 2020–2027", Fortune Business Insights (www.fortunebusinessinsights.com, accessed 31 August 2022).
11   https://datareportal.com/reports/digital-2022-july-global-statshot (accessed 31 August 2022).
12   www.statista.com/statistics/272014/global-social-networks-ranked-by-number-of-users/ (accessed 31 August 2022).
13   For example, "Build a Web Scraper (Super Simple!)", by Ania Kubów: www.youtube.com/watch?v=-3lqUHeZs_0 (accessed 7 September 2022).
14   www.cartier.com (accessed 1 September 2022).
15   Hootsuite/We Are Social, www.hootsuite.com/resources/digital-trends (accessed 1 September 2022).
16   www.gucci.com (accessed 1 September 2022).

17 Alice Cary, 2021, "Bottega Veneta's Puddle Boots Are Key to Rosie Huntington-Whiteley's Lock-down Looks", Vogue.co.uk (accessed 2 September 2022).

18 Positiveluxury.com

19 Robbreport.com

20 Caviarandcashmere.com

21 Upscalelivingmag.com

22 https://bellandblytravel.com/luxury-travel-insider/podcast/passalacqua/ (accessed 30 August 2022).

23 https://bellandblytravel.com/luxury-travel-insider/podcast/passalacqua/ (accessed 4 September 2022).

24 As a courtesy, we sought and obtained permission to use the podcast as a case illustration for this book from the two protagonists. Students of luxury would not generally be expected to do the same if their research is only going to be presented in their dissertation, but, if copyright material such as illustrations, charts, tables, images and text is going to be reproduced from previously published sources, permission to use the material should generally be sought from the original rights holder, typically the publisher. This can sometimes be managed online using RightsLink (www.copyright.com/solutions-rightslink-permissions/), which most of the major publishers are signed up to. A use fee may be payable.

25 Experiential luxury "creates a rich and dynamic environment by indulging the senses on multiple levels, beckoning us towards an immersive experience, beautiful details and delightful sensations", www.kohlerasiapacific.com/articles/experiential-luxury-defined.html (accessed 4 September 2022).

26 https://gdpr-info.eu (accessed 28 July 2022). The GDPR applies to all countries in the European Economic Area. The UK currently follows the GDPR in domestic law, enshrined in the 2018 Data Protection Act, but, following its departure from the European Union, has the right to amend this in future.

27 Watchuseek.com (accessed 5 September 2022).

28 E.g., www.calculator.net/sample-size-calculator.html; www.surveymonkey.co.uk/mp/sample-size-calculator/ (both accessed 6 September 2022).

29 A *research panel* is the group of people who have been selected to take part in a survey or some other means of obtaining data from research participants. The panel will typically be the tangible manifestation of the sampling procedures that are implemented by the researcher. Thus, if the survey requires a 5% probabilistic (random, stratified cluster) sample to be drawn from a known population of 5,000 people, and the researcher has the means to access this sample (e.g., an adequate sampling frame and a way of communicating with the selected individuals), the resultant 250 participants will make up the research panel for this particular survey.

30 The crowdsourcing platform Amazon Mechanical Turk (MTurk) had around 500,000 MTurk workers in 2018, and some 250,000 MTurk workers had completed at least one human intelligence task in 2019, 225,000 of whom were based in the USA (www.cloudresearch.com, accessed 6 September 2022). The market research firm Field Agent claims currently to have 2 million "Agents" in the USA alone (fieldagent.net; accessed 6 September 2022).

31 Aguinis, Villamour and Ramani (2021, 826) reported that 10% of MTurk workers account for 40% of all completed studies.

CHAPTER 6

Methods for Luxury Research

WHAT IS THE DIFFERENCE BETWEEN METHOD AND METHODOLOGY?

'Method' and 'methodology' may often be used interchangeably, but it is important to draw a clear distinction between the two words so that the student researcher can understand how they fit together. In essence, everything we have covered in the book up to this point forms part of the methodology of research, while what follows from this point is principally concerned with method. *Methodology* concerns the overall approach to the research, which includes the theoretical framework that is built by the researcher, their epistemological position and the rationale that underpins this (e.g., realist, idealist; positivist, interpretivist; deductive, inductive), the research focus and questions, and both the design and justification of the strategy to be used to engage and answer these questions. *Methods* are the instruments that the researcher will use in order to obtain, organise and analyse the data that are needed to engage and answer their research question(s), although the choice of method and the evaluation or interpretation of research findings are likely to be influenced by the wider methodology and thus the researcher's intellectual standpoint. Method is an integral part of methodology, but only a part; methodology is the whole.

The choice of method(s) to be used in the research should emerge organically from and be determined by the methodology and the nature of the investigation and should certainly not be predetermined before the intellectual process of building a research enquiry has even begun. In reality, students often select from a 'menu of methods' based on what they are familiar with or confident about using, rather than systematically and incrementally identifying the right tools for their particular task and learning new techniques as appropriate. The aim of this chapter is to provide student researchers with knowledge and insight about a wide array of research techniques so that they can make an informed choice in selecting the most suitable methods for their particular research investigation.

RESEARCH METHODS: THE PROFESSIONALS

Before we start building our 'menu of methods', it is worthwhile gaining a sense of how professional academics specialising in luxury approach their research investigations. Based on our

DOI: 10.4324/9781003295372-6

survey of the methodologies employed in 160 academic articles on luxury published in 2021, we found that, of the studies that reported on the research tools they had used (79 studies made no mention of research methods), 58 studies used questionnaires/surveys as their principal research tool, 23 studies used interviews or focus groups, and 1 study used both a questionnaire and interviews. Of the studies that used questionnaire surveys, 57 (98.3%) adopted a quantitative methodology (1 did not state which approach had been adopted). In contrast, 18 (78.3%) of the studies that used interviews/focus groups adopted a qualitative methodology (an additional 3 were unstated, 1 used quantitative techniques, and 1 used mixed methods). So, there would appear to be a very close link between method and methodological approach. We also found that there was a significant difference in methodological approach according to the fields of luxury in which researchers were specialising: brand management, purchase behaviour, self-perception, social media and digitalisation, and sustainability (this will be discussed in more detail as an example of analysis in Chapter 7, Figure 7.8).

SURVEY RESEARCH

A social survey is a *systematic study* of a particular issue, subject or social/demographic group (for example, consumers, consumerism, sustainability, social media users, millennials, sub-cultures, KOLs, etc.). The word 'systematic' is important here. It involves devising a methodical system for obtaining data that are standardised and consistent in design and execution, which will thereby yield consistent results – inconsistency and fluidity are the enemy of systematic analysis. Fundamentally, a survey involves the *collection of data/information by asking questions* of your target population or sample (referred to as 'participants') and recording the answers they give to these questions. A survey can be conducted *face to face* (physically or online, by yourself or using an interviewer) or from a distance (by post, via the internet or using a crowdsourcing agency). The more *remote* the researcher is from the actual administration of the survey, the less control they have over its conduct and the way that participants understand and respond to the questions. This places considerable importance on the clarity and logic of survey design and on the precise wording of questions, as well as the training of any interviewers or briefing of a third-party survey facility. A survey may involve a cluster of respondents within a given locality or be almost limitless in its geographical reach. The researcher must give careful thought to *who their target population is, how to reach it, how to obtain a sufficiently representative sample, what sorts of questions* it will be ethically and operationally appropriate to ask their participants, and also whether the survey instrument is *sufficiently well designed* to yield the kinds of information they need for their analysis and to answer their research questions.

QUESTIONNAIRES

The *questionnaire* is the most commonly used method for conducting standardised or structured surveys. A questionnaire is a document containing a series of questions which are designed to yield standardised information that is of use to the researcher in addressing and helping to answer their research questions. Beyond this generalised description, a questionnaire can contain a very wide variety of design components and formats. We will introduce some of these in the following paragraphs.

As a standardised survey instrument, it is important that all questionnaires, and the questions they contain, *are administered identically for all participants*, in a rigid sequence, in order to yield consistent and systematic data amenable, typically, to statistical analysis. This way, differences in responses can be attributed to differences of opinion rather than to the question being phrased in a different way for different participants. This rigidity is essential for standardised responses, but in the process the researcher sacrifices the opportunity spontaneously to deviate from the core questions if an interesting case or response emerges, or to add insightful nuance, or to draw out the individuality of the respondent. This trade-off can be softened by using different question styles or formats, as we shall discuss shortly.

There should be *no room for ambiguity* in a properly designed questionnaire, especially if the researcher is not going to be present to clarify any misunderstandings. Wording is very important: vague questions will lead to vague answers, no answers at all or the respondent guessing what is meant or intended. Alternatively, the researcher/interviewer may need to explain to the participant what was actually meant, which could result in them leading the respondent and the questions not being asked in an identical way for all participants. None of these situations will yield reliable data.

Can I use a questionnaire that someone else has designed for a similar purpose? No. Part of the objective of postgraduate research is for the researcher to gain and develop the requisite skills for the task and transferable skills that may be useful in the future. Simply borrowing someone else's survey instruments negates this possibility and may be considered similar to plagiarism in the ethics of research. Can I learn from the way that other people have operationalised (e.g., psychological, attitudinal or behavioural) abstract concepts when formulating questions to include in a questionnaire? Yes. This is actually standard practice in several branches of luxury research.

It is essential to *pre-test* a survey questionnaire. Once it has been designed, it should be tested out on people similar to those who will be included in the final survey, in order to check for meaning and comprehension, how long it takes to administer and so on. The pre-test phase should last for as long as is necessary to ensure that the researcher has the right instrument for the task in hand; when the pre-test reaches '*saturation point*', where no additional insight is gained from further pre-tests, then the pre-test has run its course. This is also the stage to test for and eliminate superfluous questions: participants generally have limited time and patience, and so it is important to keep the questionnaire as short as possible. An interesting questionnaire is more likely to strengthen the enthusiasm of the participant. Mix it up a bit using different styles and formats: uninspiring or monotonous questions often elicit short or scant responses.

The questionnaire should always be highly *professional* in appearance – impressions are very important. It is conventional for the student researcher to include a *copy* of their questionnaire in an appendix at the end of the dissertation. This will allow the examiners to evaluate the instrument's efficiency and efficacy and will also provide valuable insight into the clarity of the student's thinking; it can even provide a lens to their research design. The questionnaire must obviously have a clear connection with the research questions and the overall objectives of the research.

When administering a questionnaire, the researcher should, at the outset, *introduce* the objectives of their survey to the participant (either as a written statement at the beginning of an online or postal survey or verbally where the interview is face to face), so that their thought processes are in tune with the survey focus. But, depending on circumstances, the researcher should be cautious about giving away so much about the aims of the survey that they may begin to influence or preprogramme the participants' responses so that the latter give the answers they think the researcher wants rather than what they think themselves. As with the research questions that we discussed in Chapter 4, each question in a questionnaire should contain only one question, not multiple elements in the same sentence. The researcher should also avoid the use of leading questions – questions phrased in such a way that it prompts the participant to answer in a specific manner. When administering a questionnaire survey, the researcher should be conscious about how *refusals* and incomplete questionnaires can influence their *sampling* frame, if they are using one.

The researcher should pay very careful attention to *question phrasing and syntax* and think carefully about the *order* of the questions. The questionnaire might be structured in sections, each with a thematic title or heading, to help guide the participant through the document. The use of *continuity statements* such as 'now I'm going to ask you about …' or 'the next section is concerned with …' will also be more user-friendly than simply asking a series of questions. If the questionnaire *flows* smoothly and logically, the respondent is less likely to be puzzled or confused, which will both save time and elicit the participant's full attention. There are two schools of thought on the ordering of questions: one suggests that factual background information (age, sex, education, income) should be collected at the beginning in order to help ease the participant into the process; the other suggests that the 'meatier' questions should be put up front as they are usually the most important to the researcher's investigation. Sensitive or personal questions might be kept towards the end for fear of losing the participant's co-operation by jumping straight into them.

The researcher should give clear *instructions* about how to complete the questionnaire, especially when the researcher will not be present during its administration. These instructions might include: the document is to be completed by the target participant only, not 'by committee'; the questions should be completed in sequence rather than reading the questionnaire through before commencing; the fullest answers possible should be given to the open-ended questions; what to do with the questionnaire when it is completed; and so on. It is also courteous to the participant to indicate how the data are going to be used, and it is essential that the researcher should be in full compliance with the ethics of research and with data protection legislation (which we discussed in Chapter 5).

QUESTION FORMATS

First, we draw a distinction between 'open' and 'closed' questions. The *closed* or *semi-closed* question format offers the participant an array of *pre-populated* response options (*multiple choice*), from which they choose one or several depending on the rubric of the question, or they can be asked to list them in their perceived order of importance (*rank order*). It is usually advisable to include a 'none of the above' option for where their answer does not fit the options available. An illustration of the closed format is provided in Box 6.1 (with three options for how the participant should answer the question). An advantage of the closed format is that it delivers to the researcher a consistent and standardised body of data, which is one of the main aims of the questionnaire as a research tool. However, a danger with the closed format is that participants may tend to tick the box that comes closest to their position, or indeed any box at random, because there is not a box available that matches their true opinion or position, thereby introducing *bias* or inaccuracy into the survey. Alternatively, an option can be made available for the participant to provide an explanation/choice other than those offered by the researcher (*semi-closed*; shown as an extra line at the bottom of Box 6.1). The closed format might be used where the researcher needs precise and concise answers to questions – effectively data over detail – but its effectiveness is only as good as the researcher's knowledge of the topic being addressed. A *pilot test* of the questionnaire (in its semi-closed form) would reveal whether the response options adequately match the views of the research participants, and which if any options need to be added (or removed) before the final questionnaire is administered.

BOX 6.1

Closed and Semi-closed Format Questions

Which of the following best describes why you purchase second-hand luxury fashion items? (Please tick only one box/please tick any box that applies/please list your choices in order of importance.)

I believe, by purchasing second-hand luxury items, I am putting less pressure on the natural environment (Ethical)	☐
Buying second-hand stuff is cool (Social)	☐
I can't afford the same item brand new (Financial)	☐
I am already a regular purchaser of second-hand luxury things (Ethical)	☐
I like fashion items that already have a worn look/feel to them (Personal)	☐
I buy second-hand luxury items because I want to show myself to be a Responsible consumer (Social)	☐
By purchasing second-hand luxury items, I am getting better value for money (Financial)	☐
I feel happy when I find a luxury item in a second-hand shop (Personal)	☐

Other (please specify): _____

_____

The participant can also be asked to fit their response to a *rating scale*, as shown in Box 6.2.

BOX 6.2
___

The Scale Format

On a scale of 1–10, with 1 being extremely poor and 10 being extremely good, how would you rate the efforts being made by the Kering Group, LVMH, Richemont and the Swatch Group to mitigate the environmental impact of their constituent luxury brands?

Kering Group:

Extremely poor	1	2	3	4	5	6	7	8	9	10	Extremely good
	☐	☐	☐	☐	☐	☐	☐	☐	☐	☐	

LVMH:

Extremely poor	1	2	3	4	5	6	7	8	9	10	Extremely good
	☐	☐	☐	☐	☐	☐	☐	☐	☐	☐	

Richemont:

Extremely poor	1	2	3	4	5	6	7	8	9	10	Extremely good
	☐	☐	☐	☐	☐	☐	☐	☐	☐	☐	

Swatch Group:

Extremely poor	1	2	3	4	5	6	7	8	9	10	Extremely good
	☐	☐	☐	☐	☐	☐	☐	☐	☐	☐	

An advantage of the closed format is that the responses can very readily be converted into data: in Box 6.1, we have suggested four thematic categories for the responses – ethical, social, financial and personal – and accordingly the responses could be coded A–D or 1–4 (note these are *ordinal* not numerical assignations: they identify categories of response, and so, if using numbers, cannot meaningfully yield summary statistics such as mean and standard deviation). If the researcher chooses to include an 'other' category, they would need to find discrete codes to cover any additional responses that emerge, and/or fit the responses into the four coding categories already identified. In Box 6.2, the rating scale translates directly into numerical data.

A third option is the *semi-open* format, where the researcher offers a number of response categories to choose from, as above, and then follows this up with a question such as 'why did you say this?' or 'is there anything you would like to add about why you purchase second-hand luxury?' to elicit further detail and insight. This approach negates the precise and concise rationale of the closed format to some extent but has the advantage of seeking an explanation for the participant's response – the 'why' as well as the 'what' – rather than relying on the researcher's own (assumed) explanation. Clearly, for the purposes of analysis and interpretation, more effort will have to go into coding or processing such responses, but they might allow the researcher the opportunity to include both quantitative systematisation and qualitative insight at the same time.

The *open* format gives the participant much more freedom to express their answer or view, with less predetermination of response possibilities by the researcher. Open-ended questions encourage a conversation, because *they cannot be answered with a single word*. In order to initiate a conversation, and thus avoid single-word responses, you need to be creative about both the wording of your questions and the way that you engage with the respondent. Questions prefaced by 'what if?', 'why?' and 'how?' are more likely to solicit expansive responses. Questions starting with 'do you …?' are more likely to lead to simple yes/no/maybe/don't know responses. How open and responsive someone is to an open-ended question may depend on the time pressure they face, the rapport you have managed to establish with them and so on. An example is given in Box 6.3: use of the word 'why' is more likely to elicit a narrative response; use of the phrase 'the reasons why' may yield a list of reasons without a fuller explanation. The number of lines offered to the participant could be used either to restrict the voluminosity of their response or to encourage a voluminous response. The response information is likely to be more challenging to handle analytically, both in its volume and variety, but it offers the possibility of incorporating some qualitative depth and insight into the presentation of findings and further provides reassurance that the response has not been steered by the researcher's own preconceptions.

BOX 6.3

Open Format Question

Please tell me [the reasons] why you purchase second-hand luxury fashion items:

_____

_____

_____

_____

LIKERT-STYLE QUESTIONS

One of the most frequently-used question formats is the *Likert scale* (pronounced Li-kert not Ly-kert). Introduced in 1932 by the American social scientist Rensis Likert as "a technique for the measurement of attitudes" (Likert, 1932), the scale is used to ascertain participants' level of concurrence with statements proffered by the researcher and offers the researcher a more nuanced or granular set of data than that provided by simple yes/no answers. The Likert scale is often used where the researcher aims to solicit the opinions, perceptions, attitudes, preferences or behavioural tendencies of the participant.

Likert-style questions typically employ a five-point or seven-point scale between two polar extremes (e.g., strongly agree/strongly disagree, always/never, highly satisfied/highly dissatisfied, extremely important/totally unimportant), with a neutral (or undecided) option in the middle (Box 6.4). Some researchers prefer to use a four-point scale, which forces the participant to make a choice in one direction or another rather than seeking refuge in a non-committal response; this is linked to the possibility of *central tendency bias*, where people may naturally gravitate towards a middle or neutral point and may be disinclined to express extreme positions, regardless of what they actually feel. Other potential shortcomings that the researcher should be aware of (these are not exclusive to Likert-style questions) include *social desirability bias*, where people seek to adopt the 'right' position (a socially normative stance) rather than the position they actually hold; *affirmation bias*, where they provide what they perceive to be the 'correct' answer if they have worked out or been told the underlying objectives of the survey; *favourability bias*, where they seek to present themselves in a favourable light through the answers they choose; and *acquiescence response bias*, where people are more inclined to agree with something than disagree. These potential biases tend to be less evident where responses are anonymous rather than attributable to a particular participant.

BOX 6.4

Likert-Scale Permutations

	The Likert Scale					
	7-Point	Score	5-Point	Score	4-Point	Score
Strongly Agree	x	7	x	5	x	4
Agree	x	6	x	4	x	3
Somewhat Agree	x	5				
Neither Agree nor Disagree	x	4	x	3		
Somewhat Disagree	x	3				
Disagree	x	2	x	2	x	2
Strongly Disagree	x	1	x	1	x	1

Likert-scale responses can readily be converted into numerical data by substituting the response categories into numbers: for example, 1–7, 1–5 or 1–4, depending on the scale used (Box 6.4). However, students should be aware of certain assumptions and caveats that accompany this conversion process. Converting categories (ordinal data) into numbers (numerical data) may be based on an assumption that the response categories, or the intervals between them, are linear and equidistant and thus that it is acceptable to allocate sequential numerical values rather than weighting them differentially. Is the categorical 'distance' between 'strongly agree' and 'agree' the same as that between 'agree' and 'neutral'? (Indeed, is neutral even an opinion?) The researcher can help to mitigate this issue through careful and logical phrasing of the response categories in relation to the statements that the participant is being asked to evaluate. For instance, it is illogical for a scale to range from 'greatly enamoured' to 'grossly disappointed' when evaluating someone's reaction to a luxury brand pop-up, as the two extremes are not necessarily congruent and thus linearly related.

Data derived from Likert-scale questions can be used descriptively – for example, showing the distribution of participants' responses across the four, five or seven scale points to demonstrate a finding from the research – but in luxury research they are frequently used to populate what are called 'latent variables' – abstract concepts, such as 'need for uniqueness', which are not directly measurable but which can be made tangible by using measured responses to various behavioural statements plotted on the Likert scale, as we discussed in Chapter 5 and will explore in more detail in Chapter 7. In the remainder of this section, we will demonstrate how to use a series or *matrix* of Likert-scale questions to create a *composite variable*, following a similar logic to the operationalisation of latent variables and, arguably, creating a more accurate or representative indication of a particular phenomenon than from a response to a single statement.

The example involves generating a composite variable for the concept of 'materialism', which arguably is an important socio-psychological factor in people's desire to consume luxury goods (a quick search of the Web of Science reveals 140 articles written in the last five years that include both 'luxury' and 'materialism' in their subject fields).[1] Materialism can be defined as "people's endorsement of values, goals, and associated beliefs that center on the importance of acquiring money and possessions that convey status" (Dittmar *et al.*, 2014, 880). We might wish to undertake an analysis of the influence of materialism, allied to other factors such as the need for uniqueness, conformity avoidance and hedonism, on luxury purchase intention or behaviour, or the tendency towards conspicuousness/inconspicuousness in consumption choices, or even attitudes and behaviour towards luxury sustainability. Whatever the investigative and analytical framework, a solid and reliable measure for materialism (and all other variables) will be key to the validity of the research findings. We could use the yes/no answer to the simple question "are you materialistic?", but this would be fraught with limitations. We could, as is typically the case in luxury research, take three or four indicators and use these as a proxy for a latent variable in an analytical model (discussed in Chapter 7). In our example, we take 18 indicators of materialism and combine the results into a single variable. The point is that 'materialism' is a very complex concept that cannot readily be boiled down to a handful of identifiers. It is simultaneously social, psychological, behavioural and often deeply personal, and people may display materialistic tendencies in particular aspects, but not all of them simultaneously or to the same extent. Creating a composite variable out of a large array of factors holds the prospect of revealing a much greater degree of nuance and variation between participants than a simplified variable based on a handful of rather similar indicators, which we often find in luxury analysis.

Following established practice, we create our composite variable by using the Likert-scale responses to an array of statements relating to materialism that have been developed and tested across time in the literature. The statements we include here were used by Zici *et al.* (2021) in their exploration of the influence of materialism, individualism/collectivism and self-expression on luxury purchase intentions in South Africa, but these in turn were developed from Marsha Richins's (2004) work to develop a 'material values scale'. Rather than simply operationalising materialism as the desire to possess material goods, the indicators were clustered into three groups – success, centrality and happiness – which cover aspects of materialism that are personal, aspirational and concern satisfaction. Box 6.5 lists these 18 statements. Some of the statements ask the participant to confirm or refute materialistic tendencies, whereas others refer to non-materialistic values and behaviour (designated as ★ in Box 6.5, meaning that the scale is reversed). It is sometimes good to mix up the statements so that they do not become too monotonous, risking the participant losing focus. However, it is important that the researcher remembers the directionality of the statements when it comes to coding.

BOX 6.5

Statements for Creating a Composite Variable for 'Materialism'

Success:
(1) I admire people who own expensive homes, cars and clothes
(2) Some of the most important achievements in life include acquiring material possessions
(3) I don't place much emphasis on the amount [*sic*] of material objects people own as a sign of success*
(4) The things I own say a lot about how well I'm doing in life
(5) I like to own things that impress people
(6) I don't pay much attention to the material objects other people own*

Centrality:
(7) I usually buy only the things that I need*
(8) I try to keep my life simple, as far as possessions are concerned*
(9) The things I own aren't all that important to me*
(10) I enjoy spending money on things that are not practical
(11) Buying things gives me a lot of pleasure
(12) I like a lot of luxury in my life
(13) I put less emphasis on material things than most people I know*

Happiness:
(14)   I have all the things I really need to enjoy life*
(15)   I wouldn't be any happier if I owned nicer things*
(16)   It sometimes bothers me quite a bit that I can't afford all the things I'd like
(17)   My life would be better if I owned certain things I don't have
(18)   I'd be happier if I could afford to buy more things

Note: *the Likert-scale scores for these indicators should be reversed: 1 (strongly agree) to 7 (strongly disagree) instead of 7 (strongly agree) to 1 (strongly disagree).

Source: Derived from Zici *et al.* (2021), which draws from Richins (2004).

Box 6.6 adds a seven-point Likert scale to these statements (reproduced as the number equivalent to the statements in Box 6.5). In terms of converting answers into scores, this is up to the researcher, but here we have allocated a score of 7 to the answers that indicate the highest degree of materialism ('strongly agree', or 'strongly disagree' in the reverse statements) and a score of 1 to those that indicate the lowest degree of materialism. By way of an example, one of the co-authors has indicated (shown by 'X') their personal response to each of the statements, yielding a composite materialism score of 39 on a scale that ranges from 18 (unmaterialistic) to 126 (extremely materialistic), which places them at the lower end of the materialism spectrum. The other co-author scores 70.

BOX 6.6

Creating a Composite Variable for 'Materialism' Using the Seven-Point Likert Scale

	Strongly Agree	Agree	Somewhat Agree	Neither Agree nor Disagree	Somewhat Disagree	Disagree	Strongly Disagree	Score
Success:								
(1)	☐	☐	☐	☐	☐	X	☐	2
(2)	☐	☐	☐	☐	☐	☐	X	1
(3) *	X	☐	☐	☐	☐	☐	☐	7=1
(4)	☐	☐	☐	☐	☐	X	☐	2
(5)	☐	☐	☐	☐	☐	☐	X	1
(6) *	☐	X	☐	☐	☐	☐	☐	6=2

Centrality:

	1	2	3	4	5	6	7	
(7) ®	☐	X	☐	☐	☐	☐	☐	6=2
(8) ®	X	☐	☐	☐	☐	☐	☐	7=1
(9) ®	☐	X	☐	☐	☐	☐	☐	6=2
(10)	☐	☐	☐	☐	☐	X	☐	2
(11)	☐	☐	☐	☐	X	☐	☐	3
(12)	☐	☐	☐	☐	☐	X	☐	2
(13) ®	X	☐	☐	☐	☐	☐	☐	7=1

Happiness:

	1	2	3	4	5	6	7	
(14) ®	☐	☐	X	☐	☐	☐	☐	5=3
(15) ®	☐	☐	☐	☐	X	☐	☐	3=5
(16)	☐	☐	☐	☐	☐	X	☐	2
(17)	☐	☐	☐	☐	☐	X	☐	2
(18)	☐	☐	X	☐	☐	☐	☐	5

Composite Score	39/126

THE ARCHITECTURE OF A QUESTIONNAIRE

Sometimes, not all the elements of a questionnaire will apply to all participants, and so the design should incorporate a structure that guides the respondent to the appropriate questions or sections, rather than obliging them to answer irrelevant questions. The use of *filtering* or *branching* questions is a useful device in this regard and should be accompanied by clear instructions to the participant to ensure their efficient navigation through the appropriate routes or channels. A schematic illustration is provided in Box 6.7, with filter questions and instructions about where in the questionnaire to go to next depending on the participant's answers to certain questions.

ARE YOU PAYING ATTENTION?

Complete the question in Box 6.8.

Because a questionnaire is often an imposition on the participant's time, there may be an inclination to race through it as quickly as possible, not giving questions the attention they require. One consequence of this, from a data gathering point of view, is that the questions may not be answered as fully or as accurately as desired. Accordingly, it is advisable to insert an *attention check* midway through the questionnaire. This either serves to help the participant to refocus when they realise the purpose of the question, or, if the question is not answered appropriately, it flags to the researcher that the data provided by this participant may not be reliable and should either be eliminated from the sample or treated with caution. With a large sample, the percentage failing the attention check can be fed in to assessing the overall validity of the research

BOX 6.7

The Architecture of a Questionnaire

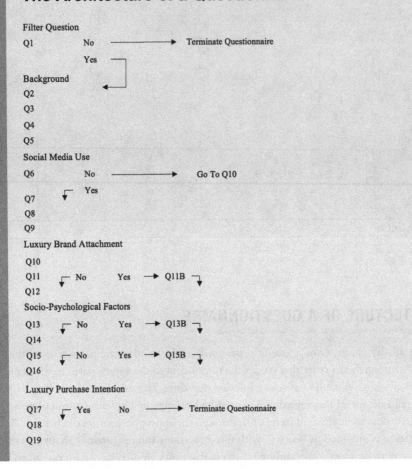

Filter Question
Q1   No ────────────→ Terminate Questionnaire
            Yes ┐
Background   │
Q2   ◄───┘
Q3
Q4
Q5
Social Media Use
Q6   No ────────────→ Go To Q10
            Yes
Q7
Q8
Q9
Luxury Brand Attachment
Q10
Q11   ┌ No   Yes → Q11B ┐
Q12
Socio-Psychological Factors
Q13   ┌ No   Yes → Q13B ┐
Q14
Q15   ┌ No   Yes → Q15B ┐
Q16
Luxury Purchase Intention
Q17   ┌ Yes   No ────────→ Terminate Questionnaire
Q18
Q19

BOX 6.8

Which Luxury Brand Do You Like Best?

Based on the text below, what would you say is your favourite luxury fashion brand? This is a simple question designed to check that you are paying attention. The correct answer here is none of the above.

Burberry	☐
Hermès	☐
Louis Vuitton	☐
Chanel	☐
Dior	☐
Gucci	☐
None of the above	☐

findings (response error) based on questionnaire responses. An example of an attention check was provided in Box 6.8. The researcher might also seek to maintain the participant's attention by mixing up Likert-style questions, as we did in Boxes 6.5 and 6.6.

THE RESEARCH INTERVIEW

In the previous section, we drew a distinction between closed and open question formats: the former intended to solicit short, staccato responses that can be readily processed into data; the latter allowing a more voluminous response which can help the researcher better understand a participant's response or provide information or insight that might help to personalise the resultant data. The *research interview* takes the open framework to a new level, being intended to yield detailed and insightful information which will usually form the basis of a qualitative enquiry. The degree of structure taken by the research interview can vary considerably, ranging from a fairly rigid, *structured* set of predetermined themes for discussion, to a *semi-structured* exchange that has 'stage posts' that the researcher should aim to pass, to a highly fluid and largely *unstructured* conversation around a research topic, theme or issue. The researcher should choose the point along this continuum between structure and fluidity that suits the needs of their investigation and analysis, their style as an interviewer and the capabilities of the interviewee. It is important to see the questionnaire and the interview as two discrete research methods, otherwise the interview may have so much rigidity that it ends up as little more than a questionnaire full of open-ended questions. The interview is intended to yield depth, detail and insight, and so conducting an interview as a series of questions risks failing to realise the full potential of this research instrument.

Because the research interview can often be quite fluid in structure and spontaneous in direction, the information gained from one research participant may not be directly *comparable* with other individual cases, because not all questions will have been posed, and not all conversations will have evolved in the same way; certain themes may have emerged from some interviews which were not present in others. Direct comparability is not an essential requirement in qualitative research, although the researcher will nonetheless have to build some form of organisational structure when preparing their data for analysis, interpretation and the presentation of findings. It may be helpful to think of qualitative data collected in this way as a mosaic from which, as it is carefully assembled, a clear picture starts to emerge.

The key advantage of fluidity in the approach to interviewing is that it allows the researcher to be spontaneous in responding to storylines that emerge from a conversation which may not have been anticipated at the outset or which are specific to the person being interviewed. The risk of too much fluidity is that the thematic focus of the research might become overly blurred, allowing the investigation to bleed beyond its operational boundaries and creating greater challenges for the structuring and processing of research information. The best compromise solution is for the researcher to operate with an *interview schedule or guide* – a series of themes, points, issues and questions (the 'stage posts') to be covered during the course of the conversation that clearly connect to the core research objectives, but without so much rigidity that it stifles spontaneity and turns the exercise into an interrogation more than an interview. The key attributes that the research interviewer needs to possess are the ability to think and act nimbly 'on their feet' so that they can process information, link themes and map out responses simultaneously; the ability to read (gauge) and establish rapport with the interviewee so that they feel relaxed and willing to divulge sometimes quite personal information; and the capability to exert discipline over the topics being discussed to ensure their research objectives are met.

Juggling all these tasks within a finite time frame while acting as a facilitator and taking detailed notes is beyond the capabilities of most researchers, and so, unless a third-party note-taker is also present, the researcher should ideally seek permission to (audio- or video-) record the interview, subject to the ethical and data-protection principles that we discussed in the preceding chapter. In addition to freeing up the researcher's mind for the task in hand, recording interviews gives the researcher (after transcription) a full body of data to work with at the analysis stage and also allows the possibility of using verbatim quotations from the interviewee in their presentation of research findings, [2] which is often very important in qualitative research, not least in allowing the voice of the participant to be heard in the overall research narrative. We are assuming that the researcher is also the interviewer, as they are likely to be most in tune with the research topic and purpose than someone engaged to conduct the interview on their behalf.

When planning an interview, it is often advisable to send the interviewee(s) an outline list of themes to be discussed in advance. This allows them the opportunity to give some thought to how they will respond to each of the themes and not only saves both parties time during the actual interview but also helps to ensure that the research participant is able to give fuller responses than might be the case if their answers are spur-of-the-moment. In Box 6.9, we have presented the list of themes that we sent in advance to participants for the interviews that provide the basis for part of the discussion in Chapter 9. This would be considered to be an *interview schedule*, which is particularly suitable for busy people, although in reality all of the interviews were free-flowing and used these themes as starting points for a discussion, rather than a more streamlined Q&A.

BOX 6.9

Example of Pre-interview Communication with Research Participants

Interview Themes

(1) How long have you worked in the luxury industry, and what roles have you have taken within this sector?
(2) How do you keep up to date on developments within your sector of the luxury industry?
(3) What aspects of your operations (could) benefit from primary research-derived information/data?

(4) When you have to conduct research, what are the principal steps you usually follow?

(5) Do you think your organisation is adequately set up to solicit, conduct, analyse and interpret research-based information?

(6) Can you please give me a typical example of your research experience?

(7) What constraints does your organisation face in regard to using research to strengthen/develop its business operations?

(8) Regarding 'doing research', what kind of advice would you like to give to young professionals who wish to enter the luxury industry?

The *in-depth interview* is a qualitative research approach which *substitutes depth for breadth*. It lies somewhere between the *semi-structured interview* and the *case study* (which we will discuss shortly). Indeed, the results from an in-depth interview might be used as a case study or one of several case studies. It is a way of obtaining what is called '*thick description*'[3] in the writing-up of the research, although findings should be analysed and interpreted rather than simply described. There is a debate as to whether the participant should be allowed to 'speak for themselves' through the extensive use of verbatim quotations, with the researcher a passive communicator of participants' own worldviews, or the researcher should control the orchestration of the narrative, actively drawing meaning through interpretation.

An in-depth interview may commonly focus on *feelings*, *attitudes*, *perspectives* and *viewpoints*. It is structured in the sense that the interview/conversation has clear research objectives and focus, but the means of reaching these are *fluid* and *flexible*. Fresh lines of enquiry emerge from respondents' responses. It seeks not just facts but also meaning, interpretation, explanation and understanding. The researcher's role is principally as a facilitator and listener. It centres on a *loosely structured conversation* which is focused on a clear and identifiable theme/question/set of objectives, but can head off in unanticipated directions depending on how the conversation unfolds. The in-depth interview is discovery-oriented (and thus principally inductive): *it aims to uncover material that is helpful to the research, in the form of either new knowledge or evidence which can be used to support a particular research interpretation* (see Box 6.10).

BOX 6.10

The Luxury Research Interview: Fine Wines

This research project is looking at the fine wine sector in the up-and-coming regions of France. The aim is to develop an alternative perspective to research that tends to focus on the star regions such as Bordeaux, Burgundy, the Loire Valley and so on. Of particular interest are the local and personal stories that young, innovative producers have to tell, and, by interviewing key actors, the researcher hopes to construct narratives on localism, provenance, personality, generational shift, vision and entrepreneurship. The researcher aims to use these interviews to build a holistic overview of three emerging fine wine-producing regions: St-Péray, Cairanne and Condrieu, all in the Rhône region of southern France.

Ahead of arranging a series of interviews, the researcher immerses themself in the research area. They start in each place by attending a *dégustation* (wine-tasting) in some of the local *châteaux* and *caves coopératives* (wine-producing co-operatives). They have an excellent command of French and a reasonable prior familiarity with the region, but spending a couple of days in each of the study sites allows them the opportunity to identify the most appropriate people to interview, while introducing themself to the people in the area. It quickly becomes apparent that the locals are as interested in the researcher as the researcher is in them: they are enthused that someone has taken the trouble to venture 'off the beaten track', they quickly come to trust the researcher and they are almost falling over one another to share their stories with them. This shows the advantages of contextual immersion and understanding, whereby the researcher is not just a pursuer and extractor of data, but a person whose research reflects a deep personal interest in the topic they are investigating.

They manage to set up six face-to-face interviews (with owners/viticultural-ists, vintners, workers – formal and casual – locals, the *maire* and traders/pro-moters) in each of the three study areas, and, such is the rapport that they have managed to establish with the locals, the interviews proceed as 'conversations with a purpose' rather than a formal extraction of information. The aim is to try to understand the world from the interviewee's point of view – the deep contextual meaning of their lived experience (Mann, 2016, 48). Themes touched on include background, history, motivation, connections, familiarity with the market, raising awareness, hopes for the future and so on. Each interview lasts more than an hour – the research is timed to coincide with a less busy period in the viticul-tural cycle – and yields a considerable volume of qualitative information. There was a clear correlation between trust gained and insight shared. The researcher agrees to share the results of their research with the study areas by sending a copy of their dissertation (with appropriate acknowledgements and attribution) to the local mayors. The researcher also willingly agrees to share with the wine producers some of their knowledge of luxury brand development and marketing gained from their course of study.

An in-depth interview should ideally be conducted *face to face* as it relies on the interviewer establishing a rapport with the interviewee and possibly also being able to monitor the body language of the respondent. It should be a 'guided conversation' rather than a Q&A session. Its fluidity allows new avenues of discussion to be opened up, *follow-up* questions to be asked, clari-fication sought, recapitulation as a means of double-checking, and even on-site validation of the researcher's interpretation of the research findings from the interview. It therefore requires the researcher to be *skilled* at identifying and engaging interviewees who are relevant to their research, establishing a rapport, making the interviewee feel at ease, steering the discussion in an appropriate direction, processing findings on the go, summarising findings and interpretations to the participant, and analysing a large body of qualitative and verbal data. In-depth interviews should be recorded (with appropriate permissions and assurances) in order to minimise the risk of data loss. They can be quite time-consuming: data from a one-hour interview can take one day to transcribe and at least half a day to analyse.

How many interviews should I conduct? There is no hard and fast rule. The researcher needs to find a balance between the information requirements of their particular research project and the time available for interviewing, transcribing, processing and analysing this information. If the objective of the interviews is to obtain a limited amount of standardised information from a quite rigidly structured interview format, which would also be relatively quick to process, a larger number of interviews should be attempted than for the pursuit of in-depth narratives which offer rich insight and detail on the real-world experiences of research participants, which can be quite voluminous and time-consuming to process. As a very general rule of thumb, a 30-minute interview may yield a transcript that runs to approximately 3,150 words of text.[4] Audio recordings are quite easy to transcribe these days – an online interview via Teams can even be transcribed live as an interview progresses – and, although transcription software is remarkably good, tidying up transcriptions to make them useable as research data (e.g., when the participant has a strong accent) can still be a quite tedious and time-consuming task. Our analysis of research methodology employed in recent publications on luxury identified 19 studies that used interviews as their main investigative tool, with an average number of interviews per study of 19.74 (range, 2–56; standard deviation, 13.75; coefficient of variation, 69.7%). Considering these 'sample sizes' were achieved by professional academic researchers, it may be reasonable to suggest that the student researcher should aim for between 10 and 15 semi-structured interviews or 5–10 in-depth interviews for their dissertation research. The key criterion is not the number but the quality and sufficiency of the information the interviews yield.

FOCUS GROUPS

Focus groups are often used by marketing firms to ascertain consumer preferences (market research) or people's reactions to advertising campaigns, for example. They are a useful device for exploring the 'why' of a topic as well as the 'what'. A *focus group* centres on the gathering together of a group of people (five or six may be most manageable) who form a *panel* from whom information and insight may be obtained relating to a particular research theme or issue. It is *not* a group interview of five or six people at the same time and in the same place; it is the collectivity of people and the cross-fertilisation of ideas and perspectives that distinguish the focus group from other research methods. Of course, the researcher may gain individual perspectives during the course of the focus group meeting, but it is the group dynamic and the way this contributes to emerging perspectives that the researcher should particularly aim to encourage – otherwise, why not just interview six people individually? Deeper and more diverse viewpoints may emerge from effectively choreographed group interaction than might be the case with research interviews. However, it is also important to note that people may say different things (particularly 'the right thing') in the presence of others to what they would say if interviewed individually (see Box 6.11).

BOX 6.11

A Focus Group for Luxury Brand Management: An Example

We are interested in the localisation strategies of luxury brands and have chosen five South-East Asian countries for a multi-nation investigation. The first part of the study involves identifying to what extent and how a cross-section of luxury brands adjust their strategies for individual Asian countries to suit local contextual circumstances: many do not, some do this poorly, and others are very creative with their localisation efforts; for some consumers this is important, and for others it is unnecessary. In addition to using survey and interview research instruments, the research finishes off the investigation with a series of focus group meetings in the target countries.

For the focus group meeting in Thailand, we sought to gather together a cross-section of members of society in order to obtain a diversity of viewpoints on luxury brands' localisation strategies. Accordingly, the six-member focus group was made up of the following individuals: a student from an elite Bangkok university (24,♀); a commentator on luxury who has a large online presence (27,♀); an official who works in the Ministry of Foreign Affairs (45,♂); a hotel manager from an up-market district of the capital (52,♂); a luxury store manager from Bangkok's premium shopping plaza (32,♀); and a person who runs an online shopping platform for imported luxury fashion goods (37,♂).

The focus group coordinator had established that localisation activities included: the production of special edition products (using Thai motifs, local materials, craftsmanship, etc.) to mark important annual events in Thailand, such as the Songkran new year festival (for example, the brand Jo Malone had a special line in April this year featuring traditional '*mud mii*' tie-dying) and the Thai Mother's Day, which coincides with the birthday of Queen Sirikit (a long-time patron of Thai silk), the present king's mother; and luxury brands' use of LINE Official Accounts in recognition of Thai consumers' high predilection for shopping through 'chat'.

The focus group participants had a lot of opinions and perspectives to share with the moderator, but it quickly became apparent that the group had, almost subconsciously, organised itself according to the hierarchies that permeate Thai society, along lines of age, seniority, position and gender. The moderator had to be highly sensitive and diplomatic in ensuring that all participants had an equal voice, and also that they were expressing their own opinion rather than an 'appropriate' viewpoint given prevailing narratives in Thailand on nationalism, localism, monarchy, sustainability and so on.[5] Keeping the conversation on track required considerable dexterity and tact on the part of the moderator, informed by their deep contextual understanding of local power dynamics and their ability to navigate towards true insights through very 'Thai' ways of dealing with such situations.

Circumstances and the objectives of the research should determine whether the participants in the focus group all share similar characteristics (*homogeneous*: e.g., gender, age, economic status, association with a particular aspect of luxury, etc.), the synergy of which will yield information and insight which are greater than the sum of the individual parts, or are a diverse group (*heterogeneous*), which will allow the emergence of diverse perspectives on the same issue. A homogeneous focus group may be a little easier to manage in terms of encouraging a group dynamic, but the facilitator must work harder to tease out heterogeneous responses. A heterogeneous focus group may be a little more difficult to manage, because disagreements and even clashes may dampen the group dynamic, but it may be more valuable to the research as a wider array of positions may become apparent than may originally have occurred to the researcher. Little is to be gained by selecting a panel of, say, six people at random; the researcher should invite people who are sufficiently familiar with the aspect of luxury to be discussed, who will be willing to express their views and who represent a relevant cross-section of social groups (see Box 6.11). There is also little value in inviting six people and then only three having the opportunity or confidence to participate.

The role of the researcher, in addition to assembling the group and organising the logistics, is to act as a *facilitator*: someone with good interpersonal skills who can ensure that rapport is established and people feel comfortable, that participants open up about the issue in focus, that *all voices are heard* and everyone feels they have made a contribution, and that the conversation flows freely and covers the territory desired by the researcher. The aim is to create an *interactive group dynamic* which leads to the revelation of shared opinions, attitudes, experiences or reactions. The researcher may have a loose interview schedule to ensure that the focus group passes the intended stage posts, but this should not be so rigid that it stifles spontaneity. The facilitator should immediately recognise any tangents in the discussion and either shut them down or pursue them if they appear worthwhile. The researcher or facilitator should be aware of any power dynamics that exist within the focus group and find ways of ensuring that they do not influence the free flow of opinion (see Box 6.11). The researcher should encourage people to discuss an issue among themselves rather than simply answer questions provided by the researcher. Attention should be given to arranging a comfortable setting for the focus group meeting that may be conducive to people feeling relaxed and willing to open up. A circular seating arrangement would be preferable to a classroom-style set-up.

The focus group is typically *qualitative* in form and outcome. It requires the researcher to be skilful at organising, facilitating, keeping the conversation going and moving in the right direction, thinking on their feet, analysing as things progress, and perhaps digesting the results in time to present them back to the group for validation at the end. A focus group might be used at an early stage of a research project (a starting point rather than a finishing point) in order to identify core issues from different interest groups, which can then be explored in more depth and/or more systematically using other research methods. A focus group could also be organised at the end of the research as a means of presenting research findings to an interest group, either validating the researcher's interpretation or allowing the opportunity for errors or misunderstandings to be rectified. Material from a focus group might be used to build a case study that could complement the presentation of more systematic data in a mixed methods approach.

The challenge with organising focus groups, which may also have resonance with other research methods, is finding people who are willing to give up an hour or so of their time to contribute to the research. Commercial companies will often incentivise participants in some way (payment, discounts, etc.), but this option is unlikely to be available to the student researcher. The natural inclination may be to invite people with whom the researcher is already familiar, such as family, friends, fellow students or other peers, but these are unlikely to represent the optimal set of people to discuss the given topic. Plugging into and drawing participants from (online) social or professional networks that are engaged with different aspects of luxury would appear more likely to yield an appropriate mix of informed and willing participants. People are also often quite willing to contribute to a student project and may also feel motivated by the belief that they are helping to make a difference to an important challenge in the field of luxury; however, ethically, it is important that the researcher does not lure people into their research investigation with promises of impacts and outcomes that they are unlikely to be able to deliver, or by making the participant feel sorry for the researcher.

As with the research interview, it would be advisable to let the group know in advance what the topic of discussion will be so they can think through their own personal perspectives, but it might also be sensible to remain a little vague about the precise focus so as to allow more scope for perspectives to emerge spontaneously from the discussion rather than being predetermined. The focus group meeting(s) should ideally be (audio- or video-) recorded, with appropriate permissions and assurances, or at the very least there should be a designated note-taker so that a comprehensive record of the conversation is made. Recording the focus group allows the possibility of incorporating verbatim quotations in the research report, which may be an important device for conveying contextual realism and giving 'voice' to the participants. However, some participants may feel a little self-conscious if they know they are being recorded and may be less willing to speak out or to communicate controversial opinions. A balance therefore needs to be struck between creating an encouraging environment and obtaining rich and usable data.

A *consent form* should also be prepared for all focus group participants (see Chapter 5); this has to be properly explained to the group members because the formality of the consent process may affect the intended informality of the group discussion. In line with the ethics of research, the researcher/facilitator should ensure that no focus group member feels discomforted psychologically from their participation – for example, systematically criticised, bullied or humiliated by other group members, or even the researcher! There should be no need for the researcher to obtain and keep personal information pertaining to the focus group members. Assurances of confidentiality can be given with regard to the use of the resultant material/transcript, but focus group members need to understand that their views will be expressed in front of others, and that confidentiality may be difficult to assure in this situation; perhaps a set of 'group rules' needs to be agreed whereby nothing that is said in the meeting is taken outside the context of the meeting, and everyone respects everyone else's opinion and their right to express it. This may also free up some people to participate more fully.

The product of a focus group may well be a transcript of 6,000–10,000 words (they yield a large amount of information in a relatively short amount of time), ideally with individual contributors identified so this can be worked into the analysis. Processing is likely to take the form of content analysis, which we will discuss in Chapter 7, but will be more complicated than with a single interviewee because it contains multiple voices.

CASE STUDIES

A *case study* is a means of studying phenomena or issues through the presentation, exploration and/or analysis of an individual case – be that a person, a social group, a brand, an institution, an event, a process, a problem, a country – with a view to deepening our understanding of an aspect of the research topic. It involves a *detailed, in-depth examination* of a real-world phenomenon or situation. The case study is typically a particularistic research device, meaning that its value lies in the insight it provides rather than its generalisability. The in-depth case study is usually an instrument of qualitative research. A case may be chosen because it typifies the topic being discussed, or even because of its unusual or distinctive character. Presentation of the case does not have to be only through words: it can include images, artwork, photographs and even audio-visual material to be submitted alongside the dissertation. A decision about whether to include the case study approach might be taken at the stage of formalising the methodology for the research, or it might emerge at a later stage of the research as the nature of the research data becomes more apparent. An effective case study not only tells a story but also reaches a conclusion that fits into the analytical framework of the dissertation.

A case study can be presented at three different scales. It might (a) be a short case illustration, or several illustrations, of a particular issue or situation, included to give a real-world flavour or example, a little like the boxed case studies we have used in this book. It could (b) constitute an empirical component of the presentation of research findings (e.g., ethical and sustainability issues with diamond jewellery and a case study of 'blood diamonds', or electric vehicle sustainability and a case study of cobalt extraction); or (c) the entire piece of research might focus on a particular country, brand or dynamic as a way of exploring a theoretical, conceptual or practical aspect of luxury industry development (e.g., a focus on luxury consumption in an emerging market, the influence of the K-pop phenomenon on Asian luxury marketing, the role of the Kering Group in the corporatisation of luxury, etc.). The case study can thus be an illustrative *device*, an aid to writing that gives the discussion a feeling of depth and realism, or it can be a research technique in its own right.

We might differentiate case studies as follows:

- *Illustrative*: used to highlight or exemplify a point being made (e.g., case studies of how and why individual consumers purchase counterfeit luxury goods).
- *Investigative*: an in-depth case study presented as data to be investigated, for example through content analysis (e.g., a forensic examination of the case of Dolce & Gabbana's controversial advertising campaign in China in explaining failed localisation strategies).
- *Exploratory*: introducing a case as a starting point to an enquiry and then drawing from it a framework for investigating the phenomenon or problem further (e.g., first present a variety of case studies of the growing presence of NFTs in luxury as a precursor to formulating research questions and an investigative framework for understanding their impact on perceptions of luxury value).
- *Explanatory*: a real-world example to emphasise or reinforce a point being made (e.g., a case study of web forums and/or luxury auction houses and/or investment brokers as an illustration of how prices for fine wines/whiskies are sustained).

- *Grounded*: included with the intention of rooting a conceptual discussion in a contextual reality (e.g., the use of case studies from a diverse variety of sites in Mauritius or the Maldives – perhaps derived from interviews – to 'ground truth' the concept of sustainable luxury tourism).
- *Stylistic*: a device to balance the presentation of research material, to add interest or variety (e.g., the insertion of occasional boxed case studies of people's personal stories about their passion for vintage luxury or their journey into pre-loved luxury).
- *Multiple*: a collection of case studies which illustrate multiple facets of the research subject (e.g., case studies of how different luxury brands have responded to the expansion and changing characteristics of social media).

In line with our earlier discussion of contextualisation in this book, it is important that a case study is not simply included as a descriptive embellishment, but that the setting for the case study is fully developed and explained (see Box 6.12). For instance, if the dissertation is going to focus on a single country as a case illustration (either the entire study or a section in the presentation of findings), the reader will need to know key aspects of this research site (as appropriate: social organisation, culture, politics, demography, attitudes towards luxury, etc.) in order for the discussion to have situational resonance. Simply choosing a country as an empirical focus for an investigation without rooting the discussion in the contextual particularities of this research site would not, in our opinion, constitute a case study.

BOX 6.12

A Luxury Case Study and Thick Description

Here is a seemingly axiomatic statement: "wealthy people buy luxury goods and services". If you are entirely happy with that statement, you can return to the main text. If you feel this statement is a bit of an oversimplification, continue reading.

When compiling empirical evidence to test a particular research idea, we might wish to use a case study, either as the sole focus of the research or as part of an array of techniques for presenting research findings. In this instance, we are using London as a test case for the way that wealth influences luxury consumption. London is one of the wealthiest cities in the world and is also a very important market for most luxury brands. We might think in terms of a questionnaire survey of a random sample of, say, 350–500 Londoners – a figure that most sample size calculators will deem appropriate – to obtain data which we can use to evaluate various questions about consumption behaviour, brand preference and so on. However, the more discerning researcher will realise that the wealth profile of London, or any city for that matter, is far from homogeneous. A properly contextualised case study would first explore the complexities and characteristics of the wealthy stratum of society in London and either use this as the basis for a more nuanced systematic sampling procedure (stratified random sampling or quota sampling) or a series of in-depth interviews with members of the various socio-economic groups that populate London's wealth mosaic, or both.

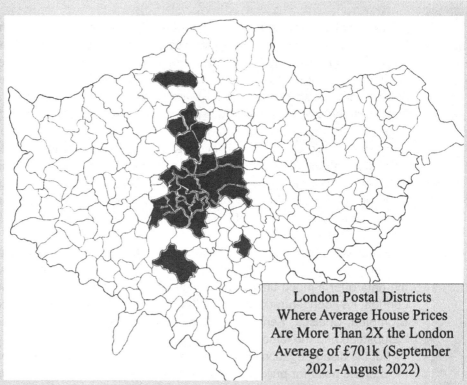

London Postal Districts
Where Average House Prices
Are More Than 2X the London
Average of £701k (September
2021-August 2022)

FIGURE 6.1 Hand-Drawn Map of the Districts of London.

Postal District	Average House Price (£m)	% of London Average		Postal District	Average House Price (£m)	% of London Average
EC4A 4	37.5	5347		W10 3	3.3	471
W1K 1	23.0	3279		W1U 4	3.3	471
W1K 4	16.0	2288		SW1W 8	3.2	452
W1K 6	14.1	2010		SW3 5	3.2	452
W1K 3	14.0	1990		WC1A 1	3.2	452
SW1A 1	11.9	1702		SW1X 7	3.0	423
W1F 8	6.1	870		NW8 6	3.0	421
SW1X 8	5.7	817		W1S 1	2.9	413
SW5 0	5.2	745		EC3R 6	2.8	405
SW7 3	5.1	731		W10 4	2.8	400
SW1W 9	4.8	679		W1H 6	2.8	400
W1K 7	4.7	668		W8 4	2.8	400
W1D 6	4.6	650		NW1 4	2.7	388
SW7 2	4.5	635		SW3 3	2.7	383
W1J 8	4.4	630		W1U 5	2.6	370
SW1H 9	4.3	612		W1J 6	2.6	368
W8 7	4.1	578		W8 6	2.6	366
WC2A 2	3.5	497		W1G 0	2.6	365
W1K 2	3.4	485		WID 4	2.5	364
W8 5	3.3	474		SW1X 9	2.5	362

FIGURE 6.2 Part of the Excel File Showing House Prices by London Postal District.

We start by producing a wealth 'heat map' of London. There are many of these available online, but we decided to create our own by way of example. We first sought to identify the spatial distribution of wealthy citizens in the capital city. We opted to use house price data as a proxy for wealth (the merits and demerits of so-doing – such as the price discrepancy between houses and apartments and whether house prices are an adequate indicator of wealth or disposable income – would ordinarily also be discussed in the methodology section). We obtained publicly available data on average house prices by postal district from Plumplot.co.uk (a partial view of the data, transcribed to Excel, is shown in Figure 6.1: Hand-Drawn Map of the Districts of London. Used with permission from Microsoft.)[6] and then plotted these data on a hand-drawn map (Figure 6.2: Part of the Excel File Showing House Prices by London Postal District).

Used with permission from Microsoft.).[7] The map shows a clustering of wealthy households in the central and western zones of London, whereas the data offer a much finer-grained view of the wealthiest neighbourhoods in London. Key concentrations of wealth in London include Knightsbridge, West Brompton, Chelsea, Kensington, Mayfair, Fitzrovia, Belgravia, Holland Park, Hampstead and the famous Bishop's Avenue.

But the disaggregation of London's population by wealth and location is just the starting point for building a more nuanced profile of the city's wealthy. Further analysis will show that there are diverse clusters of wealthy people scattered throughout the city, some closely associated with the wealthy districts the house price data have revealed, others less so. Without going into detail here, we can further stratify the wealth heat map using economic, social and cultural identifiers. There is old money (elites, aristocrats, other long-established monied groups, etc.) and new money (stockbrokers, people at the top of the financial and legal sectors, successful hipsters, upwardly mobile millennials, etc.); there are clusters of wealthy Jewish families (e.g., Golders Green), Russians (e.g., Mayfair, Belgravia), Arabs (e.g., Knightsbridge), South Africans (e.g., Mill Hill, Wimbledon), Chinese (e.g., Hampstead, St. John's Wood) and so on; as well as tourists who flit in and out of the capital.[8] And, of course, there are smaller pockets of wealth scattered throughout those districts that do not feature in the high-cost residential areas of London. If we stratify London spatially and according to various socio-economic criteria, we end up with a highly complex mosaic of wealth as a starting point for an investigation into how wealth connects with various facets of luxury consumption. Finding a way of incorporating a deeply nuanced wealth profile into an empirical investigation of luxury is a starting point for developing a highly contextualised case study as a component of a research enquiry, or its entirety. This contrasts very sharply with studies (and there are very many in the academic literature on luxury) that sample 350 people from the UK, China, Korea, Paris, New York or wherever and call it a case study of this location.

OBSERVATION

Observation is a research technique whereby the researcher seeks meaningful data by intelligently observing, recording, analysing and interpreting some form of activity or behaviour. There are two principal observation approaches: *participatory observation* is where the researcher gets involved in the activity they are observing and is thus immersed in the whole process within a natural setting (also referred to as *naturalistic observation*);[9] *non-participatory observation* is where the researcher observes an activity without becoming directly involved, in either a natural (real-world) or an artificial (experimental) setting, and is thereby less likely to influence the phenomenon or process being observed.

Participatory observation can be *overt*, where the researcher reveals the objectives of their involvement and participants are aware of their presence, or *covert*, where the researcher inserts themself into a situation without revealing their presence as a researcher and their intentions for being involved. The advantage of covert observation is that it allows the appraisal of an authentic situation which is not distorted by the researcher's known presence, and this may be particularly useful in risky situations, such as observing illegal activities – for instance, the manufacture and trade of fake luxury products. However, there are ethical issues associated with covert participatory (and even non-participatory) observation, where people may feel they have been exploited or used or deceived. It is also difficult to follow certain ethical principles such as obtaining informed consent from the (unwitting) participants in the research. Overt observation can help to overcome these dilemmas, but at a risk of introducing the so-called *observer effect*, where people change their behaviour when they know they are being observed.[10]

Observation is generally associated with qualitative research, where the researcher gains deep insight and understanding through immersion in the setting being observed, but, when used in experimental situations or with a systematic approach, it can also provide data for quantitative analysis (see Box 6.13). Participant observation offers the added opportunity for the researcher to validate their findings or interpretations by discussing these with members of the group they are working within. On the other hand, covert participation makes it extremely difficult to record observations for fear of 'blowing their cover', meaning they have to rely on the slightly more flawed technique of *recall*. The more deeply the researcher gets involved in the situation being observed, the greater is the risk that they will lose the detached objectivity that is important for interpreting observations within the context of their research framework. It is difficult to assure the representativeness of observational research, as each observed situation is likely to differ from any other, and the way the researcher interprets their observations may also be highly personalised in the absence of a systematic and repeatable set of guidelines.

BOX 6.13

The Systematic Use of Observational Data

Although many luxury brands have beefed up their online retailing channels in recent years, not least since the global pandemic, in-store retailing remains important, not just for selling products but for giving customers the chance to see, touch and sense luxury goods, even if they may eventually purchase them online. Considerable investment goes into designing flagship, retail and pop-up stores, with careful attention paid to *store atmospherics*. The 'feel' of a store is influenced by a great many factors, including: lighting, aroma, ambient sound, colour, use of space, furnishings, artwork, staff attire, pricing information and so on. Luxury brands often use various permutations of such atmospherics and aesthetics to form or reinforce their brand identity. The challenge is to match atmospherics to the kinds of customers the brands wish to draw to their stores or encourage to stay a while, or to convert a visit into a successful sale or a favourable impression.

Observing how customers interact and engage with the various manifestations of store layout and atmospherics is a vitally important tool for brand managers, but also a useful investigative method for the student researcher of luxury. Notwithstanding the ethical issues that we have already discussed in this section, access to in-store CCTV recordings could potentially yield a very rich source of data for the observant and suitably trained student to ascertain how consumers are influenced by which store atmospherics and to what effect. If this is ethically problematic, the researcher could position themselves inside the store, clipboard in hand and identifying tag on lapel, so that it is fairly evident to customers what the purpose of their presence is. Brands already use 'mystery shoppers' for a similar purpose (customer experience evaluation). Individual shoppers' journeys and touch points within the retail space, from entry to exit, could be mapped, analysed and interpreted as a starting point in the research, and hypotheses could be formed which could provide the basis for a more personalised phase in the investigation where the researcher interviews customers to ascertain – 'ground truth'[11] – why they followed particular routes and what they were thinking or feeling at different points during their in-store journey.

A crucial tool for observation research is the *field diary*, in which the researcher notes their observations (watching, listening, reading people's behaviour) and their in-process interpretations. Observation will typically tend to focus on behaviour and actions rather than narrative, but will need to be converted into words and then systematically organised in order to attempt an analysis of the phenomenon being observed. As with other forms of research, the researcher needs to decide whether to enter the observation phase of their investigation with a clear and fairly rigid set of ideas, variables and structures (deductive: for example, testing the idea that Gen Z and millennial luxury consumers respond differently to the use of VR [virtual reality] and AR [augmented reality] by luxury brands) or to let these emerge organically as this research phase evolves (inductive: for instance, the observation that Korean celebrities and influencers have considerable leverage in several Asian countries, and the need to make some organisational sense of this socio-culturally). The same applies to the processing of the resultant information: should they have a clear coding framework from the outset into which observations are fitted, or should the analytical structure and categories emerge after the observation phase has ended? The danger with the latter is that the framework for the analysis may become larger and more unwieldy than the researcher had originally envisaged, but, with the former, important new interpretations may be missed because of the rigidity of the researcher's reasoning, and the interpretation of observations may be used for little more than confirming the researcher's preconceived ideas.

Observation can be random and happenstance, but good observational research should be replicable; this may be harder to achieve with naturalistic observation, where each circumstance may be unique, than with observation in a controlled or experimental setting, where the researcher has more influence on the phenomenon and how it is observed. It is important for the student researcher to provide the reader with a clear and detailed explanation of how they have approached this aspect of their research and why they opted for this particular technique. Observation could even provide an added dimension to focus group research, particularly if the meeting is video-recorded: the researcher can look at how people interacted and how they presented their opinions (cf. Box 6.11), in addition to what they actually said. Observational data can be collected in real time, as the event unfolds, or in suspended time, such as by interpreting recorded data (such as from CCTV – Box 6.13).

A final form of observational research is *photovoice*, which came to prominence as a qualitative methodology in the 1990s. Here, the researcher present photographs on a topic and gets participants to communicate their reactions; these can then be used as the basis of observational data. A similar technique might involve giving people disposable or digital cameras and sending them out to record something related to luxury, and then discussing their results in a group situation when they return, which might be considered a form of *participatory photovoice*.

SUMMARY AND CONCLUSION

This chapter has offered some advice on a variety of research methods that students researching for a Master's dissertation are most likely to encounter. Another very important research method, content analysis, will be explored in the following chapter on data analysis. Students of luxury operating from within specialist departments or disciplines may need to undertake further investigation of research methods such as netnography (see Kozinets, 2010, 2014, 2020; Kozinets, Scaraboto and Parmentier, 2018), experimental research (Coleman, 2018; Druckman, 2022), archival research (Moore *et al.*, 2020), visual research (Spencer, 2022) and documentary research (Tight, 2019).

While we have presented each of the research methods separately, several can be used in tandem as part of a *mixed methods* approach, although this might depend upon the philosophical and methodological foundations the student has settled on for their own investigation. 'Mixed methods' has two meanings in this regard: the use of different methods based on a methodological (and philosophical) desire to incorporate both quantitative and qualitative research principles; and the combination of research techniques to suit the needs of individual components of the research enquiry, or even to add some variety to the exploration and presentation of research themes. One research method (e.g., interviews, observation) might be used to provide the information the researcher needs to be able to build and populate their main research instrument (e.g., a survey).

The reality facing many students researching luxury is that it is generally much easier to survey consumers than it is luxury brands. Accordingly, a systematic survey might be considered to explore consumers' perceptions of luxury brands within their chosen sector, and this could be complemented by insight from a small number of interviews with actors within luxury brands (brand managers, store managers, human resource managers, marketing managers and so on). Similarly, an exploration of the role played by celebrities and KOLs in influencing consumer sentiment and luxury brand attachment might start, on the one hand, with the systematic observation of influencer–consumer/follower interaction via social media, followed by a survey of consumers and/or the social media followers of these influencers, maybe supplemented by interviews or focus group meetings with particular interesting individuals who emerged from the survey, and, on the other, with a series of in-depth interviews with particularly influential celebrities or KOLs. In both examples above, the aim is to obtain information from two sides of an interaction between different parties or actors (Plan A). Should access to one side of the story turn out to be too challenging, or impossible, there should still be a rich and diverse body of data for analysis from the other side of the story, which might have to be beefed up to compensate (Plan B).

NOTES

1   Web of Science database, accessed 9 September 2022.
2   Conversations reconstructed – for the sake of note-keeping - *after* the interview has been completed cannot be used as verbatim quotations in the dissertation.
3   'Thick description' as a concept has its roots in ethnography (Geertz, 1973), where the researcher is expected to immerse themself deeply in the socio-cultural context within which they are operating and to communicate a rich, insightful and contextualised 'feel' for the study area and research participants in the presentation of their findings.
4   This figure is based on an average time–text conversion rate of 105 words per minute, calculated from the ten interviews that we use as the basis for the discussion in Chapter 9.
5   Indeed, all four of these narratives coalesce within the 'philosophy of the sufficiency economy' that was proposed in the late 1990s by the highly revered late King Bhumibol Adulyadej and with which, even today, Thai citizens want to demonstrate their compliance, even when it runs counter to many of the core underpinnings of luxury.
6   www.plumplot.co.uk/london-house-prices.html (accessed 20 October 2022).
7   We selected those postal districts where average house prices were more than 200% of the London average of £701,000. The map is for illustrative purposes only: the data are at sub-district or street level, but the divisions on the map are at postal district level.
8   See, for example, Atkinson (2020).
9   A variant of the participatory approach is participatory action research, where the investigator does not just passively observe a phenomenon 'from within' but actively sets out to bring about change through their involvement with research participants – for example, seeking the empowerment or unionisation of female piece workers who are sub-contracted to produce components for luxury goods from their homes in developing countries.
10 The observer effect is also referred to as the Hawthorn effect after secondary research by Henry Landsberger in 1958 relating to earlier studies on worker efficiency at the Western Electric factory in Hawthorn, Chicago, between 1924 and 1932 (Landsberger, 1958).
11 The concept of 'ground-truthing' is important in research. Derived from satellite imaging, where it

is necessary to gather information at ground level to ratify or calibrate an image taken from space, its application in research centres on the validation of interpretations gained from remote observation. In the present example, we may be able to map a customer journey through a store and make certain assumptions about the choices they made and the reasons for these, but ratifying these interpretations through follow-up conversations not only allows the opportunity to check that they are valid but also provides the opportunity to 'calibrate' further observations.

CHAPTER 7

Analysing Luxury Research Data

Data may typically be collected in numerical or categorical form. *Numerical data* consist of numbers that represent the true values of something that is measurable, such as income or age. *Categorical data* relate to qualities that are allocated to mutually exclusive groupings, such as a person's ethnicity or their preferred luxury sector. Categorical data may be *ordered*, such as income group (10,000–19,999, 20,000–29,999, etc.) or age group (1–19, 20–29, 30–39, etc.), or *unordered*, such as a preferred social media platform (Facebook, Instagram, Twitter, YouTube, Snapchat, etc.). Both types of data are valuable to the researcher and both are amenable to manipulation and analysis, but in different ways and with different provisos. A key distinction between the two types of data is that an arithmetic mean can be calculated for numerical data but not for categorical data, and thus statistical manipulation is more common in the former than the latter. In this chapter, we will explore some of a multitude of ways of presenting or analysing research data. We start with categorical data.

PRESENTING CATEGORICAL DATA

There are multiple ways of presenting summary categorical data in a way that allows visual perusal, including pie charts, bar charts, scattergrams, tables and so on. We will look briefly at just three of these here: pie charts, bar charts and tables, all of which will be produced with Excel. Using data from our survey of 81 brand managers in the luxury industry (see Chapter 2), we asked how their brand typically goes about satisfying their need for primary research data. Participants were offered four response categories: they undertake primary research using in-house research capabilities, they employ external consultants to undertake the research for them, they use a combination of internal and external mechanisms or they only rely on secondary data sources. The frequencies presented in Figure 7.1 were calculated from the main data set, which substituted numbers (1–4; these have no numerical value per se) for each of the response categories; these were then arranged in ascending order to make calculating frequencies straightforward. The pie chart was then constructed in Excel using Insert > Charts > 2-D Pie (using greyscale so that it could be reproduced here). An alternative way of presenting the data graphically, the bar chart shown in Figure 7.2, was created from the original data set (81 data points) using Pivot Chart in Excel (Excel > Insert > Pivot Chart), which requires the data

DOI: 10.4324/9781003295372-7

field(s) to be specified, together with a location in the Excel worksheet for the result. These descriptive data can also be presented in tabular form (Table 7.1).

Tables are also a useful way of presenting data that have been processed from their original form. In the following example, we demonstrate how we combined two slightly more complicated indicators of research in the luxury industry using the Pivot Tables function in Excel.

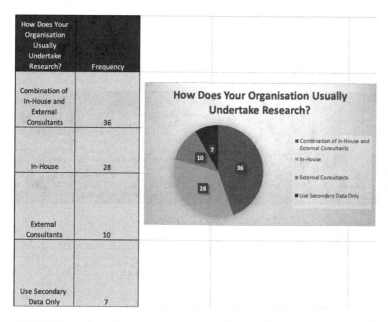

How Does Your Organisation Usually Undertake Research?	Frequency
Combination of In-House and External Consultants	36
In-House	28
External Consultants	10
Use Secondary Data Only	7

FIGURE 7.1 Pie Chart on Luxury Industry Research Source, Produced Using Excel Charts. Used with permission from Microsoft.

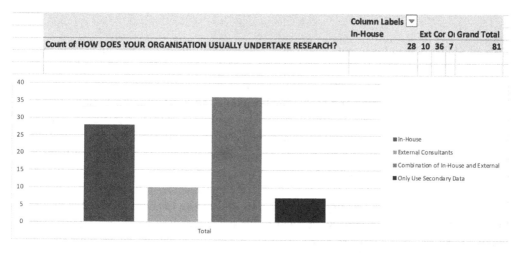

FIGURE 7.2 Bar Chart on Luxury Industry Research Source, Produced Using Excel Pivot Chart. Used with permission from Microsoft.

TABLE 7.1 Tabular Presentation of Data on Luxury Industry Primary Research Sources

Luxury Industry Primary Research Source	Frequency	Percentage
In-house	28	34.6
External consultants	10	12.4
Combination of in-house & external	36	44.4
Only use secondary data	7	8.6
Total	81	100

Data source: Authors' Luxury Industry Survey, July 2022

LUXURY SECTOR FASHION (A)	LUXURY SECTOR BEAUTY (B)	LUXURY SECTOR JEWELLERY (C)	LUXURY SECTOR HOSPITALITY (D)	LUXURY SECTOR FOOD AND DRINK (E)	LUXURY SECTOR OTHER	LUXURY SECTOR	WHAT KIND OF MARKET RESEARCH METHODS DO YOU TYPICALLY ADOPT? Secondary data for quantitative analysis	WHAT KIND OF MARKET RESEARCH METHODS DO YOU TYPICALLY ADOPT? Collect primary data	WHAT KIND OF MARKET RESEARCH METHODS TYPICALLY ADOPT? One-to-one interviews	WHAT KIND OF MARKET RESEARCH METHODS TYPICALLY ADOPT? Focus groups	WHAT KIND OF MARKET RESEARCH METHODS DO YOU TYPICALLY ADOPT? Mix of qualitative and quantitative methods	WHAT KIND OF MARKET RESEARCH METHODS TYPICALLY ADOPT?	QUANT, QUAL OR BOTH
1	1						A, B	1	1	1		A, B, C	3
1	1						A, B		1			B	1
1							A	1		1		A, C	3
1							A		1			B	1
1							A			1		C	2
											1	E	3
			1				D	1	1	1	1	A, B, C, D	3
											1	E	3
1	1	1					A, B, C		1	1	1	1	B, C, D, E	3
		1					C					1	E	3
1		1					B, C	1	1	1		1	A, B, C, E	3
										1		1	B, D	3

FIGURE 7.3 Segment of the Raw Data Set on Luxury Sector and Research Method, Showing Original Results and Disaggregations. Used with permission from Microsoft.

We asked luxury brand managers which methods they typically used when undertaking market research for their brand. They were offered the following categories: obtained secondary data for quantitative analysis, collected primary data for quantitative analysis, used one-to-one interviews, used focus groups and used a combination of quantitative and qualitative methods. Participants were able to indicate any category that applied to their case (Figure 7.3 presents the first 12 data points from the data set, and the penultimate column shows that participants often ticked several boxes). These data were disaggregated, as shown in columns 8–12. For our analysis, we were particularly interested in the relative use of quantitative and qualitative methods, and so we summarised the data in column 14, merging columns 8 and 9 into a quantitative category (denoted 1) and columns 10 and 11 into a qualitative category (denoted 2), in addition to a mixed methods category (denoted 3). We wanted to assess choice of method against luxury industry sector. However, brand managers had also been able to choose more than one category when indicating which luxury sector their brand served (column 7 in Figure 7.3: A: fashion, including apparel and small leather goods; B: beauty products and services; C: jewellery and watches; D: hospitality, including hotels and tourism; E: food and drink). These data were also disaggregated (columns 1–5; we excluded other luxury sectors in this exercise).

The entire data set was then activated, including the label field, and a pivot table was created (Excel > Insert > Pivot Table), with a cell in the existing worksheet identified in which the table was to be situated (Figure 7.4, A). We then designated the composite research method variable (column 14) as the column and, one at a time, the luxury research sector (columns 1–5) as the row, with research method as the values to be obtained, summarised by count (Figure 7.4, B), and presenting data as a percentage of row total (Figure 7.4, C and D). We repeated this exercise for each of the five luxury research sectors, which yielded the frequencies that are presented in rows 2–7 in Figure 7.5. We then repeated this exercise to show percentage distributions instead of frequencies (Figure 7.5, rows 8–12). The percentage breakdown of research method by luxury sector was then calculated manually (Figure 7.5, rows 14–18). We have thereby been able to present a sector-specific profile of luxury brands' approach to market research from data that might initially have appeared to be too highly aggregated. One of the remarkable findings from these data, and their tabular summary, is the extent to which luxury brands make use of qualitative research data, at least in part; this contrasts quite sharply with the overwhelming predominance of quantitative methods in academic research on luxury, which we touched on in Chapter 2 and to which we will return later in this chapter and in the discussion in Chapter 9.

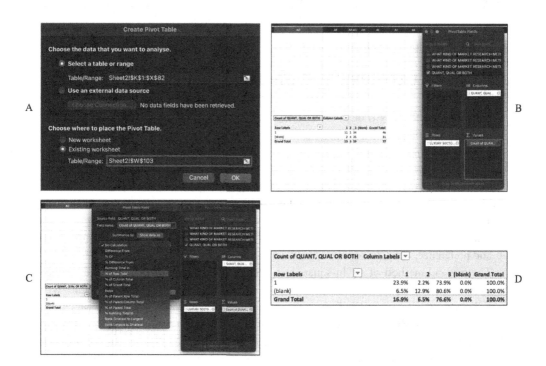

FIGURE 7.4 Creation of a Pivot Table in Excel. Used with permission from Microsoft.

	Quantitative	Qualitative	Mixed Methods	Total
Fashion	11	1	34	46
Jewellery	2	0	10	12
Beauty	5	2	29	36
Hospitality	0	0	10	10
Food & Drink	0	1	5	6
	18	4	88	110
Fashion	23.9	2.2	73.9	Luxury Sector Research Approach (%) [Row Percentages]
Jewellery	16.7	0.0	83.3	
Beauty	13.9	5.6	80.6	
Hospitality	0.0	0.0	100.0	
Food & Drink	0.0	16.7	83.3	
Fashion	61.1	25.0	38.6	% Distribution of Each Research Approach By Luxury Sector [Column Percentages]
Jewellery	11.1	0.0	11.4	
Beauty	27.8	50.0	33.0	
Hospitality	0.0	0.0	11.4	
Food & Drink	0.0	25.0	5.7	

FIGURE 7.5 Summary Categorical Data for Research Method by Luxury Sector. Used with permission from Microsoft.

ANALYSIS OF CATEGORICAL DATA: CHI-SQUARE TEST

A step further in the analysis of pairs of categorical data is to evaluate data distributions. One of the most commonly used techniques for this is the Chi-square test (usually written x^2). The researcher is able to use the test to see whether or not the distribution of findings differs from a theoretical normal or independent pattern. As a simple example, in a sample of 50 men and 50 women, half of each indicated that they preferred the brand Hermès, while the other half of both genders preferred Louis Vuitton. There would, therefore, be no significant difference in brand preference between men and women. If, however, 40 men preferred LV to Hermès, and 40 women preferred Hermès to LV, we would expect there to be a significant gender difference in brand preference. The Chi-square test is a way of evaluating the data pattern statistically.

The use and method of a Chi-square test are best illustrated with a real-world example. Here, we use some data derived from the analysis of research methods used by academics writing on luxury, which was touched on in Chapter 2 and to which we will return later in the present chapter. In early 2022, we used the Web of Science database to identify the 200 most-recently published academic research articles that included the word 'luxury' in the title field. Of these, 40 were excluded because their use of the word 'luxury' was not connected with the luxury industry. The ultimate aim of the present exercise is to ascertain whether different fields of study in luxury adopt similar or different methodological approaches to their research.

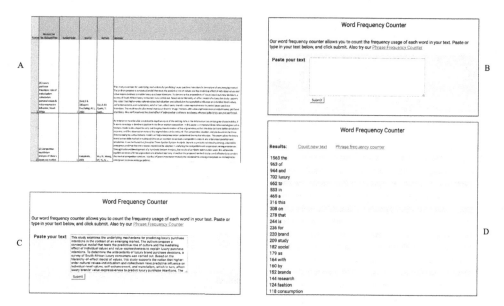

FIGURE 7.6 Undertaking a Word Frequency Analysis. Used with permission from Microsoft and Write Words (http://www.writewords.org.uk/word_count.asp).

To achieve this, we first had to identify thematic research clusters. The approach we settled on was to identify prominent keywords through a *word frequency analysis* of the abstracts provided by the Web of Science for each of the 160 papers we included in this exercise (which totalled 26,000 words). These were originally collected in an Excel worksheet (Figure 7.6, A), but for this exercise they were copied into a single Word document. We then used a web-based word frequency counting tool to process these data (Figure 7.6, B–D).[1]

We manually sifted through all the word frequency results to identify keywords, which we allocated to cognate clusters. It should be emphasised that the clustering was a subjective judgement made by the researchers; others might have classified the keywords differently. We also need to treat word count data with a little caution: in this instance, one abstract making repeated use of a single keyword may have distorted the overall picture. However, we deduced that, because the abstracts provided by the Web of Science are all of a similar length, this potential distortion was considered relatively trivial. From our clustering exercise, we identified five more or less discrete subject fields (Figure 7.7). It could be argued that 'social media and digitalisation' and 'sustainability' might have been subsumed within the other categories, but in this particular instance we were interested in these two themes as being important contemporary topics in the field of luxury. There were some 'outliers' that did not fit our chosen categories, and these were excluded from the exercise. After a slight adjustment in the allocation of keywords related to 'perception', the final distribution of keyword clusters is presented in Figure 7.7. Having identified our five thematic clusters, we then went through all 160 articles in order to allocate each to one of the five groups. This was surprisingly straightforward, although judgement calls had to be made for some papers that straddled two or more themes. The distribution of research articles according to this categorisation exercise is presented in Figure 7.7. Of the 160 papers, 10 did not fit any of the thematic clusters and so were excluded from this exercise.

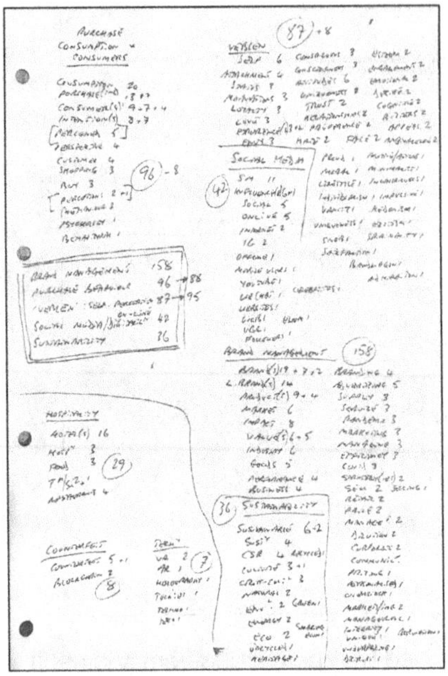

Thematic Cluster	No. of Articles	
Brand Management	158	32
Purchase Behaviour	88	41
Self-Perception	95	23
Social Media & Digitalisation	42	31
Sustainability	36	23
Other	44	
Not Classified		10

FIGURE 7.7 Creating Luxury Clusters from Keywords.

We wanted to see if there was any significant difference in methodological approach between these five segments of luxury research. The methodology sections of the 160 articles under consideration indicated whether the researchers had adopted a quantitative, qualitative or mixed methods approach. Twenty-four of the articles had no research methodology per se, either because they were entirely theoretical, conceptual, practical or literature-based in nature (14), or because they consisted of descriptive case studies without any analysis (7), or because they made no mention of method (3). The distribution of research methods against the five thematic clusters is shown in Figure 7.8. These data were then streamlined to focus solely on the quantitative *or* qualitative research approaches, omitting mixed methods (quantitative *and* qualitative) from this stage of the analysis.

The Chi-square test looks at differences in observed values from the values that might be expected if the distribution in each of the ten cells was perfectly uniform. The expected frequencies are calculated by multiplying the row total by the column total and dividing this by the total number of observations; thus, the expected frequency for brand management and quantitative would be $25 \times 99/120 = 20.625$; the expected frequency for sustainability and qualitative would be $18 \times 21/120 = 3.15$; and so on. For each cell, we then calculate the difference between the observed and expected frequencies, which is then squared and divided by the expected frequency. Thus, for purchase behaviour and quantitative, this would be $(33 - 29.7)^2/29.7 = 0.3666$. These ten calculations are then added together to give a Chi-square value of 13.337567. We now need to assess the significance of this value. To do this, we consult a Chi-square table (Figure 7.9). We must first decide on an acceptable significance level: conventionally, the threshold would be 0.05, meaning a 5% or less chance that the observed pattern occurred purely by

			Method			
		None Stated	Quantitative	Qualitative	Mixed Methods	
	None Stated	4	3	2	1	10
	Brand Management	5	15	10	2	32
	Purchase Behaviour	2	33	3	3	41
	Self-Perception	4	18	1	0	23
Subject Code	Social Media & Digitalisation	6	19	3	3	31
	Sustainability	3	14	4	2	23
		24	102	23	11	160

		Quantitative	Qualitative	
Observed Frequencies	BM	15	10	25
	PB	33	3	36
	S-P	18	1	19
	SM & D	19	3	22
	Sustainability	14	4	18
		99	21	120

		Quantitative	Qualitative
Expected Frequencies	BM	20.625	4.375
	PB	29.7	6.3
	S-P	15.675	3.325
	SM & D	18.15	3.85
	Sustainability	14.85	3.15

(O-E)^2/E	BM	1.534090909	7.232142857
	PB	0.366666667	1.728571429
	S-P	0.344856459	1.62575188
	SM & D	0.039807163	0.187662338
	Sustainability	0.048653199	0.229365079

Sum of (O-E)^2/E		13.33756798
		Critical value at p=0.05 and 4 df is 9.488 and for p=0.01 is 13.28
		p=.01
		Significant Difference in Distribution of Values Compared to a Perfectly Even Distribution

FIGURE 7.8 Conducting a Chi-Square Test on Luxury Research Methodology Data. Used with permission from Microsoft.

chance, or, put another way, we would have 95% confidence that any inference we make about an observable distribution is valid. We also need to calculate degrees of freedom – the number of values in the calculation that are free to vary; generally, the more cells in the calculation, the harder it is to establish with confidence that there is a significant pattern in the data. Degrees of freedom here are calculated as $(r − 1)(c − 1)$, where r is the number of rows and c is the number of columns – in this case $(5 − 1)(2 − 1) = 4$. The critical value at 95% confidence and 4 degrees of freedom on the Chi-square table is 9.49. To be significant, the Chi-square value must be greater than the critical value. Our Chi-square value (13.337) is, in fact, greater than the 99% confidence level (13.28), and so we can surmise that there is a highly significant pattern in the distribution of data which differs from a perfectly even distribution. The Chi-square value does not tell us what this distributional pattern is: this requires a visual interpretation of the data. By comparing the observed and expected frequencies, we can see that the brand management cluster makes disproportionate use of qualitative methodologies, whereas academic studies of

Percentage Points of the Chi-Square Distribution									
Degrees of Freedom	Probability of a larger value of x^2								
	0.99	0.95	0.90	0.75	0.50	0.25	0.10	0.05	0.01
1	0.000	0.004	0.016	0.102	0.455	1.32	2.71	3.84	6.63
2	0.020	0.103	0.211	0.575	1.386	2.77	4.61	5.99	9.21
3	0.115	0.352	0.584	1.212	2.366	4.11	6.25		11.34
4	0.297	0.711	1.064	1.923	3.357	5.39	7.78	9.49	13.28
5	0.554	1.145	1.610	2.675	4.351	6.63	9.24		15.09
6	0.872	1.635	2.204	3.455	5.348	7.84	10.64	12.59	16.81
7	1.239	2.167	2.833	4.255	6.346	9.04	12.02	14.07	18.48
8	1.647	2.733	3.490	5.071	7.344	10.22	13.36	15.51	20.09
9	2.088	3.325	4.168	5.899	8.343	11.39	14.68	16.92	21.67
10	2.558	3.940	4.865	6.737	9.342	12.55	15.99	18.31	23.21
11	3.053	4.575	5.578	7.584	10.341	13.70	17.28	19.68	24.72
12	3.571	5.226	6.304	8.438	11.340	14.85	18.55	21.03	26.22
13	4.107	5.892	7.042	9.299	12.340	15.98	19.81	22.36	27.69
14	4.660	6.571	7.790	10.165	13.339	17.12	21.06	23.68	29.14
15	5.229	7.261	8.547	11.037	14.339	18.25	22.31	25.00	30.58
16	5.812	7.962	9.312	11.912	15.338	19.37	23.54	26.30	32.00
17	6.408	8.672	10.085	12.792	16.338	20.49	24.77	27.59	33.41
18	7.015	9.390	10.865	13.675	17.338	21.60	25.99	28.87	34.80
19	7.633	10.117	11.651	14.562	18.338	22.72	27.20	30.14	36.19
20	8.260	10.851	12.443	15.452	19.337	23.83	28.41	31.41	37.57
22	9.542	12.338	14.041	17.240	21.337	26.04	30.81	33.92	40.29
24	10.856	13.848	15.659	19.037	23.337	28.24	33.20	36.42	42.98
26	12.198	15.379	17.292	20.843	25.336	30.43	35.56	38.89	45.64
28	13.565	16.928	18.939	22.657	27.336	32.62	37.92	41.34	48.28
30	14.953	18.493	20.599	24.478	29.336	34.80	40.26	43.77	50.89
40	22.164	26.509	29.051	33.660	39.335	45.62	51.80	55.76	63.69
50	27.707	34.764	37.689	42.942	49.335	56.33	63.17	67.50	76.15
60	37.485	43.188	46.459	52.294	59.335	66.98	74.40	79.08	88.38

FIGURE 7.9 Chi-Square Table.

purchase behaviour tend to make greater use of the quantitative approach, as do studies of self-perception. These are academic studies; practitioner research is likely to differ from this, with a greater preponderance of qualitative research overall.

ANALYSING NUMERICAL AND CATEGORICAL DATA

Most students undertaking research for their Master's dissertation will need to present at least part of their research findings descriptively, using charts, tables and simple statistical tests as outlined above for categorical data or descriptive summaries of numerical data. The same will generally apply for luxury industry research outputs, which will often be designed to communicate information to managers, clients or consumers in a form that is appealingly visual and readily digestible. However, it is an expectation of many luxury brand management programmes that students will also undertake at least some analysis of their research data as an integral part of the research process and as a way of developing skills and understanding that they may take into any future employment, within the luxury industry or elsewhere. The remainder of this chapter will outline some of the principal analytical approaches associated with, first, quantitative research using numerical data and, second, various forms of qualitative investigation. It should be re-emphasised here that decisions concerning analytical approach and methods are not made after data collection is complete but must be fundamentally integrated into the design of the research at quite an early stage.

Table 7.2 gives a sense of how academic research professionals approach the analysis of their data, based on our survey of 160 academic articles in the field of luxury that were published

TABLE 7.2 Analysis Methods Used by Academic Researchers of Luxury, 2021

Analysis Method	Number of Studies
Structural equation modelling	37
Confirmatory/exploratory factor analysis	42
Regression and path analysis	27
Analysis of variance/covariance	22
Cronbach's alpha	31
Experiments/simulations	33
Case study/case analysis	14
Content/discourse analysis	23
Conceptual/theoretical, no method	16
Literature-based	6
Exploratory study	3
Online data/social media scraping	25
Thematic analysis	4
Observation	3
Total number of studies	160

Data source: Web of Science.

in 2021. Some of the analytical methods used, such as structural equation modelling, might be a little too sophisticated (but far from impossible) for a Master's-level student to consider deploying in their own research, but this method is included in the following discussion because it demonstrates valuable techniques for interrogating conceptual models, which we introduced as an organisational device in Chapter 4. We will start with a brief overview of the three most basic analytical techniques: analysis of variance, correlation and regression.

ANALYSIS OF VARIANCE

Analysis of variance (ANOVA) is a useful tool for examining variations in a numerical variable that are associated with variations in one or more categorical variable(s). One caveat is that the categorical variable must have more than three groups or categories. ANOVA is accomplished by examining the means of two or several variables and ascertaining if there is a statistically significant difference in the respective means. The variables must also be independent (unrelated), in the sense that they do not measure more or less the same thing. Like Chi-square tests, ANOVA is what is called an 'omnibus test': it does not tell us what the relationships or differences are, simply that there are differences determinable from the data. Further tests are required to explain these variations.

The conventional framework for analysis of variance is presented in Table 7.3. This is best explained by way of a worked example. From the Web of Science data discussed earlier in this chapter, we wanted to look at sample size (the dependent variable) in relation to research approach (quantitative, qualitative and mixed methods: the independent variable).

TABLE 7.3 Components of the Analysis of Variance Test

Source of Variation	Sum of Squares	Degrees of Freedom	Mean Square	F	P
Between groups	SS_B	df_B	$MS_B = SS_B/df_B$	$F = MS_B/MS_W$	(P)F
Within groups	SS_W	df_W	$MS_W = SS_W/df_W$		
Total	SS_T	df_T			

The expectation – hardly profound – was that sample size would, on average, be greater for quantitative studies than either qualitative or mixed methods studies. In their statements on research methodology in the Web of Science database, most academic authors gave an indication of the size of sample they used in their investigation. Several studies had conducted multiple surveys, and so, for the simple purpose of the present exercise, which required only a single value for each case, we selected the average of the indicated sample sizes. Five studies used web-scraped data that ran into the millions, and these 'outliers' were eliminated from the exercise because they distorted the sample size profile so significantly. For the sake of simplicity, we also eliminated cases where research method and/or sample size were not indicated, which we designated 'missing variables'. This data cleaning left us with 109 out of the original 160 cases. These data sets satisfied the requirements of the ANOVA test, including: no outliers, the dependent variable consisting of interval (continuous) values, the independent variable having two or more categorical groups, different participants in each group and no participant in more than one group, and the dependent variable being approximately normally distributed.

ANOVA was calculated using Excel > Data > Data Analysis > Anova: Single Factor (Figure 7.10): this is because we were only looking at the relationship between two groups, research method (categorical) and sample size (numerical). The null hypothesis was that sample size would essentially be the same for each of the research method categories. As per Table 7.3, the first step is to calculate the within-group, between-group and total sum of squares. Our data set has 109 cases divided into three groups within the independent variable (quantitative, qualitative and mixed). We first need to calculate the group mean for each of the three groups (sum the sample size scores for each case within a group and divide by the number of cases within this group). We then calculate the difference between each individual score and its respective group mean for each of the 109 cases. The results of each of these calculations are squared, and then all the squared values are added together to give the within-group sum of squares. The between-group sum of squares is calculated by taking the difference between the group mean and the grand mean (the sum of the sample size scores for all cases divided by the number of cases) for each case, each of which is squared, and then they are added together. SS_W and SS_B are then added together to give the SS_T, which shows the total degree of variation in the dependent variable.

Between-group degrees of freedom are the number of groups (2) minus 1 (= 1; see Figure 7.11). Within-group degrees of freedom are the total number of observations (109×2) minus the number of groups (2; $118 - 2 = 216$). These are added together to give the total degrees of freedom (217). The MS_B (mean square between groups) is calculated from SS_B/df_B (6724637); the MS_W is calculated from SS_W/df_W (82589). The F value (81.42), or ANOVA

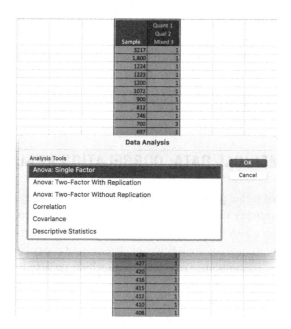

FIGURE 7.10 Procedure for the ANOVA Test Using Excel. Used with permission from Microsoft.

Anova: Single Factor

SUMMARY

Groups	Count	Sum	Average	Variance
Sample	109	38424	352.5137615	165177.8077
Quant 1 Qual 2 Mixed 3	109	136	1.247706422	0.280665987

ANOVA

Source of Variation	SS	df	MS	F	P-value	F crit
Between Groups	6724637.358	1	6724637.358	81.42287425	1.01616E-16	3.884870455
Within Groups	17839233.54	216	82589.04417			
Total	24563870.9	217				

FIGURE 7.11 Analysis of Variance in Sample Size by Research Method. Used with permission from Microsoft.

coefficient, is calculated by dividing MS_B by MS_W. The F-distribution (named after its inventor, Sir Ronald Fisher) in a one-way ANOVA test indicates whether or not the group means (i.e., the mean sample sizes for quantitative, qualitative and mixed methods) are identical. If they are (close to being) identical, which would be indicated by a small F value, we would accept the null hypothesis that sample size is essentially the same for each research approach. In our case, there is a large F value, which would suggest that we should reject the null hypothesis. We can confirm this assumption by calculating the P (or probability) value,[2] which is less than 0.001, or less than a 1 in 1,000 chance that the distribution has occurred by chance. Excel also provides an F critical value, which is the threshold value at 95% confidence, taking into account the degrees of freedom, which the F value must be above to be significant. Not unsurprisingly, given the quite different character of quantitative and qualitative research (and the fact that, for the purposes of this demonstration exercise, mixed methods research was weighted in favour of qualitative methods, given the overall balance between the use of quantitative and qualitative methods by academic researchers of luxury), sample sizes vary significantly between the two principal categories. This is not exactly rocket science, but it helps to demonstrate ANOVA with a real-life worked example from the field of luxury.

ANALYSING NUMERICAL DATA: CORRELATION ANALYSIS

One of the foundational techniques in data analytics is correlation analysis. This basic statistical method enables the researcher to explore relationships between two sets of numerical data by examining the extent to which the variables co-vary or correlate. Correlation analysis will tell the researcher about the strength of the relationship between two variables but will not explain the directionality of this relationship – in other words, which variable influences which. Thus, a correlation analysis may show that there is a strong relationship between an individual's disposable income and their propensity to purchase luxury goods; only logic will determine that the former may influence the latter, and not vice versa. Regression analysis, which makes use of correlation coefficients, can be used to infer the directionality in the relationships between variables, as we will show shortly.

To demonstrate correlation analysis, we set up a simple investigation. The eighth edition of the Deloitte Global Powers of Luxury Brands report in 2021, entitled *Breakthrough Luxury*, contains two sets of data on page 35 which highlight (a) the global locational distribution of the top 100 luxury companies (based on the location of their headquarters) and (b) the global locational distribution of luxury sales from these top 100 luxury companies. We thought it would be useful as a demonstration exercise to look at the relationship between these variables, which we summarise as 'production' and 'consumption', although, of course, we had doubts that the relationship would be strong because of the different historical trajectories of global luxury production and consumption, the different factors that influence them and the considerable globalisation of consumption in recent years. For good measure, we also explored the influence of a country's relative economic status ('wealth') on both variables, by using World Bank data on gross domestic product per capita, which is a commonly used basis for differentiating between countries in terms of economic performance moderated by population size. The data for the analysis are presented in Figure 7.12. The Deloitte data present the percentage of the global total for each variable that is accounted for by the nine countries in the table plus a 'rest of the world' residual. For the GDP data, we listed the figures for the same nine countries plus we used the global GDP per capita average for the residual nations (the true figure is likely to be lower than this if we exclude the nine countries represented here).

We will briefly demonstrate two correlation analysis methods. The more straightforward is the *Spearman's rank* technique, which, instead of using the given numerical values, ranks each of the cases (countries) for both variables and uses these rankings as the basis for the statistical test. We start by ranking both variables, from highest to lowest, and then calculate the difference (d) between these rankings. The differences are each squared, and the sum of these squares is calculated (58). The formula for the Spearman's rank coefficient is $1 - 6 * \Sigma d^2 / n^3 - n$, where n is the number of cases for each variable. The formula yields a coefficient value of 0.649 (Figure 7.13).

Country	% of Top 10 Luxury Companies (2021)	% of Luxury Goods Sales (2021)	GDP per Capita, Current US$ (2021)
Spain	3	1	30,115
Germany	3	1.2	50,801
Japan	5	4.2	39,285
Other	10	4.9	12,262
PR China	9	8.9	12,556
UK	11	9	47,334
Italy	26	11.3	35,551
Switzerland	10	12.6	93,457
USA	15	18.8	69,287
France	8	28.1	43,518
	100	100	

FIGURE 7.12 Data for Correlation Analysis of Luxury Production, Consumption and Wealth. Used with permission from Microsoft.

Country	% of Top 100 Luxury Companies (2021)	% of Luxury Goods Sales (2021)	GDP per Capita, Current US$ (2021)	Rank x	Rank y	d	d^2
Spain	3	1	30,115	1.5	1	0.5	0.25
Germany	3	1.2	50,801	1.5	2	-0.5	0.25
Japan	5	4.2	39,285	3	3	0	0
Other	10	4.9	12,262	6.5	4	2.5	6.25
PR China	9	8.9	12,556	5	5	0	0
UK	11	9	47,334	8	6	2	4
Italy	26	11.3	35,551	10	7	3	9
Switzerland	10	12.6	93,457	6.5	8	-1.5	2.25
USA	15	18.8	69,287	9	9	0	0
France	8	28.1	43,518	4	10	-6	36
	100	100				Σd^2	58
						$6*\Sigma d^2$	348
						n^3-n	990
						$6*\Sigma d^2/n^3-n$	0.351515
						$1-6*\Sigma d^2/n^3-n$	0.648485

FIGURE 7.13 Spearman's Rank Correlation Exercise for Luxury Production versus Consumption. Used with permission from Microsoft.

Correlation coefficients can lie anywhere between +1 and −1, with +1 indicating a perfect positive relationship between the variables (as one value increases, the other value also increases), and −1 indicating a perfect negative relationship (as one variable rises, the other falls). Zero indicates there is no correlation. A coefficient close to +1 or −1 indicates a quite strong correlation. With this exercise, a correlation coefficient of 0.649 indicates quite a strong relationship between the first two variables in the table. Using an online calculator[3] gives us a p value of 0.05, showing that the fairly strong correlation between the two variables suggested by the coefficient is unlikely to be attributable purely to chance: in other words, there is a valid relationship. There are two caveats here, however: first, some statisticians argue that, with small data sets where there are tied rankings (as we have for both Spain–Germany and Switzerland–Other; we used the mean of the two rankings), Spearman's rank is not a particularly reliable technique; second, by using rankings rather than raw data, we have lost quite a lot of detail in the data set, meaning that the coefficient may not be particularly reliable. We therefore have a trade-off between convenience and accuracy. To indicate this point, we now do a similar correlation exercise, *Pearson's r*, this time using the actual raw data.

Figure 7.14 presents the principal workings for the Pearson's r correlation calculation for the relationship between luxury production and consumption. The formula is at the bottom of the table. Working through the calculations by hand yields a Pearson's (r) correlation coefficient of 0.3576, which, from the same set of data, is a lot smaller than that for Spearman's rank, although it is still positive. The p value for this calculation is 0.31, suggesting that there is at least a 31% likelihood that the shown relationship occurred by chance or from random factors other than the relationship between the two sets of values. Our 'confidence' threshold is 0.05, and thus we conclude that there is not a significant correlation between the two variables.

Correlations can very readily be calculated in Excel using Data > Data Analysis > Correlation. Figure 7.15 shows the results of the three permutations of analysis possible from the original table of data. Excel does not provide p values for correlations, but a work-around is to use Data > Data Analysis > Regression, which gives both the Pearson's r correlation coefficient (in a regression of two variables, the multiple R value is the same as the Pearson's r value) and the p value (both under ANOVA significance F and the p value at the bottom of the table), as shown in Figure 7.16. None of the relationships proved to be significant, as we expected.

Country	x % of Top 100 Luxury Companies (2021)	y % of Luxury Goods Sales (2021)	xy	x^2	y^2
Spain	3	1	3	9	1
Germany	3	1.2	3.6	9	1.44
Japan	5	4.2	21	25	17.64
Other	10	4.9	49	100	24.01
PR China	9	8.9	80.1	81	79.21
UK	11	9	99	121	81
Italy	26	11.3	293.8	676	127.69
Switzerland	10	12.6	126	100	158.76
USA	15	18.8	282	225	353.44
France	8	28.1	224.8	64	789.61
Σ	100	100	1182.3	1410	1633.8
$n(\Sigma xy)-(\Sigma x)(\Sigma y)$	10(1182.3)-(100)(100)		1823		
$\sqrt{(n\Sigma x^2-(\Sigma x)^2)(n\Sigma y^2-(\Sigma y)^2)}$	√(14100-10000)(16338-10000)		5097.6		
$r=n(\Sigma xy)-(\Sigma x)(\Sigma y)/\sqrt{(n\Sigma x^2-(\Sigma x)^2)(n\Sigma y^2-(\Sigma y)^2)}$	r=1823/5097.6		r=0.3576	p=0.3103	

FIGURE 7.14 Pearson's r Correlation Exercise for Luxury Production versus Consumption. Used with permission from Microsoft.

	% of Top 10 Luxury Companies (2021)	% of Luxury Goods Sales (2021)		
% of Top 10 Luxury Companies (2021)	1			
% of Luxury Goods Sales (2021)	0.357617385		1	p=.3103

	% of Luxury Goods Sales (2021)	GDP per Capita, Current US$ (2021)		
% of Luxury Goods Sales (2021)	1			
GDP per Capita, Current US$ (2021)	0.332826508		1	p=.3473

	% of Top 10 Luxury Companies (2021)	GDP per Capita, Current US$ (2021)		
% of Top 10 Luxury Companies (2021)	1			
GDP per Capita, Current US$ (2021)	0.067174253		1	p=.8537

FIGURE 7.15 Correlation Results for Production, Consumption and Wealth, Calculated Using Excel. Used with permission from Microsoft.

SUMMARY OUTPUT

Regression Statistics	
Multiple R	0.067174253
R Square	0.00451238
Adjusted R Square	-0.119923572
Standard Error	7.142740406
Observations	10

ANOVA

	df	SS	MS	F	Significance F
Regression	1	1.8500759	1.8500759	0.03626267	0.85371759
Residual	8	408.1499241	51.0187405		
Total	9	410			

	Coefficients	Standard Error	t Stat	P-value	Lower 95%	Upper 95%	Lower 95.0%	Upper 95.0%
Intercept	9.19801105	4.778989745	1.92467688	0.0904606	-1.8223591	20.2183812	-1.8223591	20.2183812
GDP per Capita, Current US$ (2021)	1.84719E-05	9.70024E-05	0.19042761	0.85371759	-0.0002052	0.00024216	-0.0002052	0.00024216

FIGURE 7.16 How to Locate r and p Values from a Two-Variable Regression Using Excel. Used with permission from Microsoft.

It should be emphasised that analysis outcomes do not always have to be 'good' (i.e., significant): we can learn quite a lot from showing that two variables are not connected. In this case, the data suggest a separation of the concentration of production and consumption, and this could provide the basis for further exploration.

REGRESSION ANALYSIS

Regression analysis goes one step further than correlation by exploring the directionality of relationships between variables and thereby allows inferences to be made about causality. Regression thus centres on something to be understood or predicted, termed the *dependent* or *response variable* (RV), and the factors that help us to understand it, called *independent* or *explanatory variables* (EVs). Regression can measure statistically the level of influence of EVs on an RV, as well as the influence of one or more variables while controlling for the influence of others. *Path analysis*, a form of regression analysis, can evaluate the influence of EVs on an RV in steps or stages.

We might, for example, want to examine the influence of economic, social, cultural, psychological and demographic factors on people's propensity to purchase luxury watches. We could operationalise the explanatory variables as: disposable income, status consciousness, extent to which conspicuous displays of wealth are culturally (un)acceptable, a measure of self-confidence or insecurity, and both age and gender. Each of these variables individually might be expected to have some influence on consumption propensity, but regression analysis allows us to evaluate their collective and simultaneous influence – how much of the variation in the RV is explained by variation in the EVs. We might also arrange the EVs in a theoretical model (Figure 7.17, Model A) which posits that cultural factors have the strongest foundational influence, which in turn may influence social and psychological factors, which may influence consumption propensity moderated by disposable income (which may be related to age) and gender. Multiple linear regression allows us to test the explanatory strength and validity of this model when the influence of variables is tested in sequence rather than simultaneously. The strengths of the individual, incremental and collective paths in this model given by regression analysis might suggest a revised model where cultural factors influence the way that gender moderates social factors, and age moderates psychological factors (Figure 7.17, Model B). It is conventional to put directly measurable variables in rectangular shapes and indirectly inferred or latent variables in oval shapes, as we will discuss further in the next section.

The key to understanding regression is what is called the *regression line*. When two variables are plotted against each other on a graph – the RV always on the *y-axis* and the EV always on the *x-axis* – a scattergram is formed. If there is no relationship between these variables, the individual plots should be scattered seemingly at random across the graph. But, if there is a relationship between the variables, it should be possible to make out a line, or curve, which runs through the highest concentration of paired values. The stronger the relationship, the less scatter there is likely to be around this line or curve, and the greater the certainty that the regression line we plot through the paired points will be the best fit. The regression line is best calculated statistically. If all plots on the graph occur precisely on the regression line, there will be no *residuals* – gaps between the plots and the best-fit regression line – and thus no likely error in predicting values for x from values of y. The larger the residuals, the greater the likely error and the less confident our predictions will be.

The example in Figure 7.18 is taken from 1 of 25 studies in our evaluation of luxury articles (Table 7.2) which used regression analysis. The study by Ma *et al.* (2021) looked at the influence of several social variables on luxury fashion purchase intention, comparing the

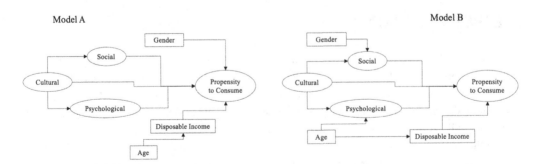

FIGURE 7.17 Theoretical Model of the Influence of Economic, Social, Cultural, Psychological and Demographic Factors on the Propensity to Purchase Luxury Watches.

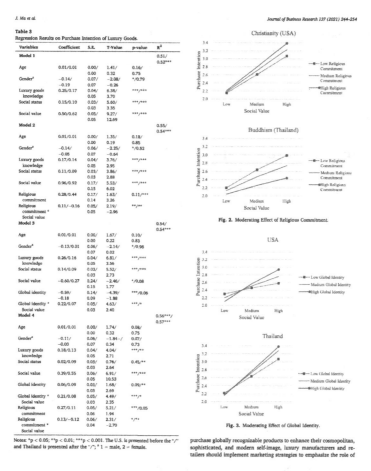

FIGURE 7.18 Example of the Use of Regression Analysis in Luxury Research.
Source: Ma *et al.*, 2021, p. 251.

situations in the USA (where most people are Christian) and Thailand (where most people are Buddhist). The key explanatory variables were religious commitment, global identity and luxury social value, but there were also indicators for social status, knowledge of luxury goods, age and gender. The latent variables in the equation (everything except age and gender) were created based on Likert-scale answers to between three and seven questions, such as "I feel like I'm living in a global village" as one of five questions for global identity, and "my religious beliefs lie behind my whole approach to life" as one of five indicators of religious commitment. The study found significant positive correlations between both social value of luxury and social status with luxury purchase intention, but the link between religious commitment and luxury purchase intention was strongly positive for the USA but strongly negative for Thailand, where Buddhism cautions against extravagant materialism. This is reflected in the regression lines in Fig. 2. in Figure 7.18, which shows the link between social value and luxury purchase intention, controlling for religious commitment: in Thailand, there was a greater propensity to consume with lower religious commitment, whereas the opposite was true for the USA. The overall explanatory power of the RV provided by the EVs contained in the analysis was around 50 percent, as indicated by the R^2 values for each model. It should be noted that five variables (age, gender, luxury knowledge, social status and social value) explain 51% and 52% of the variation in the RV for the USA and Thailand, respectively, and the addition of further variables (religious commitment, global identity and some combination variables) does not add significantly to the explanatory power of the overall model.

STRUCTURAL EQUATION MODELLING

Regression is frequently used to test the strength of theoretical models, but, in recent years, structural equation modelling (SEM) has tended to supersede regression analysis as the go-to technique for more or less the same purpose. In the following discussion, we will briefly outline some of the core principles and procedures of SEM before describing a worked example taken from the recent literature on luxury, 1 of 37 that was revealed by our perusal of recent publications (see Table 7.2 above).

SEM contains a suite of elements. At its heart are the construction and statistical evaluation of a model which diagrammatically represents hypothesised relationships between theoretical or observable phenomena, referred to as 'factors' and 'variables'. Much like a regression model, the hypothesised relationships would indicate a path flow between EVs and an RV, with an inference of causality in these directional relationships. SEM typically requires the development of two models: a *theoretical model*, which posits relationships and flows, and a *measurement model*, which substitutes measured variables for conceptual factors. The components of the model may consist of *observed variables*, which are conventionally indicated by rectangular containers, and *latent variables* or *factors*, for which oval containers will be used. An observed variable would be something tangible and measurable, such as luxury brand sales figures or footfall in the vicinity of a luxury pop-up. A latent variable is something abstract or conceptual, something we believe to exist but which is difficult to measure, such as brand attachment, social envy, purchase intention, exclusivity, the 'essence of luxury' and so on. The literature on luxury is replete with research (e.g., Balabanis and Stathopoulou, 2021; Monfared, Mansouri and Jalilian, 2021; Park, Hyun and Thavisay, 2021) which seeks to explore the influence of latent variables on various aspects of luxury consumption behaviour or brand perception, and SEM is a popular analytical method for exploring and quantifying such relationships.

A very important step in SEM is to find a way of converting latent variables into something that can be measured and thus evaluated statistically. A latent or unobserved variable is referred to as a *factor*, and the challenge for the researcher using SEM is to build the best-possible representation of a factor from observable or measured variables. Taking a random example, Jebarajakirthy and Das (2021) wished to explore the influence of different aspects of social comparison on luxury purchase intention and included a factor for 'materialism' as a control variable in their analysis. A measured variable for the abstract notion of materialism was constructed based on the extent to which respondents agreed/disagreed with four statements that tested for their materialistic tendency.[4] Responses were placed on a seven-point Likert scale. As is typically the case with researchers who construct measurement models for SEM, the measures for materialism and all the other variables in the equation were based on established operationalisations derived from the literature. The extent to which the measures fit the factors can be ascertained statistically using *confirmatory factor analysis* (CFA), which also helps the researcher to streamline their model (for example, reduce the number of measures which define a factor) by identifying which measures have the greatest explanatory power. Jebarajakirthy and Das had originally taken six measures of materialism from an article published by Marsha Richins in 2004, but CFA suggested that two of these should be eliminated from the measurement model (Jebarajakirthy and Das, 2021, 6). A similar process, called experimental factor analysis (EFA), is used when the researcher is seeking to build a hypothetical model from factors and variables, rather than evaluate and confirm a structural model, as in the case of CFA. As with regression analysis, SEM will also identify statistically the degree of error that is integral to the model (e.g., imperfections in the operationalisation of factors) and thus the degree of confidence the researcher may have in its accuracy and its power to explain the strength of relationships contained within the structural model.

Having established that the measurement model is a valid operationalisation of the theoretical model, the relationships between the factors in the model are established statistically in the form of *path coefficients*, which identify the strength and directionality of all theorised relationships in the model. The true relationships between factors can be identified by statistically controlling the influence of other variables that are included in the analysis – as in the case of materialism discussed above. Unlike regression analysis, where relationships between factors and variables are calculated sequentially, these are assessed simultaneously in SEM. SEM is considered to have greater statistical power than regression analysis (Beran and Violato, 2010), which helps to explain why it is now the preferred statistical technique used by quantitative researchers in the field of luxury.

The intricacies of SEM are best explained by way of a factual example. Here, we use a paper by Chen *et al.* (2021) to outline the use of SEM and associated analytical techniques. Their paper is concerned with the extent to which luxury fashion brands' use of internet celebrity endorsement of their products influences impulsive buying. Of particular interest to the researchers was the way that celebrity endorsement underpinned consumers' trust in the product and brand, which in turn potentially made them more likely to impulse buy. They further hypothesised that the endorsement–trust–purchase connection might be moderated by the extent to which consumers identified with the celebrities in question (in other words, how 'relatable' they were) and their perceived social distance from the celebrity endorsers (in other words, how socially similar or dissimilar they and the internet celebrities were perceived to be). China provides the context for the paper, which uses data from a survey of 585 followers of internet celebrities in that country which was conducted using Survey STAR, China's largest survey platform. It should be pointed out that the definition of 'luxury' used in this research was more akin to 'accessible luxury' than high-end luxury.

The relationships and influences to be investigated were summarised as seven key variables which are presented in their theoretical model (Figure 7.19), with impulse buying as the dependent variable to be explained by the combined influence of several independent variables. The structural model also suggests the sequencing or path structure of these variables – all unidirectional – with impulse buying tending to be explained by the posited influence of the popular internet celebrities, who help build trust in the brand, although possibly moderated by identification, perceived fit (the extent to which the celebrity used is perceived to be a credible

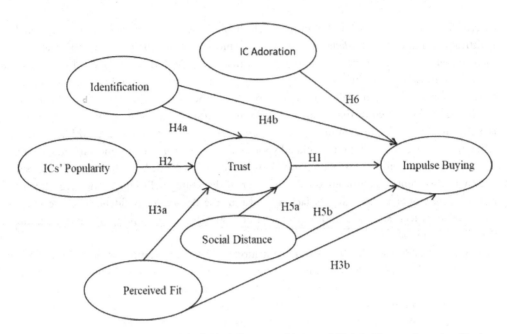

FIGURE 7.19 Theoretical Model of the Influence of Internet Celebrities on Impulse Buying of Luxury Fashion Items.

Source: Chen *et al.*, 2021, p. 2477.

endorser of particular products: they and the brand are a good match) and social distance. There is also hypothesised to be a direct connection between consumers' adoration of internet celebrities and impulse buying which is not moderated by the other variables: in other words, people love the celebrities so much they will buy anything they endorse, regardless of other factors. Six main hypotheses (including three sub-hypotheses) were developed relating to the directional permutations or relationships/influences in the model, as shown in Figure 7.19. Hypothesis 2 (H2), for instance, states that "the popularity of internet celebrities has a positive influence on trust" (*ibid.*, 2474), and, in turn, "trust has a positive effect on impulse buying for luxury fashion brands" (Hypothesis 1; H1). Note that the variables in the model are presented in oval containers because they all contain what are called 'latent variables': phenomena or abstract concepts that are meaningful for analysis but not observable in the sense of being readily measurable, unlike age. Observable variables tend to be presented in rectangular containers.

The next challenge for the researchers was to obtain data relating to each of the seven variables in the structural model. This is a quantitative (deductive) investigation which deals with social, psychological and behavioural phenomena, and so it was necessary to find ways of measuring participants' actions and perceptions, thereby yielding a set of numerical data which could be subjected to statistical analysis. As we discussed in Chapter 5, there are various ways of converting the social into the numerical. Chen *et al.* used tried and tested measures drawn from several literature sources (their own past research was also used) to create validated scales to use in their research constructs (variables). By way of an example, internet celebrity popularity was ascertained through five measures: levels of fandom, level of fame in society, level of sharing and discussing products endorsed by the celebrity, level of popularity on the internet, and the

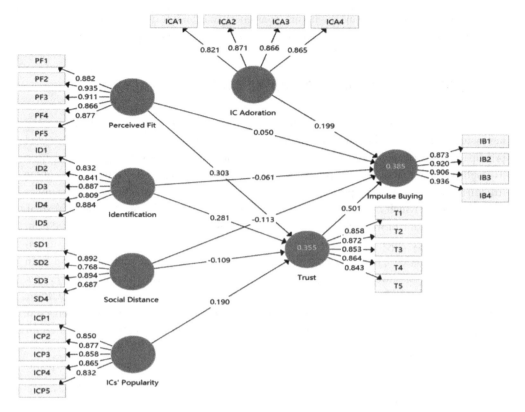

FIGURE 7.20 Measurement Model for the Influence of Internet Celebrities on Impulse Buying of Luxury Fashion Items.

Source: Chen *et al.*, 2021, p. 2482.

number of active followers (Chen *et al.*, 2021, 2477, 2478). Social distance was ascertained by four measures concerning the perceived difference in personality, appearance, taste and style, and living standard between the participant and the internet celebrity (*ibid.*, 2478).

From the structural model we move to the measurement model (Figure 7.20). Each latent variable (in oval containers) is explained by several observed variables (in rectangular containers): these are the actual measurements derived from questions posed to participants in relation to the seven variables included in the theoretical model; perceived fit is explained by five measurements, trust by five measurements, [5] impulse buying by four measurements and so on.

The results of the analysis showed that the model as a whole was sufficiently robust, and that a number of the path coefficients showed strong levels of covariance. For instance, trust in internet personalities had the highest mediating influence on the impulse buying of luxury fashion products. Trust itself was strongly influenced by the popularity of the internet celebrity, the extent to which the consumer felt they identified with the celebrity, and the perceived fit between the internet celebrity and the products they were endorsing. However, the authors cautioned that, in general, internet celebrities carried less credibility and influence than 'traditional celebrities' such as film stars and pop icons. The research was useful in exploring the tripartite connection (not always positive) between a source of information (the internet celebrity), the receiver of this information (the luxury consumer) and the information itself (concerning luxury fashion brands), which clearly has significance for luxury brand management.

ANALYSING NON-NUMERICAL DATA: CONTENT ANALYSIS

'Content analysis' is a generic term which covers an array of techniques for extracting meaning systematically from fluid or unstructured textual and other data sources. It is presented principally as a qualitative research tool, although historically, and still today in many instances, its results are often presented quantitatively. More accurately, it should be viewed as a tool for structuring and interrogating qualitative data in order to identify and extract concepts, meanings and relationships which might otherwise be difficult to visualise from large volumes of textual, audio, visual and other forms of non-numerical data. These qualitative data may be derived from a myriad of sources, including some of the methods that were discussed in Chapter 5, such as open-ended interviews, focus groups, case studies and observations, as well as material from magazines, blogs, talks, websites, company brochures and advertisements, brand stories, reviews, social media posts, films, artwork, exhibitions and so on. These are all means of communication. Content analysis explores not only *what* is communicated but also *how* messages are conveyed. For instance, an analysis of reportage from the European heartlands of luxury might search for bias in the depiction of luxury brands from emerging economies.

Different qualitative researchers may adopt different approaches to content analysis depending on the nature and objectives of their investigation, but we can distil the analysis process down to a few key stages.

(1) The analysis stage of the research will clearly have to be consistent with the research questions and investigative framework that will have been developed much earlier in the research process. These should also help to determine the purpose of the content analysis: is it to be used to supplement and add contextual depth to the findings of prior quantitative analysis, or is it the principal focus of the investigation? Are the results to be presented as a quantitative summary (e.g., word counts or frequency of concepts), or does the researcher wish to allow the data to 'speak for themselves' in the sense of using choice fragments of text to illustrate the interpretation of findings? The research questions will also help to define the thematic orientation of the analysis.

(2) The researcher will then have to identify and obtain the data to be analysed, which will include making judgements about the medium to be interrogated (textual, visual, audio, etc.), the date range, location and other parameters, and also the volume of data that might be considered sufficient for the purposes of their research.

(3) The researcher should then check the quality of their data to ensure they are amenable to further analysis. Some data cleaning might be necessary at this stage: for instance, tidying up automated interview transcripts or removing superfluous elements.

(4) The actual analysis stage typically commences with a thorough read-through (or watch-/ listen-/look-through) of the body of data in order that the researcher can familiarise themself with its content and commence the process of 'immersion' in the data, which is a very important component of qualitative analysis.

(5) A second read-through begins the process of identifying keywords, themes, concepts, ideas and other content from the body of data, which in turn will become the core building blocks of the analysis. At this stage, the researcher needs to decide whether to approach the data with predetermined categories into which the data will be placed or to allow these to emerge organically as the perusal of the data progresses. This choice can be likened to a deductive or inductive approach to content analysis. The former might be used where the investigation is linked to a clearly defined theoretical formulation which the content analysis is intended to test, and where the researcher (or the literature they are following) has a clear vision of the structural components of their investigation; the latter might be used where the researcher is investigating a new phenomenon about which little is presently known, and where new concepts or theories are the intended outcome of the content analysis. In practical terms, having a clear, predetermined categorical framework might help the researcher keep the scale of the investigation under control, whereas the organic approach might risk the array of categories getting out of hand, even though they might more closely reflect the true nature of the data. Primary qualitative data from interviews, focus groups and so on might have a predetermined structure by virtue of the planning that went into the meetings, matching the analytical framework of the researcher, whereas textual data derived from secondary sources are likely to be more fluid in nature and thus require more organisational input from the researcher.

(6) A useful organisational device that can be used at this stage of the investigation is to conduct a word frequency analysis (where textual data are being used). We have already demonstrated how this can be done, in Chapter 2, and will provide a further illustration of computer-aided word frequency analysis shortly. This can help the researcher to identify the most dominant keywords in the text, which might provide the basis for at least an initial identification of themes and concepts. Some textual content analyses end at this point: showing the frequency with which certain words are used might be sufficient to demonstrate a key point, such as the broad orientation of reviews of luxury brands, products or services.

(7) The next stage – which might be concurrent with the previous one: it might require several iterations – involves coding the data. The best analogy here is the sense of 'attacking' the data with a colourful array of highlighting pens, each colour identifying a particular theme that is of relevance and interest to the researcher, including not just what is written but how a view is expressed. Where the theme recurs throughout the text, the same colour is used. At the end of the exercise, there should be multiple segments of text which have been highlighted in multiple colours. This is the process of coding the text, with a label attached to each, perhaps in a coding book or using a software package, as we will discuss shortly. It may be useful at this point for the researcher to specify a number of coding 'rules' which explain the rationale for allocating particular themes to certain codes: this is especially important where multiple researchers are working independently on the same body of data. Codes might be attached to both explicit/overt and implicit/covert concepts: the former are transparent and obvious, such as an influencer positioning a particular luxury product; the latter require more subjective interpretation, such as the subliminal messaging that brands might use to foster an emotional attachment to their brand values.

(8) Assuming the researcher, figuratively, has a sufficiently wide array of highlighting pens, the data might have been separated into upwards of 100 codes. The next stage of the analysis is to attempt to consolidate these codes into a smaller number of cognate clusters or categories, which will become the core structural foundations of the analysis and the reporting of findings.

(9) Depending on the scale and character of the content analysis, and thus the number and range of codes and clusters, it may be possible and worthwhile to arrange the core categories either schematically, in a conceptual diagram which shows how they all relate or connect into an integrated whole, or hierarchically by importance, in the form of a 'category tree'. Here, we can draw a parallel with the 'nested hierarchy of research questions' which we presented in Chapter 4: for analytical purposes, it is useful to break the data down into various, nonetheless linked, cognate clusters; but, for the purpose of reporting findings, it is helpful to invert the 'tree' so that, ultimately, all data point to a core investigative outcome which, obviously, should be consistent with the research questions which guided the analysis.

(10) The final stage of the analysis, particularly where the researcher wishes to convey contextual and naturalistic richness, depth and insight, is to identify exemplars from the text (Hsieh and Shannon, 2005, 1279), typically in the form of direct quotations, which can populate the writing-up of the analysis to give it a real-world feel and dilute the sense that the findings are purely a researcher-written text.

Content analysis can be quite time-consuming and arduous, particularly when large volumes of data are involved, but the effort is necessary if the researcher is to extract meanings, patterns and relationships from fluid qualitative data that would not otherwise be apparent from a superficial perusal of these data – in much the same way that statistics reveal patterns and relationships in quantitative data which the human mind would otherwise struggle to see. However, an important difference between quantitative and qualitative research, as we discussed in Chapter 5 (Table 5.1), is that, in the former, the researcher is distant (they gather data systematically and rely on statistics to extract meaning) whereas, in the latter, the researcher is close (immersed in both data and context and centrally involved in the determination of meaning). The researcher is pivotal to content analysis in that they determine the categories, codes or other devices which are used to interrogate the data, as well as being key to the interpretation of outcomes. Subjectivity of judgement is thus a potential weakness in content analysis, most particularly in terms of the replicability of findings: different researchers might interpret the same body of data differently and reach quite divergent conclusions. Communicating choices and rules transparently will help with replicability, while being systematic, consistent and as objective as possible should help to strengthen the validity of interpretations.

One of the challenges of content analysis is to find a way to sift meaning out of a complex body of data without losing naturalistic depth, insight, nuance and context, which are the fundamental calling cards of qualitative research. Content analysis is often criticised for being reductionist – analysing complex phenomena through their simple constituents – which is almost inevitable given the core methodology that was described above. This can be rectified at the writing-up stage by including excerpts of real-world language, quotations, illustrations and so on which will help to add naturalistic flesh to the organisational skeleton of systematic analysis, as we do in Chapter 9. Also, we should not lose sight of the fact that a great deal of quantitative analysis is also fundamentally reductionist.

USING NVIVO TO FACILITATE CONTENT ANALYSIS

NVivo is one of several software packages (collectively referred to as computer-assisted qualitative data analysis software; CAQDAS) that can be used as an aid to content analysis, although it should be emphasised that it is principally an organisational device that cannot substitute for the intellectual processes that are integral to processing qualitative data. In other words, NVivo is an aid to analysis, not data analysis per se. NVivo provides a variety of mechanisms to help the researcher organise their qualitative data, most particularly nodes and cases to identify and codify emerging themes, concepts and words, as well as arranging the textual evidence to populate these key analytical structures. The following example is based on textual data – an interview transcript – but NVivo can also be used to organise audio files or video by using time ranges as the basis for coding and annotating, and collecting audio or video excerpts in the same way as blocks of text are gathered to populate various nodes.

As part of the background research that the authors conducted in support of the present volume, ten semi-structured interviews were conducted with industry professionals across a range of sectors and roles in order to explore how primary research fitted into their routine activities. Some of the findings of this qualitative enquiry will be discussed in more detail in Chapter 9. The example below illustrates the preliminary organisation of the first of these ten interviews, conducted with a luxury industry consultant of 15 years' standing who also has an academic and teaching background in luxury management. The transcribed interview ran to 5,000 words and, to some extent, was already structured around broad thematic blocks as the discussion had been prompted by the researcher (and co-author) asking themed questions. The data can be approached in many different ways: the researcher can note key themes from an initial read-through of the transcript, which then become the top-level nodes, to be populated or added to in subsequent perusals or when new data are added; or they can create and populate a hierarchy of nodes (and cases, which identify potential case studies) as they progress though the text in-program. In our case, we preceded the 'nodification' stage by conducting a word frequency enquiry (NVivo > Query > Word Frequency). The results can be presented either as a summary or in the form of a word cloud (Figure 7.21). The word frequency data were cleaned up by eliminating words which were superfluous to the enquiry.

We then went through the transcript to identify the key thematic nodes which emerged from the interview and which were relevant to the topic of luxury industry use of primary research data. The top-level nodes that emerged from our preliminary appraisal of this document can be seen in the left-hand column in Figure 7.22. The right-hand column illustrates the body of text that is allocated to one particular node. At this early stage of the analysis, three entire paragraphs, and the prompting question from the researcher, are included in this particular node. As further interviews are added, this nodal coding will be further refined and, of course, expanded. The allocation of text to nodes can be displayed as a treemap (Figure 7.23).

FIGURE 7.21 Word Cloud from an NVivo Query, Interview Transcript, Participant 1. Copyright QSR International.

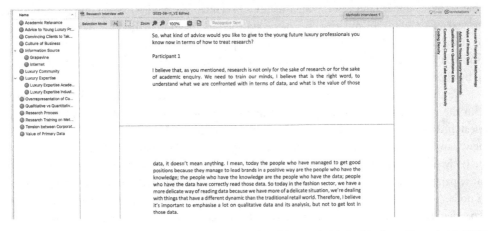

FIGURE 7.22 NVivo: Organisation of an Interview Transcript into Nodes. Copyright QSR International.

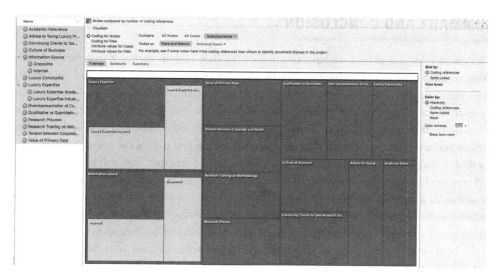

FIGURE 7.23 NVivo Treemap: Allocation of Text to Top-Level and Subsidiary Nodes. Copyright QSR International.

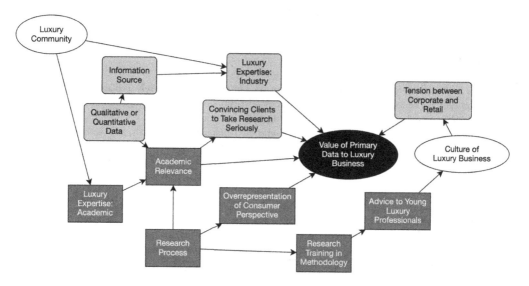

FIGURE 7.24 NVivo: Concept Map Based on the Nodes Allocated to the First Interview.

Having identified and allocated nodes to relevant segments of the textual transcript, we wanted to add some structure to this thematic organisation. NVivo offers the opportunity to construct mental maps and concept maps. Figure 7.24 shows a concept map that we created to accommodate the thematic nodes that emerged from the first of the ten interviews, which touched, inter alia, on the relevance and application of academic research for luxury brands in Europe. We created an industry flow and an academic flow, while the model as a whole was oriented towards the interface between the two. This concept map provides an organisational framework which can be consolidated and built upon as the qualitative data processing advances. We will return to discuss some more of the findings of this exercise in Chapter 9.

SUMMARY AND CONCLUSION

This chapter has introduced students to some of the data analysis methods that they are most likely to encounter in researching luxury, building in levels of sophistication and complexity from the more descriptive means of presenting research data to rather more challenging multivariate statistical analysis and qualitative content analysis. Data analysis comes easily to some and is quite daunting to others, but learning how to understand, handle and analyse data, and to present and interpret the findings of one's analysis, is an integral part of the research process and a valuable transferable skill to take into one's future career, whether that will be in the luxury industry or elsewhere. We would like to reiterate the point made much earlier in this book, that all aspects of the research process should involve choosing and using the right tools for the job, rather than restricting one's options through lack of knowledge or confidence. In some ways, it might have been useful (but illogical) to have placed this chapter on data analysis much earlier in the book so that students could familiarise themselves with the array of techniques available, and the rationale that lies behind them, to help them make an informed choice about analysis while at the stage of designing their research investigation. We hope we have explained data analysis sufficiently clearly that it appears slightly less intimidating to students who genuinely fear this stage of their research.

NOTES

1   We used writewords.org.uk and online-utility.org, but other tools are freely available.
2   This can be calculated online; we used www.socscistatistics.com/pvalues/fdistribution.aspx
3   https://geographyfieldwork.com/SpearmansRankCalculator.html
4   The four statements were: "I admire people who own expensive houses, cars, and clothes"; "I like to own things that impress others"; "the things that I own say a lot about how well I am doing in life"; and, reverse-coded, "I try to keep things simple, as far as possessions are concerned" (Jebarajakirthy and Das, 2021, 7).
5   The five indicators for trust, for example, were seven-point Likert scale responses to the following statements, derived from Xiao and Benbasat (2007): "I believe this IC [internet celebrity] has the ability to provide professional information"; "I believe the IC is honest about the product and describes it objectively"; "I believe this IC won't just recommend the product just for business interest"; "I believe this IC can provide unbiased recommendations"; and "I believe this IC recommends for helping others" (Chen et al., 2021, 2478).

CHAPTER 8

Writing Up and Presenting Luxury Research Findings

Having put so much effort into designing and conducting an investigation, it is important that the researcher communicates all aspects of their research to their audience, clearly, engagingly and effectively. This chapter will touch on several aspects of writing up and presenting research findings in the hope that the student researcher may gain some useful advice for showcasing their work. The discussion is principally aimed at the postgraduate student producing a dissertation in an academic setting, but we will finish by considering some of the points of connection and difference in the presentation of academic and practitioner research.

WRITING UP

The aim of writing up is to *communicate* to a wider audience what you have done, why you have done it in a particular way, what you have found out and what the value of this is to our wider understanding of luxury. Inevitably, the principal audience for a Master's dissertation will be the examiners, and most institutions specify the criteria against which the document will be evaluated, and so it is important to ensure that all the relevant boxes are ticked in this regard. But the thesis should also be written as if it is going to be read by an interested and informed general readership. As such, the narrative should be accessible to all readers, specialist and non-specialist alike, being authoritative, confident, informative and accessible, without being either too flowery or too jargonistic (especially if jargon and opacity are used to mask the researcher's incomplete understanding of a topic or concept). There is a particular academic style of writing of which the student should be aware and which can be picked up by paying close attention to how the books and articles that are used in the literature review are presented. With this in mind, we present in Box 8.1 an "anatomy of an academic article" to cast some light on the style and structure of the academic approach. Convention usually dictates that the narrative should be presented in the third person, although you will have noticed throughout this book that we prefer to use the first person (plural, in our case).

DOI: 10.4324/9781003295372-8

BOX 8.1

An Anatomy of an Academic Article

To exemplify what we mean by 'academic style', we decided to dissect an academic article to gain a sense of how leading authors in the field of luxury present their research. With literally thousands of articles to choose from, we decided to select the paper in the field of luxury that has the most citations, which deduction suggests is among the most authoritative articles in this field. According to the Web of Science at the time of writing, an article on social media marketing and customer equity in the field of luxury, published in 2012 by Angella Kim (University of Minnesota, USA) and Eunju Ko (Yonsei University, South Korea), had 766 citations by October 2022 (and 973 citations on Scopus), and so we chose this one.[1]

The article is a quantitative analysis that tests ten hypotheses relating to the influence of social media marketing activities on four kinds of equity (value, relationship, brand and customer equity) in the realm of luxury, which in turn may influence purchase intention (Kim and Ko, 2012, 1482). Louis Vuitton was chosen as the brand that best represented luxury brands, in part because it was among the best-recognised luxury brands in South Korea, which is the focus of the empirical component of the study (*ibid.*, 1482).

The presentation of ideas, theories, concepts, methodology, investigative model and research findings follows a conventional structure that is found in most such quantitative studies. The paper commences with a short introduction which, first, outlines some of the challenges facing the luxury market and, then, positions social media marketing as one strategy that can help to meet these challenges. Academic articles typically face quite tight word limit constraints, and so there is little space here to expand on key statements, such as "[t]he luxury market has attained maturity" (*ibid.*, 1480) and "[a] decrease in sales related to a global economic downturn drives luxury businesses to change" (*ibid.*), which ordinarily (and, one would hope, in a Master's dissertation that faces fewer word constraints) might be more deeply nuanced. The statement "[w]ith the increased use of SMM [social media marketing] by luxury brands, it has become highly necessary to quantitatively analyze the effects of the social media" (*ibid.*) appears to be the principal justification for the authors' research, which again could have been more fully explained and justified – why wasn't a qualitative investigation even considered, for example?[2] But, in general, the introduction is expressed succinctly and with authority and very quickly gets to the heart of the investigation. No references are used in the introduction: it is the place where the authors make a pitch for the relevance and value of their piece of research.

There follow three sections where the authors expand on the literature-informed conceptual foundations of their research, looking in turn at social media marketing activities and how they affect both the performance of firms and the activities of luxury brands (*ibid.*, 1481), the drivers of customer equity, and consumer purchase intention. In the section on social media, the authors cite their own previous work on the influence of social media on the reputation of luxury brands, further reinforcing the sense of confidence and authority in the arguments they are developing.[3] Again presumably owing to constraints of space, some of the concepts are introduced quite superficially: 'purchase intention', which is so often a dependent variable in quantitative research on luxury, is only afforded around 100 words of explanation, even though statements such as "measuring purchase intention assumes consumers' future behavior based on their attitudes" (*ibid.*, 1481) might arguably have been more critically dissected. In the section which outlines the hypotheses which will guide the empirical investigation, the statement "a primary goal of any marketing strategy is to increase sales and profitability" (*ibid.*, 1482) could also be much more deeply nuanced within the context of luxury, where marketing may have important, and even paramount, non-commercial functions as well. One would hope, in a Master's dissertation, that ten hypotheses would be afforded more than 250 words of explanation and justification, although it is often the case with academic publications that authors 'write in code' to other authors who 'get it' without the need for a lengthy repetition of acknowledged and frequently used concepts and ideas. A Master's student should make no such assumptions.

As we saw in the discussion of structural equation modelling in Chapter 7, the authors succinctly and precisely introduce the measures which will be used to operationalise and populate their structural model, all of which are based upon established ways of measuring the constituent variables drawn from a wide literature (*ibid.*, 1482). The data were collected from a convenience sample of 362 citizens in Korea who had purchased a luxury fashion item in the last two years and who were also familiar with Louis Vuitton's social media sites (*ibid.*, 1483). The data were based on a questionnaire survey carried out in two of Seoul's main luxury shopping districts. The discussion at this point is succinct, factual and informative, without being particularly reflexive. At no stage is contextualisation discussed in this paper, other than a short profile of the Korean shopper towards the end of the paper. The demographic profile of the sample participants is described, and the characteristics of the various constructs used in the model are outlined, before the strength and direction of the various measures are introduced and explained to the reader.

The study ends with a section which draws conclusions from the research findings. It is interesting to observe, given our comment above, that the authors concluded that their study "indicate[d] the great difficulty in measuring customers' future [purchasing] behavior" (*ibid.*, 1485). The authors also make the following concluding statement: "SMM activities perceived by consumers were significantly efficacious to luxury brands' future profits" (*ibid.*, 1484). This is curious, because the study focused on consumers, not brands, and on present behaviour (future behaviour was difficult to measure) and perceptions of brand equity and value. There was no measurement of brands' profits, either current or in the future. What we think the authors meant was that social media marketing helped to enhance brand equity and value, which in turn may help to increase brand stability or even profitability in the future. If this is correct – and we apologise if this is not the case – it emphasises the importance of careful and precise wording throughout. The authors do not reflect on how a convenience sample of 362 Koreans can speak to the role of SMM in enhancing luxury brand equity in general, although they do concede that a wider cross-section of contexts should yield a more representative picture of the wider situation.

This short 'anatomical investigation' has identified some key pointers concerning the style and structure of academic writing that student researchers of luxury might take on board as they nurture their own stylistic approach to presenting their research findings. It has also picked up on several critical points simply to reiterate some of the advice we have given in earlier chapters.

Different people have different styles and practices, of course, but it may be useful to avoid the notion that 'writing up' is a task to engage with once all other stages of the research have been completed. Writing is a task that should be undertaken throughout the research process, not only to avoid writing pressures building as the submission deadline looms, but principally because it provides opportunities for the student to reflect on their work as it progresses and avoid shortcomings that might become amplified as the research develops. It is certainly recommended that the student complete at least a tidy draft of the 'literature review' and research design narrative before embarking on the data gathering process. Indeed, the concept of a 'tidy draft' is a useful one to work towards: for many people, editing is usually easier than writing, and so seeking to achieve absolute precision in writing right from the start can significantly slow the writing process.

Institutions vary in whether the supervisor is allowed to read and correct drafts of a dissertation before it is submitted. In our experience, this is not good practice, as it may be construed as 'pre-marking', where the input of the supervisor may start to mask that of the student. It is also a practice that can disadvantage those who do not receive the same level of support.

READING AND TAKING NOTES

One of the challenges of reading to build a foundation for the research within the existing body of knowledge, and to inform the various practical stages of the research process, is to be able to identify what material is essential, what is relevant, what is interesting but tangential, and what is superfluous. One of the reasons why the research-based dissertation is placed at the end of a postgraduate course of study is that it allows the student to build their investigation upon a platform provided by their earlier coursework and to deepen their engagement with a particular issue or question related to one aspect of luxury management. In this sense, students should already be quite familiar with a relevant body of literature prior to embarking on their research project. If they follow some of the advice offered in previous chapters of this book – for example, using keywords and keyword searches, mental maps and layered research questions – they should also be able to pinpoint the most relevant and up-to-date sources that they need to build the foundations for their research and construct clear topical boundaries around their research investigation. Of course, in an ideal world, the inquisitive researcher can never read enough: there is always something fresh to learn. But, in a time-limited project, it is important to keep literature-based exploration to the parameters that are strictly relevant to the task in hand. Clear thinking from the beginning will underpin efficiency throughout. Hoping to stumble on a relevant seam of knowledge risks charting a meandering path towards an uncertain destination.

Building knowledge and understanding through reading the literature is an incremental process. When you set out, new theories and concepts can appear to be quite dull and dry, and you may gain, and note down, only a few sparks of inspiration after reading a long article. This is quite normal. As your reading progresses and your notes become richer, you will soon be able to connect the inspirational 'dots' into 'lines' and later 'patterns' of thinking. These can even be presented graphically, along the lines of the mental maps that we introduced in Chapter 4. Your reading notes, properly organised, start to inform the various components of the theoretical discussion with which your dissertation will commence, and the mental map can help to give this discussion a logical structure.

Having a clear structure, direction and understanding is also crucial when it comes to taking notes from one's reading. Different people have different techniques, but practice can range from a precise series of bullet points with occasional direct quotations on the one hand to effectively rewriting the bulk of what is being read on the other. The latter is not only time-consuming and inefficient, it can also inadvertently contribute to plagiarism: verbatim notes, poorly referenced, may over time be reproduced in the student's dissertation as their own words. The fundamental aim of writing up is for the student to communicate, in their own words, the essence of their research: its theoretical foundations, the research framework, design and methodology, the findings, and an evaluation of their value and contribution to existing knowledge in their chosen research field. *Collating* a literature review from a combination of snippets drawn from their reading and including a copious number of direct quotations is rather bad form and does little more than showcase the writer's ability to cut and paste. A researcher should bear these pitfalls in mind when note-taking while reading. It may be advisable to read an article first and then note down key points and observations afterwards, together with reflections on how this source will fit into the wider picture the student is creating. This will certainly speed up the process of reading and should also hone the student's skills at sifting, digesting, evaluating and summarising those elements that are relevant to their own research. Proper referencing is essential, and it is also sensible to compile a list of references as the reading and writing progress in order to avoid the need to scurry around finding (sometimes obscure) missing items at the last moment before submission. The same applies to all web-based materials used in the thesis: these are best flagged in a footnote with the full URL (uniform resource locator) and an indication of the date the material was accessed online, as we have done consistently in this book.

TIME MANAGEMENT

Reading, researching and writing a thesis are tasks that must be completed within a set time frame. It is therefore crucial that the student tailor the scale of their ambition to a level that is achievable within the time available. Having done so, they should map out a clear timeline that takes them from beginning to end within the allotted time, and they should exercise disciplined time management to ensure they stay on track. This is not just because failure to complete the thesis on time leads to all kinds of problems for the student, but also because discipline, time management and completion of tasks on time are qualities that will be expected of any graduate entering the world of luxury business. Excuses such as "my dog ate my work" simply will not wash in the real world. Researching and writing a thesis are usually first-time experiences for most students, and so it is difficult at the outset to envisage the timescale required to complete the various stages of the research process or to foresee the impediments that may lie in its path. Getting advice from one's supervisor and/or someone who has already been through the process should be invaluable in this regard. But the student can also help themself by having a very clear idea of the structure and direction of their project and the boundaries of their research (as we discussed in Chapter 4), by seeking to be efficient and disciplined throughout, by avoiding procrastination and indecisiveness, by building in a margin for unforeseen eventualities and by leaving time for proofreading and copy-editing. If they are planning to enter the luxury industry on completion of their thesis, it makes sense to treat the research and thesis-writing as they imagine a professional would when undertaking research for a luxury brand.

WORD LIMITS

As with the need to demonstrate time management capabilities as a precursor to entering a career in luxury business, compliance with word limits is also a discipline that students need to master. Precision and succinctness are qualities a student is expected to demonstrate in all their written exercises. When a student embarks on their research-based dissertation, the need to write anything between 12,000 and 20,000 words (50,000 words in continental Europe) may appear to be quite a daunting prospect, but, as the project progresses gradually, the word limit starts to be seen as a constraint. It then becomes a question of ensuring that every word has a place and a value, with an appropriate balance being struck to ensure that each component of the thesis is given the prominence it deserves. It would be misleading to be prescriptive about how many words should be allocated to each section and component. Very general guidance might be as follows, with the researcher deciding on the relative balance of these (and possibly other) components: introduction, 5–10%; literature review, 30–40%; research design and methodology, 10–20%; introduction to research site, 5–10%; presentation and discussion of findings, 30–40%; and summary, conclusions, reflections, limitations and recommendations for future research, 10–15%.

PLAGIARISM

Plagiarism is the taking of someone else's words or ideas (including images and diagrams) and presenting them as if they are one's own. It is a form of intellectual dishonesty. At its worst extreme, it may be a deliberate attempt to deceive; at its mildest, it may involve an innocent or unintentional failure to acknowledge sources in the appropriate manner; but, in all cases, it is a serious transgression of accepted academic practice to assure academic integrity. *Ignorance is not a defence*. The principles of plagiarism apply equally to published and unpublished sources, including lecture notes, and it is even possible to self-plagiarise by using, without formal attribution, words or work that has previously been prepared and submitted for another purpose.

Deliberate plagiarism is cheating, but there are several circumstances that can lead to accidental plagiarism. As we mentioned above, poor note-taking practice (for example, not consistently noting documentary sources and page numbers) can lead to students incorporating direct quotations or paraphrased sections from another author, thinking these are words they have written themselves. Paraphrasing others' work also risks accusations of plagiarism: the words may be slightly different, but the essence is the same, and the fundamental ideas have been drawn from someone or somewhere else. Paraphrasing may fool plagiarism-detecting software (such as Turnitin, EasyBib and Unicheck), but that is not the point: one of the key objectives of a postgraduate education is to enable the student to find and express their own voice; collating other people's words and ideas, perhaps through a lack of confidence or experience in expressing one's own argument in one's own words, signifies a failure to achieve ownership of the writing process, however creative one's paraphrasing may be.

HOUSE STYLE

Check what your institution requires in terms of referencing conventions, font and font size, line spacing and spacing between paragraphs, indentation, margins, pagination, headers/footers, justification, footnotes/endnotes. It is very important for the thesis to be neat, uncluttered and professional in appearance. You may need one day to show it to a prospective employer in the luxury industry!

CRITICALITY

Being critical does not simply mean learning to criticise everything. It requires the student to tune their critical eye in reading, appraising and evaluating statements, debates and ideas expressed in the literature on luxury and some of the disciplinary fields that feed into this. Much of what is written about luxury in the academic literature is proposition rather than fact; all authors, to a greater or lesser extent, have an argument, a position, a perspective, an angle, a standpoint, an ideology, a tradition to which they belong, perhaps even a vested interest in the statements they contribute to the wider world. The more you read, the more you should be able to identify the flavour and ideological orientation of someone's argument or their identity as an author. And, the more you read, the more you might find that different people are focusing on different things within the same field, or even that their arguments, when seen *in toto*, might appear somewhat contradictory. You, as a researcher and the author of your dissertation, have the privileged position of being able to stand apart from these debates and, to some extent, pass judgement on them, or at the very least orchestrate their discussion in a way that helps build your own argument, making sense of ongoing debates for the purposes of laying a platform, or a point of departure, for your own study. Seeing the tensions and contradictions in the literature for what they are, speaking up about them and mapping your own discursive path through them are all key to adopting a critical stance.

DISSERTATION STRUCTURE AND CONTENTS

While the structure, contents and overall style of a dissertation may be determined to some extent by the student's institutional or disciplinary requirements and conventions, there are certain component elements that are almost universally required. These are listed in Box 8.2 and are discussed individually below.

BOX 8.2

Conventional Components and Structure of a Master's Dissertation

Title Page
Acknowledgements [optional]
Abstract
Table of Contents
List of Figures, List of Tables and so on
Introduction
Problem Statement
Literature Review, Including Theoretical Context
Research Questions, Design and Methodology
Introduction to the Research Site [contingent]
Research Findings, Discussion and Argument
Conclusions, Implications [including for luxury brand management], Recommendations, Suggestions for Further Research, Limitations
References
Appendices

Title Page

Your dissertation starts with a title, and this is your first chance to explain to a potential reader what your research is about. Think of the title as a logo: something catchy, creative, communicative and memorable that forms an impression on the observer and leaves them curious to investigate further. The title should be concise, precise and informative and should communicate the essence of your dissertation in fewer than 20 words. It makes sense for the title to be consistent with the primary research question, but simply using this question as a title seems unlikely to tick many of the boxes suggested above and will not be very appealing to the lay reader. Many writers solve the appeal–detail conundrum by preparing a title in two parts, separated by a colon. The first part should be a pithy engagement of the issue or problem in the field of luxury with which the research is concerned (e.g., sustainability); the second part should be a brief encapsulation of the main research question (e.g., corporate greenwashing) and possibly also the research approach (e.g., case study, empirical investigation, qualitative enquiry, critical analysis, etc.). An example based on the above might be: "Sustainable Luxury? A Critical Investigation of Corporate Greenwashing". This is only eight words. The use of the question mark in the first part actually says a great deal without the need to flesh out the issue. The second part makes clear what the focal point will be and also informs the reader of the author's likely standpoint. This does not necessarily imply that the researcher will only look for evidence of greenwashing by brands and corporations – that would not be sufficiently objective and balanced. But it does offer the prospect of a critical engagement with the notion of sustainability and rather triumphant claims about sustainable luxury. Should your dissertation be good enough to be published, a catchy and alluring title which also incorporates some of the keywords that are the focal point of your research would seem likely to figure quite prominently in search engines and literature databases.

In addition to the title, the title page should also provide the name of the author, the degree for which their thesis is being submitted, their institutional affiliation (department, university), the date of submission and the word count.

Abstract

The abstract provides a condensed overview of the study and would usually consist of a single paragraph of around 150–250 words. It makes sense to write the abstract once the research is finished and the thesis completed. For guidance, academic articles published by the Emerald Publishing Group[4] require authors to cover the following areas in their abstracts: research purpose, research design/methodology/approach, research findings, research limitations, practical implications and originality/value. The first part identifies the issue, problem, challenge or theme within the field of luxury with which the research aims to engage, perhaps including the main research question, and might also contain a justification which shows why this piece of research is valuable. A brief summary of methodology should follow, which might mention whether the study is quantitative or qualitative in orientation, or uses mixed methods, before specifying what methods were used. If the research focuses on a particular location or group of people, this should be mentioned and also justified. A succinct summary of the principal research findings should follow – enough to give the reader a sense of where the study ended up, without giving away too much of the detail at this early stage. The abstract should finish with a statement about the value, possible applications and implications of the research findings to the field of luxury management, and/or wider scholarly debates, and any constraints the research encountered which may have had a bearing on the validity of the research findings. Academic writing, including a PhD thesis, is usually expected to make an original contribution to knowledge, but it is reasonable to expect that the findings from a Master's-level project may be relatively modest in this regard, and so it is best not to make stronger claims in the abstract than can be supported by the evidence presented. Several universities publish the abstracts of theses completed under their auspices on their websites, and so it is important to take care to ensure that this document is clear and concise and communicates the essence of the research accurately.

Acknowledgements

Over the course of the research process, students may benefit from various kinds of support, be that financial, intellectual, practical or even emotional. A short acknowledgements section gives you the opportunity to recognise and express your appreciation for this support. It is particularly important to acknowledge the support given by stakeholders in the luxury industry, be they brand managers, heads of departments or retail outlets, industry associations and so on. However, if brands and actors are to be anonymised in the thesis, care should be taken not to compromise this principle in the acknowledgements section. If a student has received a grant or other financial support from an organisation, or even leave of absence to allow them to undertake their postgraduate programme, this should also be formally acknowledged. Supporting bodies may ask to receive a copy of the thesis when it is completed (subject to institutional regulations), and so they would like to see their contribution to the research formally acknowledged. The acknowledgements section should be no more than a single paragraph and can be written in a less formal and more personal style, using the first person.

Table of Contents, List of Figures, List of Tables and so on

The table of contents will communicate to the reader your dissertation's organisational structure and, by including page numbers, can actually show the reader (and the examiner!) how, proportionally, you have allocated space to its constituent parts. As a minimum, the table must contain all chapters and substantive sections; the student must choose whether or not to include a complete list of sub-sections where these are particularly numerous (this is an 'all or none' decision). Sectionalising a thesis is generally a useful technique that helps to guide the reader through the discussion thematically. However, over-sectionalising the dissertation can disrupt the flow of the discussion and make it appear too 'bitty'. The preliminary pages should also include lists of tables, figures, images and so on, each with precisely the same title as is given in the text (the same applies to chapter and section headings). These should be completed at the very end, once definitive page numbers are known.

Introduction

The introduction is an important part of the thesis which has four main objectives. It sets the research within the context of a topical issue in the field of luxury and certain problems or challenges that this gives rise to: for example, the 'democratisation of luxury' or the 'massification of luxury' and the challenges it poses for maintaining the fundamental essence of luxury as an exclusive domain. Thus, after introducing the reader to the way that the luxury industry has been metamorphosing in recent years, the author makes a clear *problem statement* which specifies the focus of their investigation. The same principle applies if they are looking at the *process* of change rather than its impact. This first section of the introduction should also identify a gap in our existing knowledge and show how the study will help to fill this gap.

The second objective is to contextualise the research. The likelihood is that the research investigation will not look at the entire luxury industry, globally and involving all groups of consumers, and so it is important at an early stage to give an indication as to which segment of the industry, which country or region, which demographic or socio-economic group and so on will provide the focus of particular attention for the investigation, and why (manageability is a reasonable justification here). At this point, the writer should also reflect a little on the distinguishing characteristics of this target group or location, where it or they fit in to the process and problem being described, and indicate their awareness of the constraints that a particularistic investigation poses when drawing wider conclusions for the luxury industry more broadly. This gives an early indication to the reader of the writer's awareness of some of the potential limitations of their chosen approach.

The next objective is to give the reader a clear indication of how the writer plans to approach their research. There is an important distinction to be drawn between the introduction and the abstract in this regard: the latter is a *post facto* statement that is informed by what actually happened; the former is an *ex ante* indication of what is intended and why. As such, it is important not to give the impression that aspects of the research approach have been predetermined. As we will see below when we discuss the literature review at length, the intellectual and practical bases for the research investigation should emerge organically and incrementally as the discussion evolves. Thus, a decision about methodology and method should follow the process of *problem development* (informed by theoretical and other debates drawn from the existing body of knowledge), the statement of research questions and the mapping out of an investigative framework. For this reason, we would advise against listing the various research questions (primary, secondary and possibly tertiary) in the introduction, but instead recommend incorporating their gist in a broad *problem statement*. We are not being prescriptive here: ultimately, the student must choose which approach best suits their enquiry and their personality. This section might conclude with an overview of the thesis in terms of structure (e.g., chapters) and content.

Finally, the discussion might reflect on the potential value of the investigation they have in mind, perhaps in rising to the challenges of luxury brand management or in terms of informing our understanding of an important process within the field of luxury. There should be no statement of findings in the introduction, only the possible applications of any research results that the student may be able to come up with. This may also be a good place to add a further reflexive statement which shows that the student is aware of the constraints of their investigation and its limited scope to make a major and original contribution to knowledge. We prefer modesty and humility to bravado and overconfidence, but this too is the personal choice of the author of the thesis.

Literature Review

The aim of the literature review is to situate the research investigation within the existing body of knowledge and the debates contained therewithin, at the same time laying a theoretical foundation for the research enquiry. It should be borne in mind that 'knowledge' consists of more than just 'what we know': it also comprises 'how we come to know' – intellectual processes as well as facts. The literature review also provides the student researcher with an opportunity to demonstrate that they have identified, engaged with and thoroughly understood the current state of research in their chosen field.

The widespread use of the term 'literature review' can be quite unhelpful to the novice researcher. Certainly, at some point, the researcher will peruse, process, evaluate and organise a discussion of arguments and ideas based on a healthy range of literature sources – intellectual activities that the word 'review' hardly does justice to – but the literature-based section of the thesis should also involve much more than this. The aim of this academic exercise is not simply to show what and how much you know about a certain topic, but to orchestrate this knowledge for the clear purpose of establishing a solid intellectual platform for your own research. This might take you from a somewhat broad discussion of 'luxury', via a more detailed engagement with particular arguments or debates, to a focused exposition of the precise issue/process/ challenge within the field of luxury on which you will be concentrating; from theoretical, via conceptual, to more practical ideas; and from known things to unknown matters which might usefully be expressed as research questions. To do this, you will require an array of literature sources which will allow you to write with authority about all the above elements. Your initial literature search should be guided by the 'wine glass' analogy that we introduced in Chapter 3 (Figure 3.1), flowing from broad to narrow and from generalised to specific: the aim of the literature review section of the thesis is to reach the top of the 'wine glass stem' by the time you get to the end of this chapter. All this, quite clearly, requires more than a basic 'literature review'. It requires a carefully orchestrated argument that draws from the existing body of knowledge but steers the discussion in a direction that leads towards the research problem and the method-ological means for its exploration. It is not a passive assemblage of other people's writing but a choreographed and directed discussion which showcases the intellectual DNA of the researcher.

Logically, given the discussion above, the literature review should conclude with a statement and an explanation of the research questions (or at least the principal research question) which are to guide the investigation. These should be the intellectual pinnacle of the literature-based debate and discussion that led to the identification of a gap in knowledge and an issue that is worthy of deeper enquiry. The key steps or elements of a literature review are summarised in Box 8.3.

BOX 8.3

Key Elements of a Literature Review

The literature review chapter might usefully engage with the following questions:
What is known about this topic?
What are the leading issues and ideas being discussed in the literature?
What are the intellectual structures (e.g., theories, concepts) for these debates?
Is there a universally accepted viewpoint, or is there some contention or
  argument, and a point of departure?
Who are the principal proponents of these competing viewpoints?
What are the gaps in our knowledge that might usefully be filled through primary
  research?
What are the key questions that need to be engaged with in order to advance
  our knowledge in this field?

Before the researcher can attempt to build a knowledge-based foundation for their research, they need to have a quite clear idea about the direction in which the study is aiming. This may seem obvious, but it is not uncommon for students to drift through the literature in the *hope* of stumbling on a theme or a foundation, rather than carefully orchestrating their literature search with a clear objective in mind.

McMenamin (2006) stresses the need for clarity of purpose and definable boundaries when attempting a literature review. Although luxury as a mainstream field of study has a relatively short history, the literature has grown substantially over the last decade, as we showed in Chapter 2, and, when put together with theoretical writing from other academic disciplines, it is quite easy for the researcher to get lost in countless debates, at a cost to progress with their own research. McMenamin emphasises, as do we, that the literature review is not an end in itself but a means towards an end. In other words, it is not a self-contained cell that lives and survives outside the main body of the thesis, but a key organ, almost the heartbeat of the dissertation. The conventional creation of a discrete chapter entitled 'literature review' runs the risk of convincing the researcher that this is a milestone to pass before getting down to the research proper. Nothing could be further from the truth: it is an integral and essential paving stone on the path towards building an investigation and framing research questions. *The literature review is not a self-contained essay.* The literature review is both a text and a process (McMenamin, 2006). One of the cardinal errors a student can make is to detach their literature review from their main research purpose.

If the student's first thought is to fret about how many books and articles they should consult in putting together their literature review, they have already missed the point. It is a case not so much of 'how many' but of 'how well' – how well this literature-based chapter lays a foundation for, and serves the needs and purposes of, the dissertation as a whole. Of course, they do have to convince the reader that they are sufficiently familiar with current debates in the field of luxury and are able to identify and digest the most important reference sources in this regard, but this is not the sole, or even the key, purpose of the literature review.

Research Design and Methodology

It is usually advisable to set aside a separate chapter to explain to the reader the methodological procedures that the research will follow and their supporting rationale. This is where the primary investigation begins, and the first step is to build a robust framework for the ensuing enquiry. If the literature review chapter ended with an outlining of the main research question on which the investigation will focus, the next chapter could usefully commence with a deeper exposition of this and any subsidiary research questions, and how these are going to be operationalised for the purposes of the research enquiry. As we saw in Chapter 4, a conceptual model is a useful means of identifying the key intellectual components of the investigation, and this might be developed and explained ahead of identifying and elaborating on the research framework (this could even be placed towards the end of the literature review chapter as a way of tying the discussion together and creating a clear point of transition from a secondary towards a primary focus).

The student's methodological approach should then be detailed and explained. This should not just consist of a listing and justification of the methods to be used in the research and a reflection on their strengths and weaknesses, but should be used as an opportunity to demonstrate where, and why, the study fits into the various philosophical perspectives on the nature of knowledge and how we approach knowledge generation, which we discussed in Chapters 3–5. The student might also reflect on how the chosen approach might influence the reliability and validity of their research findings.

Some attention should also be given at this point to operationalising key concepts, including explaining the measurement variables to be incorporated in a structural model if this kind of quantitative approach is being considered. This chapter should also contain information on any sampling procedure used and a brief reflection on representativeness. Details should be given about how research methods were used in the research, who the target participants were and why, and any difficulties that were encountered 'in the field'. For instance, was it necessary to 'change tack' at some point when faced by insurmountable difficulties, and how did the student rise to this challenge? The student should also reflect on any ethical dilemmas they encountered in their research and how they overcame them. One purpose of the methodological discussion, beyond convincing the examiner that the research has been done 'properly', is to inform other researchers about the procedures followed in case they want to replicate or build upon this piece of research.

Introduction to the Research Site

This might be incorporated in the methodological discussion, as detailed above, or included as a small section in the literature review chapter, or given its own discrete section in the thesis. Contextualisation may be more important to some pieces of research than others (hence our use of the word 'contingent' in Box 8.2), but it is always useful to demonstrate to the reader that you are in tune with the specificities of your chosen context and aware of how they may influence both your research approach and your interpretation of findings.

Research Findings, Discussion and Argument

You will have noticed that we have presented our own research findings at different stages throughout this book – particularly in Chapters 2, 6 and 9 – and this might be used as a general guide to how results are presented, explained and woven into an evolving argument.

The way research findings are presented will, of course, be determined by the nature of the investigation and the data being presented, but there are some generic points that might apply in most circumstances. The first is that the presentation of findings should be analytical and interpretive as well as descriptive. The student may choose to present the findings descriptively first and then go on to interpret and discuss them, or these two things might be attempted simultaneously. Whatever the preferred approach, it is important that the discussion should focus not just on what was found but on what the implications of the findings are for the argument being developed and the issue being discussed. This is also where the various research questions should resurface: essentially, the findings should be evaluated against the original objectives of the research and the questions that guided it. Here we reiterate the point we made in Chapter 4: not only is the nested hierarchy of research questions a useful device for breaking an investigation down into smaller but cognate component parts, but also, when the 'pyramid' is inverted, all of these smaller 'roads' lead back to the central question. The nested hierarchy of research questions therefore provides a useful framework for structuring the presentation and discussion of research findings, as well as clearly demarcating the boundaries of your investigation and also, thus, the discussion of findings.

The approach to presenting research findings is likely to be quite different for quantitative studies – which may centre on detailing and discussing the results of statistical analysis – and qualitative studies – which may use narrative-rich data as both evidence and analysis, interspersed with commentary and interpretation. The way your report your research findings may also be predetermined to some extent by the conventions of the discipline to which you belong, if any, which might supersede the advice offered here. Clearly, the allocation of words to discussing the various findings from the research, and thus the level of depth and detail that is possible, will depend on how much space is available within an overall word limit. As with other sections of the thesis, it is obviously necessary to allocate words in such a way that allows an appropriate balance between the various elements. It is thus often necessary to be selective in the presentation of findings, especially with a tight word limit. A natural tendency is to feel inclined to include just about everything that the research has revealed; there may be a sense that you have gone to so much effort to obtain the data that you do not want to leave anything out. Here, again, judgement is required to sift the essential from the relevant, from the interesting but tangential and from the superfluous.

It is in the presentation of findings section of the thesis that the 'wine glass' shape starts to turn back from narrow to broad as the 'stem' reaches the 'base'. After detailing and interpreting the findings from the investigation and analysis, the discussion should start to reflect on how the outcomes from the research connect with and contribute to the wider theoretical and practical debates with which the dissertation commenced.

One final word on analysis: there is a natural tendency to want to present a QED (*quod erat demonstrandum* – a final proof) at the end of your research. There may be a reluctance to present findings that are inconclusive or contradictory or that refute initial propositions or assumptions, especially when a final mark is at stake. But research that consciously steers findings in a particular direction is actually poor research, whereas research that reflects and tells the 'truth' is what we really need in the pursuit of knowledge. Findings are findings, and, indeed, findings that identify a line of enquiry as a 'dead end' are sometimes just as valuable to the advancement of knowledge as research with positive outcomes.

Conclusions, Implications, Recommendations, Limitations and Suggestions for Further Research

The concluding chapter is where the research is once again fully integrated with the issues and questions which provided the initial rationale and direction for the investigation: it should by this point have gone full circle – imagine, if you can, the 'wine glass' as a circular, not linear, phenomenon, where the base fits back neatly into the opening. The chapter might begin with a reminder of its underlying objectives and chosen approach, followed by a summary of the key findings. This should lead into a consideration of what the research outcomes might mean for the field of luxury and the theories that guide our understanding of the industry's dynamics, and an assessment of the implications of the research findings for various aspects of luxury management. On the basis of the investigation and findings, the student may also wish to make certain recommendations with regard to the future direction of management policy in order to ameliorate the particular issue or problem that the research was designed to engage. This would help to show that the student is aware of the practical applications of their research endeavour.

In line with the principles of reflexivity that we have referred to consistently throughout this book, the student should round off the discussion by reflecting on the limitations of their research, which may relate to its scale, depth and any compromises that were necessary in taking it through to completion. Care should be taken not to list a range of limitations that could or should have been avoided if the research had been designed and executed properly: you will simply be flagging to the examiner what the deficiencies of the thesis are. The limitations discussed should thus be unavoidable – for example, sample size, participants' refusals, problems of gaining access to luxury brands, mobility constraints and so on. Reflecting on how the research was done and how, in different circumstances, it might have been done better can help turn a discussion of shortcomings into a showcasing of the researcher's depth of understanding of the research process. Likewise, suggestions for further research, which might build upon and advance the just-completed project or which identifies important gaps in knowledge that the study has revealed, also demonstrate the student's holistic understanding of the issues and challenges currently facing the realm of luxury.

List of References

We mentioned at the beginning of this chapter the need to maintain a full record of all readings (including material gleaned from the internet). This having been done, the compilation of a list of readings should be a relatively straightforward task. We use the term 'list of references' because this section of the thesis should *only* contain materials that you have directly referred to in the text (including footnotes): nothing more and nothing less. A *bibliography* may contain additional materials that you have consulted but not directly referred to in the text; this information is not required, and indeed its inclusion may obfuscate the main purpose of the list of references – to provide details of the sources that have been cited and provide a guide to others who may wish to follow up this research. Care should be taken to remove from the list any references and citations that were taken out of the dissertation at various stages of editing and to include any that were subsequently added.

A direct quotation from a source must include page numbers as well as author and year of publication. When using or paraphrasing words from a source, as a minimum you should include the author and year of publication in parentheses, but also the page number if the use of this author's work is substantive, even without direct quotation. The convention with multiple authors is to list the names of them all if there are three or fewer, but to use *et al.* where there are four or more authors, with full details of them all in the list of references. The use of diagrams, images and so on from another source should also include the page number, or website URL if it has been taken from an online source. The systematic use of referencing of authoritative sources also helps to underpin the academic credentials and plausibility of the work you are writing. A lack of sources and sourcing suggests that the author is relying too much on their own opinions and views, which, given they are not yet an acknowledged expert in their field, could be problematic: finding one's own voice is one thing, but ignoring the voice of others is perhaps a step too far.

Care should also be taken to ensure that all references are presented using one of the formal referencing conventions. Often, the student's institution will specify which convention should be followed in the thesis, but the general rule is 'be consistent': identify a referencing convention and stick rigidly to it throughout. Referencing in the humanities tends to be placed in footnotes (which may take up more space than text on some pages) or endnotes (which can run to several pages) and is exemplified by the Oxford referencing system. In the social sciences, it is more usual to use what is called 'parenthetical citation': including the author(s), year of publication and, for direct quotations, diagrams or references to specific statements or ideas, page number(s), all enclosed in parentheses (brackets). The cited reference should then be presented in full in the list of references to appear at the end of the thesis. Business studies tends to use parenthetical citation. Box 8.4 presents an illustration of three referencing systems: Harvard, Chicago and APA (the American Psychological Association). References should be presented in alphabetical order, with a hanging indent. There are some web-based reference resources (such as citethemright-online.com) which provide guidance for students who are unsure about referencing. The well-organised student can compile their list of references as their research and writing progresses, using reference generators such as EndNote or Zotero.

BOX 8.4

Some Examples of Referencing and Citing Conventions

Harvard (Book)

Parnwell, MJG & Meng, KY 2023, *Research methods for luxury management*, Routledge, London. In-text citation: (Parnwell & Meng 2023).

Harvard (Article)

Meng, KY & Parnwell, MJG 2023, 'Luxury and sustainability: ne'er the twain shall meet?', *Philosophical Issues in Global Sustainability* vol. 1, no. 1, pp. 1–25. In-text citation: (Meng & Parnwell 2023).

Chicago (Book)

Parnwell, Michael, and Kelly Meng. *Research Methods for Luxury Management*. London: Routledge, 2023. In-text citation: (Parnwell and Meng 2023).

Chicago (Article)

Meng, Kelly Y., and Michael J.G. Parnwell. "Luxury and Sustainability: Ne'er the Twain Shall Meet?" *Philosophical Issues in Global Sustainability* 1, no. 1 (April 2023): 1–25. (Meng and Parnwell 2023).

APA (Book)

Parnwell, M.J.G., & Meng, K.Y. (2023). *Research Methods for Luxury Management*, Routledge. In-text citation: (Parnwell & Meng, 2023).

APA (Article)

Meng, K.Y. & Parnwell, M.J.G. (2023) "Luxury and Sustainability: Ne'er the Twain Shall Meet?". *Philosophical Issues in Global Sustainability* 1(1), 1–25. In-text citation: (Meng & Parnwell, 2023).

Generally speaking, when referencing an *electronic article*, the researcher should include the following details: author, date of publication, article title, journal name, volume/issue number, page numbers and the DOI (digital object identifier – a number that is unique to the item, usually found on the first page of the article). For an *item taken from a website*, include details of the author, date of publication, item title, website URL and the date the item was accessed by the researcher.

Appendix (Appendices)

Any material that the student feels it would be useful for the reader to be able to access but which is not deemed essential to include in the main body of the dissertation can be added in an appendix, to be placed after the list of references. Different institutions may have different rules regarding appendices, including whether or not they count towards the word limit, and so it would be advisable to check before adding and submitting one. The general rule with appendices for dissertations is that they will not count towards the word limit, but they will also not be consulted by the examiner as a substantive piece of work and, therefore, included in the assessment. They are appended for information only. An appendix might contain a copy of a questionnaire or interview schedule, invitation letter, consent form, sampling frame, *selected* interview extracts (not whole transcripts), evidence of coding procedure or analysis process and so on. Discretion needs to be exercised over how much material to consign to an appendix or appendices. As a rule, only the most important and informative material should be included.

PRESENTING THE FINDINGS OF PRACTITIONER RESEARCH

Although this chapter is aimed principally at Master's-level students who are working on presenting their theses or dissertations, throughout this book we have sought to ensure that the ideas being discussed also have relevance to and resonance with luxury industry practitioners. Part of the rationale behind this is the expectation that many students of luxury brand management will take up positions within the industry upon completing their studies. A further motivation for treating these as integrated rather than separate worlds is the belief – which is supported by some of the evidence from our own research that we have presented in this book – that the training and experience students gain in conceiving, designing, managing and executing their own research project will potentially be valuable to an industry that relies on research for at least part of its functioning and that often struggles to find competent (in-house) researchers from within its ranks. But students making the transition from academia to the luxury industry need to be aware that the way research is used and presented can be quite different from the somewhat formulaic approach that we have outlined above. Accordingly, we want to finish off this chapter by taking a brief look at how luxury brands present the results of their research to the wider public, as this is of relevance to graduates who are seeking to enter the profession.[5]

The fundamentals of research are the same regardless of the practitioner and the purpose, but the audience for the results of the research may influence how research findings are presented. Leaving aside some of the more popular writing by scholars, academic research is principally written for an academic audience and must therefore comply with certain conventions within the academy. This means, among other things, that it is expected to demonstrate a deep grounding in the existing body of knowledge and should include detailed information about the chosen methodology. In a sense, it is written by experts, for experts. Practitioner research may be undertaken by experts, but the target recipients of the research might not match this level of expertise, and so results have to be presented in a way that they can be readily absorbed by a lay audience. This is not to downplay the capabilities of the recipients; it is simply a statement of business realities, where time is often very pressing, and thus information needs to be communicated in a succinct, accessible and digestible manner, largely unencumbered by superfluous details about process. At a risk of overgeneralisation, the methodological competence of the researcher (be they in-house or syndicated) is underwritten by their reputation and past experience, rather than having to be spelled out in detail in a research report. In Box 8.5, we provide an example of research reporting within the luxury industry, by professionals, for professionals.

BOX 8.5

The (In)Visibility of Practitioner Research Methodology

In 2020, Statista, a globally leading provider of market and consumer data, produced the *Luxury Goods Report 2020* (Statista, 2020). This consisted of 101 pages of luxury market analysis, ranging from an overview of market drivers, sales channels and key players to the identification of market trends for each of five luxury sectors, as well as insights derived from consumer surveys. The report consisted mainly of colourful charts which summarised the results of the company's research and analysis, accompanied by bullet point explanations and elaborations. Our survey of luxury industry practitioners (reported in Chapters 2 and 9) indicated that reports such as the ones produced by Statista are vitally important sources of up-to-date information and insight on luxury industry trends and characteristics.[6]

Direct mention of methodology in the *Luxury Goods Report 2020* is quite limited. In addition to identifying the various sources of data and clarifying certain definitions, only a handful of charts are accompanied by an explanation of research method. For example, on page 38, data on consumers' luxury watch brand preferences are accompanied by the question that was used to solicit this information ("which of these luxury watch brands would you like to own?") and some information about the number of people who were asked this question (900 in the USA, 1,015 in Germany). Similar clarifications are provided on pages 39 and 40. However, most of the data contained in the 2020 report is actually derived from the much larger *2020 Statista Consumer Market Outlook*, based on the Statista Global Consumer Survey, which is accompanied by an 81-page clarification of research method (Statista, 2021). This is an extremely detailed document which gives information, *inter alia*, on the methodologies used in forecasting, modelling and market sizing for each segment of the market (mass as well as luxury) that was included in the survey.

So, in terms of *reporting* research findings, the principal instrument of communication is the presentation of a series of punchy and easily digestible charts and diagrams, accompanied by brief and essential comments and explanations. According to the luxury professionals we interviewed, this is the kind of information that luxury industry practitioners, and CEOs in particular, are looking for. Further information on methodology is also usually available, but needs to be teased out.

Research reporting by practitioners can serve several purposes and take many forms, including financial reports, evaluation reports (customer satisfaction, advertising effectiveness, product development, etc.), annual reports, market reports and deeper research reports, produced either for internal (to the brand) or external consumption or both. Some reports are rich in detail, as stipulated by institutional or legal reporting requirements, whereas others (for example, those produced by some commercial research companies such as Statista) offer a brief, alluring, publicly accessible summary report which is designed to attract customers to purchase the more detailed and research-rich full report. At risk of overgeneralisation, we may find that all these channels have certain factors in common that influence the reporting of research. These include who the *intended recipients* of the report are and the level of *expertise* they possess. There is little value in presenting a highly technical report to a lay audience or a simplified summary to industry experts. Whereas an academic writer is expected to demonstrate their competence as a researcher through their detailed exposition of theory and methodology, for instance, practitioners can often skip the forensic detail because writer and receiver communicate in the same business 'language', and expertise may be taken as 'given' because that was a factor in the commissioning of the research in the first place. A detailed explanation of the purpose of the research might be unnecessary as this might have been stipulated in the TORs (terms of reference) which preceded the research enquiry.

Perhaps the most important factor is *time*: the principal commissioners and recipients of research reports, such as managers and CEOs, are very busy people who much prefer a bullet point summary to a lengthy narrative. For this reason, the most important part of any research report will be the *executive summary*: a short, punchy overview of a larger report that identifies the purpose of the research, key findings and success matrices, and core recommendations. The length of the executive summary will generally depend on the length and complexity of the research report, but, as a rule, it should extend to not more than 5% of the total length of the report and, ideally, should be presented as a single page where everything the manager or reader needs to know is visible in one go. The executive summary can be likened to an abstract, but presented as bullet points rather than continuous narrative and centring on essential details rather than a complete overview. One of the review exercises we have suggested at the end of Chapter 10 asks students to prepare an executive summary for a piece of academic work, as we think this will be a very useful way of transitioning from academic to practitioner thinking and practice.

Effective business report writing involves the clear identification of *goals* (the purpose of the report and what information the writer wishes to convey), the nature and expertise of the *audience*, with the mode of communication tailored accordingly, and the level of *detail* that is digestible within the time frame available and is essential as background to the recommendations or conclusions that are the main deliverables of the report. Practitioner report writing requires quite a different mindset to the presentation of academic research. The challenge to the research student hoping to enter the luxury industry is to reprogramme their approach to research reporting without compromising the core principles of research itself.

SUMMARY AND CONCLUSION

This chapter has taken the student through the various stages of the writing-up process and has touched on some of the principles and considerations that underpin this. It is important that the student should develop their own style of writing which communicates their personality as a researcher, their philosophical stance on the nature of knowledge, their argument and stance in relation to key issues in the field of luxury, their understanding of the value and limitations of their research, and, ultimately, their take on the essence of luxury. The discussion in this chapter has offered guidance on the systematic processes of structuring and presenting a thesis, but no textbook on luxury research should be so presumptuous as to feel it can shape the student's individual worldview and their identity as a researcher. We have encouraged students to find their own 'voice' and to communicate this effectively through the writing-up of their research but have stopped short of being prescriptive about anything other than the 'conventions' of research.

NOTES

1 It is worth noting that the number of citations may be a function of time as well as the quality or topicality of an academic article. It can often take a year for an academic article to appear in print and, thus, for the articles cited in the paper to register on citation records. The longer the paper is in circulation, the greater its dissemination within the academic community and the higher, too, the possibility of its being cited in other cognate works.

2   The answer in this instance is quite straightforward: the article was published in the *Journal of Business Research* which, certainly in 2012, almost exclusively published the results of quantitative, reductive research.

3   It is interesting to note, in the present context, that one of the co-authors, Angella Kim, actually completed a Master's dissertation on the same topic in 2010, which presumably helped to lay the foundation for her subsequent research work (Kim, 2010).

4   www.emeraldgrouppublishing.com

5   Because information about the internal operations of luxury brands is seldom made available to the general public, not least for reasons of commercial sensitivity, it is beyond the scope of this discussion to examine in-house research reporting.

6   Our research participants also mentioned the following companies as important sources of market information: Bain & Co., the Boston Consulting Group, Euromonitor, Wealth X, UBS, Credit Suisse, Deloitte, McKinsey, Henley and Partners and Knight Frank (see also Chapter 9).

CHAPTER 9

Linking Research and Luxury Management

INTRODUCTION

The aim of this book has been to introduce an array of research methodologies and methods to postgraduate students of luxury management who, in turn, are prospective practitioners in the luxury sector. The immediate value of the book's contents should be to help students with the preparation and completion of a research-based dissertation, which is a requirement of most Master's programmes in this field. But, to our minds, there is little value in divorcing research as an academic exercise from its actual and potential application to the field of luxury management, given that this is the principal focus of these postgraduate programmes. As such, we have consistently sought, throughout the book, to illustrate why and how the methodological elements we have introduced intermesh with real-world challenges and processes in the field of luxury. It is our hope that the skills students develop through this research exercise will be valuable to their future careers in the field of luxury, both in terms of the intellectual reasoning that a research investigation demands, and through familiarisation with the techniques and principles that are required to ensure that research outcomes are meaningful, valuable and reliable.

We now want to round off the discussion in this book by exploring the interface between academic research and luxury management to see how, or to what extent, the two neatly dovetail. It would be wrong simply to assume that obliging students to undertake a research investigation in an academic setting and equipping them with an array of techniques and approaches will, in itself, deliver the kinds of people and assemblage of skills that the luxury industry needs and can make use of. To gain some insight into how and where research fits into the array of tasks undertaken by luxury practitioners, and as a follow-up to the results of our luxury industry survey that we presented in Chapter 2, we conducted interviews with ten luxury industry professionals (see Table 9.1) drawn from a cross-section of luxury sectors and activities and based in nine countries across six global regions.[1] Our findings are presented below. The following discussion might also be seen as an example of the presentation of research findings which supplements the material on writing-up in Chapter 8. We have opted to foreground the words of our participants as they are the experts in this field (see, for example, Loranger and Roeraas, 2022). We will then draw the discussion together towards the end of this chapter and evaluate how effectively academic research and luxury management harmonise in reality, and how luxury management students trained in research methods might potentially make a valuable contribution to this field.

DOI: 10.4324/9781003295372-9

TABLE 9.1 Summary Profile of the Ten Interview Participants

Participant	Region	Luxury Industry Experience
Interviewee A	N. America	Luxury fashion
Interviewee B	Europe	Luxury consulting, mainly in luxury hospitality, service and automobiles
Interviewee C	Asia Pacific & Europe	Luxury fashion and automobiles
Interviewee D	Asia Pacific & Europe	Luxury jewellery and fashion
Interviewee E	Europe & Middle East	Luxury fashion, consulting and education in luxury
Interviewee F	Worldwide	Luxury beauty, cosmetics and well-being
Interviewee G	Europe	Luxury hospitality
Interviewee H	Worldwide	Luxury hospitality
Interviewee I	Europe & Africa	Luxury concierge services
Interviewee J	Europe	Luxury jewellery and watches, consulting and education in luxury

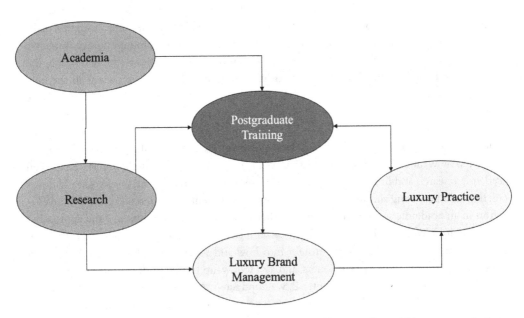

FIGURE 9.1 Schema for the Interface of Academia and Luxury Brand Management.

Figure 9.1 presents a simplified schema of the interface between academia and the field of luxury, with the postgraduate student positioned somewhere in between (we will return to a revised version of this diagram towards the end of this chapter). Universities vary in the balance they offer between academic learning and practical training, but ideally there is a strong flow of insight from both directions in a luxury student's programme of study. Training in and experience of research form just a part of the panoply of knowledge and skills that a postgraduate student will acquire during the course of their degree, but the research dissertation should represent the 'icing on the cake' where the student is able to showcase all they have learned through their coursework; it is something that should also strike a balance between theory and practical reality. On this basis, we have suggested a two-way flow of information or value between luxury research and luxury practice: a student's enquiry into an aspect of luxury or luxury management will be informed by a sound understanding of practical realities, ideally gained by practitioner involvement in their postgraduate training programme, and what the student has gained from the research process should be contributable to strategic management practice if they subsequently enter the luxury industry. Independent of their nurturing of the research capabilities of their postgraduate students, academics also engage in their own research in the field of luxury, as we discussed in Chapter 2, which, again depending on the balance between scholarly and practical emphasis, might also potentially contribute a deeper understanding of issues and processes currently affecting the luxury industry. However, our interviews with luxury industry professionals suggested that some of these flows of value are stronger than others.

THE IMPORTANCE OF RESEARCH TO LUXURY BRANDS

We started by asking our research participants where research fits into their routine activities as practitioners within the luxury industry. One of our interviewees, who helps several European luxury brands position themselves in markets worldwide, gave this fulsome response:

> To a certain degree every part of my business benefits from research-driven information and intelligence. Data is a key deciding factor in the strategy undertaken, but I also never undervalue instinct in the decision-making process … Research is on-going for me, but if I have a new client that specifically wants to enter a new market with a specific product, I will make sure I have the most up-to-date information. For this I will mix both primary and secondary research. My first steps involve competitive analysis, relevant opportunities review, market momentum, price point, commercial requirements and regulations – in other words, a full due diligence to ascertain if this is a viable market for the client, and if so, will it deliver good ROI [return on investment] and long-term sustainable growth. Secondly, I look at the broader picture on the trade, consumer and media side; I personally will look at digital platforms to get the feel of a market and a channel, as a more integrative approach is fundamental now. It also helps inform the different cultural nuances that are so vital, particularly when it comes to luxury brand profiles and messaging … On a personal level, I don't feel I experience any constraints, but I would say in general if you do not understand how to review and analyse the data you have, or the information research gives you, then it does not deliver the best value. Also, make sure to secure research through authentic channels as these data are a defining factor in the business strategy.[2]

A second interviewee added:

> I believe from a professional point of view, having primary research adds value to an organisation, and maybe puts it a step ahead of others who don't have access to that information. It's a form of added value, maybe even a competitive advantage.[3]

A third interviewee, who has worked with several luxury brands, including in the fashion and automobile sectors, suggested that the need for research data is not uniform across the luxury industry:

> I think not all luxury brands are the same. It depends on what kind of luxury it is. I think automobiles use a lot of market research, but for fashion it is relatively less relevant. I don't know if I'm right or not, but I feel this from my work experience. Because if you think about it, in fashion there are at least two big seasons or four seasons in a year, depending on different brands. It is impossible to do surveys every year, every six months, every two months. But the European automobile brands, they will not change their models very often, so they do a lot of focus groups. With a lot of research, before their product launch, they will do a lot of focus groups. Their car model will be on the market for many years, so it's worth spending the money. Fashion is impossible, because we have too many seasons and the products change too fast. So, research in fashion may only be a broad sweep related to the market. It will be a consumer market survey, not an in-depth survey of individual products. If it is a product such as a perfume, I think it is recommended that some brand companies do some surveys. But in fashion it is quite rare. We only do it in-house, our own relatively small, but very targeted surveys.[4]

A fourth interviewee suggested there is also a difference in the importance and incidence of research depending on the size of the company, as smaller brands lack the internal capacity, and also sometimes the financial resources, to undertake or commission primary research:

> *Do you think the large conglomerates and smaller jewellery brands approach research in the same way?*
> I would say the mechanism is quite different between big corporates and niche companies. For a big corporate, maybe their headquarters' management controls this aspect of what research to do, and they feed the information to us at the retail level. Like from management down to us. But for a niche company, it's the other way round. It's more like the retail side is the front line. They think, "what are we going to do? What does the head of retail think about where the market is heading? What should we be focusing on?" So, the retail team proposes the idea to the owner, up the hierarchy. Like, I just talked to the CFO, and we decided we want to go in this direction, so we need such-and-such data. We certainly wouldn't just randomly every season do research on such-and-such. We just search for data when we have a new project.[5]

Several interviewees indicated that the brands they work for have a strong need for research-derived data, but that they were constrained by their limited capacity or capability to undertake this research themselves and were put off by the often-considerable cost involved in commissioning external agencies to undertake market-related research for them. The first quotation below indicates that some brands adopt a make-do-and-mend approach to research using their own resources, but suggests that they lack the specialist expertise to accomplish this in a professional manner. Postgraduate entrants trained in research methodology could therefore prove to be a valuable asset to such firms. This view is reinforced by the second quotation, which shows how some luxury brands look first to their internal resources to undertake research, although such people may not be fully trained in research methodology.

I think the price [of research by external agencies] is very expensive today. Many brands want to do research, but they have a limited budget, so they may not do it. Because of this, we used to do 'unofficial' research. It was not done by a research company, but by the employees of our own company. We designed the questionnaire by ourselves, and then we approached two groups. First of all the media: we asked many media editors and good friends in the media to help us fill in this questionnaire. The second group was the consumer: we wanted to improve our CRM [Customer Relationship Management] Pro-gramme, so we needed to know what our customers thought about our brand, how to make them feel good about the brand, so we sought some data from them. We did things unofficially [informally], not through a [formal] research company. This is partly because it is impossible for a research company to get data on our high-end customers. Only our sales representatives can reach those customers and get them to fill out these questionnaires. This stuff is very private and confidential, but it is super effective, because these data are taken directly from our high-end customers. Based on the data, I could analyse what our clients want, and how we can improve our services from the perspective of marketing, CRM, or retail, to meet their requirements.[6]

Usually how we work with a new market is, we need to see if within our internal struc-ture we have any talents that already understand the market. If we have someone, that will be a huge step to help guide us in the new direction, rather than taking 10 steps but then finding out they were wrong. We tend to find a reputable local agency to start things off, to point us in a certain direction. There are a lot of luxury agencies [in China], a lot of luxury concierges, that provide these kinds of services. They will give a solution to a problem. We would tell them what we are trying to do here; we want to establish a market. We let them know briefly what kind of audience we're trying to reach, and what our requirements are, like we want to set up a shop or we just want to do two events to test the water. So, we give our requirements to those middle persons, and they facilitate our needs.[7]

Two interviewees indicated that brand managers often see the potential value of research and primary data to their operations, but are reluctant to invest time and resources in this endeav-our. The first quotation is from a consultant with an academic background who offers strategic research services to luxury brands:

If we were to undertake some research for a luxury brand – say 25 in-depth interviews to allow a deep and comprehensive view of some issue – we would naturally need several months to complete this task, and a further few months to process and analyse the data. But the client would neither give you a year to complete the work, nor give you the nec-essary resources to accelerate the process of data collection. The manager would say that the industry is moving too quickly to allow such a time frame to do this work. Obtaining quality data takes time and costs money, but in my experience brands either do not have the budget to cover this or they question its value.[8]

A second interviewee added:

> What I've been noticing for the past couple of years is that managers want quality first-hand [primary] data, but they don't want the hassle or headache of collecting and analysing those data.[9]

ON THE NATURE OF RESEARCH

Two interviewees addressed the disparity between brand-focused and consumer-focused research in the field of luxury:

> we see so many more papers that place an emphasis on the luxury consumer side when compared to the luxury brand perspective, because the consumer is easy to survey. I found this when I was undertaking this survey: I underestimated how challenging it would be, because I have thousands of luxury professionals in my network. I put a survey on the system and thought they would come rolling in, but no. So, then I had to end up emailing thousands of people. This finally yielded a survey of 80 practitioners and 10 interviews. Luxury brands are reluctant to divulge information which they consider to be commercially sensitive, which in fact covers a great deal of their business.[10]
>
> Everyone knows that collecting data takes time. Luxury managers won't disclose information, you have to go fish for it. Getting access to this information is very difficult, so you have to activate your network even before you start doing your job. Even as we become more older and more mature in the industry, we still don't have access to this kind of information. So, how about young people coming out of their MA's and wanting to work in this industry, but cannot access this kind of information?[11]

One interviewee also addressed the balance between quantitative and qualitative research. We have already seen in earlier chapters that the overwhelming majority of academic papers on luxury tend quite rigidly to adopt a systematic quantitative approach to research, and this is partly driven by conventional practice in their core disciplines. More qualitative research is being attempted, but, in our view, this comes nowhere near matching the highly qualitative nature of luxury. One practitioner who shares this view commented on the battle she has convincing her line manager of the value of a qualitative perspective and of getting qualitative research accepted by mainstream business journals:

> I've had this conversation with my director. He's like maybe very traditional. For him, qualitative research has no value if it's not quantified. But in areas and topics that I was researching, quantitative research killed the beauty of qualitative research that has been collected, especially quantitative research that does not fit into the context. I truly believe that there should be different layers of qualitative data, like doing your in-depth interviews. This is a great thing, and then refining your interviews by another set of interviews, maybe when needed, completing with observation, *in situ* observation on a retail level, on an office or internal level, it depends, and then on a consumer level. Today ethnographic research

has become really accessible and important, and it could be used to corroborate your data. Maybe this corroboration or relationship could be quantified, OK, but at least you've done your work and you have revealed the value of the data. But then again, I will tell you when I have presented qualitative research to many journals they directly get rejected. It's crazy.[12]

ON THE VALUE OF ACADEMIC RESEARCH

The next topic we addressed in the interviews was the value of academic research to the routine operations of the luxury brands that our participants worked with or for. We have seen earlier in this book that the scale of research attention to the broad field of luxury has grown exponentially over the last five to ten years. We wanted to know if the luxury brands derived any direct benefit from this. The first quotation suggests that, although academic research is of interest, busy businesspeople have little time to dip into academic articles on luxury and therefore tend to rely on industry reports instead.

> I think academic output is very relevant and very important. In my case, I read it from time to time, I do not read it more often because of the length of the reports. When I read a BCG [Boston Consulting Group] or a Bain & Co. report, they go straight to the point, and I soak the relevant information in half an hour. They highlight the key messages, the main facts, and I get it quickly. If I need to soak the relevant information from an academic paper, it will take me more than one or two hours to read it and to get it. I mean, in my opinion, academic reports are too long. They are much better, because they have theoretical support; they explain theory very well before they present the facts. But I don't always have time for that. That's my problem, not the academics' problem.[13]

This view is mirrored in the second quotation:

> Of course, academic books are very interesting, but the survey reports issued by the consulting agencies are much more useful. In every market you have to look at the trends of the market and their consumers. So, if you want to know how to promote a brand or build a brand, then we all know that you need to understand your products, and you need to know your target audience very well. The target audience is constantly changing. I think the information sent by the research agencies is very, very important, for business strategy as well as marketing.[14]

Another interviewee suggested that academic research was in some ways superior to that produced in industry reports or by private research agencies, which lacks breadth and balance:

> I really value academic research compared to, like, research from outside companies. I think it's more closely realistic to what's happening in the world. I think a lot of research coming from companies may be too extreme on one side or the other, you know. One story to fit their own purpose. The only thing I guess is that academic journals are too long and too complicated, especially the literature review. Once you get over that part let's get into the data and the research.[15]

For other practitioners, the issue was not one of the quality and relevance of academic research, but simply that it was hard to access:

> The issue is not whether people want to read academic articles or not, it is simply that they are not accessible to the general public. I might be interested in looking at a particular article coming from a particular journal, but all I can access is the abstract.[16]
>
> I rarely use academic materials. They are very hard to find [access]. Sometimes I look for references for books on jewellery history, but if I'm interested in market trends then I will look at recent news and recent market reports. It is much faster to get the information I want. I don't have to read through the whole paper to get the few numbers I need. Of course, in my own time, if I want to study a certain [historical] period in jewellery, say to understand the Egyptian revival, then I will do some high-end research, but for market trends I rarely use academic sources.[17]

One interviewee, who is a luxury industry consultant, offered this rather stark statement about her experience of working with two academics on a paper about an aspect of luxury:

> Recently, I've tried working with a couple of academics to edit two pieces on luxury. I was surprised to see that someone who supposedly specialises in luxury doesn't have the know-how that would make him or her eligible to be called a luxury expert within the industry.[18]

Paradoxically, another interviewee mentioned how academic institutions overlooked her 18 years' experience in luxury and her MBA from a prestigious French university when she applied to teach a Master's course in this field because she did not satisfy their rigid criteria:

> I have been declined a couple of times the opportunity to teach courses labelled as 'luxury marketing' or 'luxury' or whatever because my Master's degree doesn't have 'luxury' in the title, which is absurd.[19]

The quotations above convey the impression that academia and the luxury industry are two largely separate worlds, and that, although there is overlap between the two in the field of research, they are rather poorly integrated. Academic researchers are principally writing for other academics, following a clear set of institutionalised blueprints, including theoretical and methodological rigour. Some articles do include a section entitled 'managerial implications' in their summing up, but these have little value if luxury industry practitioners are unable to access this information. The lead-in times for the execution and publication of academic research on luxury may often be so lengthy that its topical relevance in a very rapidly changing industry may also be questioned. Luxury brand managers, as we have seen, seem principally to be interested in data that provide happening-now market intelligence, which appear to be best provided by research agencies that specialise in such forms of research. Bigger-picture research that is valuable to luxury practitioners tends to be gleaned from industry reports far more frequently than from academic papers. Our interviewees identified the following as their go-to sources for such information: Bain & Co., the Boston Consulting Group, Euromonitor, Wealth X, UBS, Credit Suisse, Deloitte, McKinsey, the *Financial Times*, the *Wall Street Journal*, New World Wealth (for

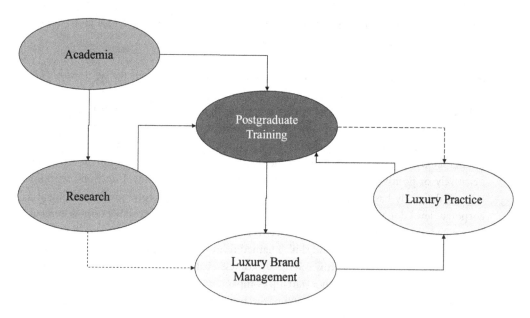

FIGURE 9.2 Revised Schema for the Interface of Academia and Luxury Brand Management.

the markets in Africa), Henley and Partners, Knight Frank, HSBC and Barclay's Wealth and the Robb Report. The only academic bodies that this admittedly small sample of practitioners mentioned in this regard were reports by Hautes Études Commerciales in Paris and the London Business School. All interviewees emphasised the importance of LinkedIn at a professional level in the luxury industry and noted that more and more brand managers are contributing content on luxury to the platforms these days.

Based on the above discussion, we would like to submit a revised version of the schema we presented earlier in this chapter. Figure 9.2 suggests that the connection between academic research and luxury management is perhaps weaker than originally suggested, and also that the connection between postgraduate research training and luxury practice has potential to be strengthened. This is not the definitive word on the balance between the academic and practical worlds, but is intended as a contribution to an ongoing conversation.

We are not suggesting for a moment that academic research should somehow be watered down to make it accessible and relevant to the luxury industry, and we recognise that many academics who contribute to luxury studies are not what we might consider luxury experts with practitioner experience so much as specialists from other disciplines who are increasingly plying their trade in the luxury realm, which is to be welcomed. But we are motivated to see how the two worlds might be brought a little closer together, and we feel that postgraduate research training for prospective luxury practitioners might potentially represent one such channel. Two of our interviewees emphasised how important their MBA training had been in enabling them to look beyond the minutiae of routine management tasks when they joined the luxury industry, but they also argued strongly that there is no substitute for grounding one's familiarity with luxury by getting real hands-on experience at the so-called 'coal face', such as on the retail shop floor:

Imagine yourself in 2012 when you joined the company and were conducting market research. How you have evolved, or changed, or developed [over the last ten years]?

I think that I definitely would not have approached it the same. I think I'd have been maybe too narrowly focused on a specific part of the business, working in retail and then in a regional position and a more corporate position, but my MBA really exposed me to kind of see the bigger picture of the business and how the external environment can either negatively or positively impact an organisation. But at the same time, I do think working in retail definitely has given me an advantage that most luxury professionals working at a corporate level don't have, and that is really understanding the day-to-day business of retail. I strongly believe there is a disconnect between the corporate team and the retail team.[20]

I think that the knowledge and skills I gained from my MBA experience have prepared me to really be successful in this role [as a business analyst with a leading luxury brand]. Because my current role is with a start-up company, we actually have more flexibility and discretion in how we conduct our own research – they do not yet have a standard process. But working closely with the retail team, and with me coming from a retail background, I understood some of the challenges that were happening at store level in terms of, like, team development, leadership training, you know a lot of learning and development, and so I took it upon myself to better understand partnering with the talent management team and HR team to see how we can really elevate the associates, equip them with the right skills, not only to serve their clients but also just to be better professionals, and to help them along their career path. That involved a lot of primary research, there was a lot of interviewing, surveys directly with the sales team, and I think my MBA helped me a great deal with this.[21]

It is our profound hope that the readers of this book will gain some knowledge of and insight into the research process, coupled with the big-picture vision that academic study nurtures, that they can take into their future careers in the luxury industry, and that in time they will help to bridge the academic and practical worlds of luxury and make a difference to how knowledge is generated and treated within the industry.

INSIGHTS FROM LUXURY PRACTITIONERS

To finish off this discussion, we thought it would be useful to students of luxury to gain some personalised insights from luxury industry practitioners. We asked each of our interviewees what words of advice they would offer to young aspiring luxury professionals. We start with some observations on research, followed by their take on the essence of luxury. This is what they had to say:

I believe that research is not only for the sake of research or for the sake of academic enquiry. We need to train our minds, I believe that is the right word, to understand what we are confronted with in terms of data, and what is the value of those data, otherwise it doesn't mean anything. I mean, today the people who have managed to get good positions because they manage to lead brands in a positive way are the people who have the knowledge; the people who have the knowledge are the people who have the data; people who have the data have correctly read those data. So, today in the fashion sector, we have a more delicate way of reading data because we have more of a delicate situation, we're dealing with things that have a different dynamic than the traditional retail world. Therefore, I believe it's important to emphasise a lot on qualitative data and its analysis, but not to get lost in those data.[22]

Have your research as close as possible to the consumers and to the retail staff. The better you can understand, specifically the retail staff, they have more insight on the consumers than any market research can tell you, because they're the ones that are directly talking to people of all walks of life. And do research close to retail stores in different areas – you know, a global flagship store is going to be very different to a resource store. The most successful retail executives – and you can just probably look on LinkedIn and do a search – started in the retail store. If they've listed their journey, you will see that they've come up in a retail shop, and ran to regional vice-president to president and CEO, and I think that's because that foundation in the retail environment really sets the standard and the tone of your journey.[23]

You are at this stage of being a student, you study and do research because you want to work in the industry, or you want to contribute more to the industry. But you have to realise that we are actually researching something every day. Even if you are comparing two different brands. You go on Google and look at the reviews, etc; which brand is better for my health? Which is tastier? Even this kind of process is a research process. So, you are conducting research, and I understand the journey is long and can be painful, but research is a must for everyday life, and is especially important when you get a job in luxury. But, if you have a brilliant idea, but you don't have supporting facts, then not everyone can visualise it, and not everyone can believe in it.[24]

Doing your homework puts you in a far stronger position as you gain insight and knowledge that help you make the best decision you can for your brand. Instinct is still important, but if you want to be successful in business, research is a vital component as with it you will find that all-important gap that opens up the future.[25]

What I would do, if I was teaching Master's students luxury, would be in the first lecture to get them to write down everything about themselves, keep it, and when they have finished their year, go back over it and reflect on how much they have grown during the course of the year.[26]

The first thing that I would do would be to clarify with myself what are my values and what is my personality, because these will naturally drive you to go to the type of luxury that fits with your personality and with your values. I did this exercise with a friend recently, writing down what kind of world do we want to live in. I was supposed to write a page with no limits. There were certain things I was certain about: I wanted a world with more natural things; I wanted a world with kindness. So naturally the type of luxury I was drawn to is not the opulent type – you know the silver shining, the gold. It is understated. Also, a more educated type of luxury that is very close to the territory and celebrates anything that has an appreciation of Mother Nature. I like this type of luxury. So, I think students should clarify these things to themselves. I think this is very important for the younger generation, and when they still have an opportunity to immerse themselves in knowledge and education, they can hopefully keep this pure mindset into their own future.[27]

When you are dealing with luxury, you must have a very different kind of mindset. You have to have in mind a dream, and it's a privilege to live out this dream with people who have the essence of luxury in their blood.[28]

It took me 25 years to reach the point I am at. The wisdom I have and the person I am come only with time. There is nothing a book or a research investigation can teach you in six months; you have to live your life in order to become wise and mature. There was no book that could tell me how my life was going to unfold. I wish there was. I wish I could write that book.[29]

Develop your interest and knowledge in a variety of subjects, from fine arts, to politics, to different cultures, to psychology. You will need them all to build the proper mindset and sensitiveness to be fluent in the language of luxury.[30]

The younger generation of younger professionals, they tend to focus on everything as a quick fix. It's not about developing knowledge, it's about – just tell me the shortcuts or a quick fix or something. Quick, grab some money … But that's not luxury; call it something else. That's the democratisation of luxury, or the so-called democratisation, which is banalising luxury, actually. Mind you, the massification of luxury will leave space for niche brands to stand out and do it in a different way.[31]

To be proficient in the language of luxury in time, you need to understand things. Because there's a philosophical sense in luxury that you need to grab: it has to do with culture, psychology to understand the behaviour, it has to do with taste.[32]

You need to understand a bit of fine art, or know a bit of ethnicity, anthropology, culture, different cultures, different peoples, because luxury is a global phenomenon.[33]

I would advocate luxury from a more cultural perspective instead of only pushing it as business, business to make money. It is not our philosophy.[34]

NOTES

1   As we have emphasised throughout this book, the information from this limited number of interviews should be treated as being *indicative* of the experience of some luxury brands rather than being *representative* of the luxury industry as a whole. They do nonetheless represent a broad cross-section of the industry in terms of brands, location, management activities and research involvement. The interviewees were drawn from LinkedIn contacts, and from people who indicated a willingness to contribute a follow-up interview when they completed the luxury research survey reported in Chapter 2. The interviewees agreed to participate on the basis that neither their identities nor those of the luxury brands they work for would be revealed.
2   Interviewee F.
3   Interviewee E.
4   Interviewee C.
5   Interviewee D.

6   Interviewee C.
7   Interviewee D.
8   Interviewee E.
9   Interviewee E.
10   Kelly Meng in conversation with Interviewee E.
11   Interviewee E.
12   Interviewee E.
13   Interviewee B.
14   Interviewee C.
15   Interviewee A.
16   Interviewee E.
17   Interviewee D.
18   Interviewee E.
19   Interviewee E.
20   Interviewee A.
21   Interviewee A.
22   Interviewee E.
23   Interviewee A.
24   Interviewee D.
25   Interviewee F.
26   Interviewee G.
27   Interviewee G.
28   Interviewee G.
29   Interviewee H.
30   Interviewee B.
31   Interviewee B.
32   Interviewee B.
33   Interviewee B.
34   Interviewee B.

CHAPTER 10

Overview and Learning Resources

OVERVIEW

In this book, we have sought to achieve two things. First, we have tried to develop a resource which not only introduces the principal elements of research methodology to students of luxury but does so in a way that will have particular relevance for people who hope to pursue their interest in luxury after completing their studies. We have rooted the discussion in the history and character of luxury as a field of study and have used examples drawn from a wide array of luxury topics, issues, dilemmas and challenges. Second, although the book is written with the Master's student (and some PhD students) principally in mind, we have been careful not to divorce academic research on luxury from its potential value to luxury professionals and practitioners. Many of the students who read this book will end up working in the luxury industry in some capacity or another, and so we have placed a strong emphasis on developing transferable skills that will have some value in the real world of luxury. There is a need for such skills. Some research from the USA that is reported by Donald Cooper (Cooper, 2019, 4) found that 60% of 63,924 business managers felt that student recruits lacked adequate critical-thinking and problem-solving skills and that, of the ten skills that employers were most keen on, four fell within the field of research: the ability to obtain and process information; creative problem-solving; the ability to analyse quantitative data (to which we would also add qualitative data for luxury practitioners); and the ability to create and/or edit a written report. In supporting students' grasp of the fundamentals of research, we hope we have helped to develop skills which are in significant demand and of particular relevance within the luxury sector.

We make no apology for evangelising on certain points in this volume, most particularly the importance of contextualisation, representativeness and reflexivity in luxury research, and the need to counterbalance the overwhelming focus on quantitative approaches with more scope for qualitative research. We have sought to draw a distinction between the reductionist worldview of much business research and the need to capture the nuanced realities of luxury. Our approach has also been multidisciplinary and multifaceted in character: luxury permeates into so many realms of life, in so many subtle ways, that it cannot be adequately explored and understood from academic silos or from an exclusive focus on luxury fashion. We hope that, in putting this book together, we may have helped to nurture people who will enter the luxury

DOI: 10.4324/9781003295372-10

industry equipped to make a difference to the challenges the industry faces. These challenges can best be summarised as a series of paradoxes and oppositions:

- The desire to remain exclusive in a world rightly pursuing inclusivity;
- The aim to be sustainable while being the epitome of non-essential consumerism;
- The drive to extend global reach while emphasising the importance of locality and provenance;
- The heralding of hand-crafted perfection while incorporating the modalities of mass production;
- The essence of luxury (culture) meeting the substance of marketisation (commerce);
- The atelier and the global division of labour;
- The conglomeration of family-owned firms;
- Old luxury meeting new luxury;
- Aesthetic tangibility facing the abstract metaverse;
- Opulence in the face of deprivation.

In addition to providing rich subject material for researchers, these are challenges that need to be faced and resolved if the luxury industry is to emerge from these testing times with robust business pathways and an enduring core essence. In, hopefully, rising to these challenges, luxury specialists versed in the modalities of research potentially have a lot to offer. It starts with critical thinking and problem identification: standing apart from the minutiae of everyday business to visualise overarching structures, forces, processes and possibilities, and possessing the intellectual confidence to imagine alternative paths and build strategies to follow them. It continues with an ability to build a holistic view of a business challenge and to organise its component parts into a logical structure that points towards an investigative framework which can lead towards one or several solutions. It involves people who know who they are and where they stand and who possess the ability to reflect on their capabilities and limitations. It fundamentally requires operatives who understand their markets, their customers, the way their brands are seen and received in different parts of the world: not as homogeneous categories or groups, but as diverse, contingent, multifaceted and complex communities. It needs people who do not hide behind conceptual generalisations and who are equally adept at handling qualities as well as quantities. The future requires talented leaders who are efficient in their use of time, expressive in their use of words, capable in their handling of numbers, creative in their building of strategies, and who gain respect through their interactions with people. It is our sincere hope that this volume has made a contribution to this essential enterprise, however modest.

REVIEW EXERCISES

We set out below ten learning exercises that students are encouraged to work through in order to review important components of the research process that have been introduced in Chapters 2–9. These exercises will also help to reinforce the intellectual and practical processes that a student needs to follow as they build their own research investigation. These exercises can be attempted independently or as class exercises, with appropriate guidance from teachers, tutors or the dissertation supervisor.

EXERCISE 1

Keywords

Create a 'keyword tree' for one of the following luxury research themes or for a theme of your choice:

Counterfeiting in luxury
Luxury and the emerging economies
Luxury digitalisation
Disruptive forces in luxury
Luxury and the circular economy
The importance of place in luxury
The influence of Gen Z on the essence of luxury
The pursuit of exclusivity in luxury hospitality
The skills shortage/talent drain in the luxury industry

An example of a keyword tree and the process of developing one can be found in Chapter 4, pages 58–59. Your keyword tree should consist of a minimum of 30 keywords.

EXERCISE 2

Conceptual Diagram

On the basis of the keywords you have identified in Exercise 1, create a conceptual diagram which includes at least 15 of these keywords and points towards a clear research focus.

Building a conceptual diagram is discussed in Chapter 4, pages 60–61.

EXERCISE 3

Research Questions

On the basis of the keywords identified in Exercise 1 and the conceptual framework developed in Exercise 2 (or the research focus chosen for Exercise 4), devise one principal research question and three (cognate) secondary research questions which can provide the basis for an investigation into your chosen research theme.

The formulation of research questions is discussed in Chapter 4, pages 62–67.

EXERCISE 4

Operationalisation

Devise five Likert-style questions that can help to operationalise one of the following concepts or a concept of your choice:

On the meaning of *luxury*
Reactions to the *'massification' of luxury*
Luxury and *post-consumerism*
Impact of *digitalisation* on the essence of luxury
Luxury and *social status*
Luxury and *cultural appropriation*
Luxury and the *metaverse*
Experiential luxury
Luxury *entrepreneurship*
Luxury *brand reputation*

Operationalisation is introduced in Chapter 3 (pp. 46–47) and demonstrated in Chapters 4 (pp. 67–68) and 6 (pp. 109–113). The use of Likert-style questions is discussed in Chapter 6, pages 109–113.

EXERCISE 5

References

On the basis of your 'keyword tree' (Exercise 1), conceptual framework (Exercise 2) and research questions (Exercise 3), compile a bibliography of at least 25 references that are centred on your core research focus. If possible, use a bibliographic database (such as the Web of Science or Scopus), or, if you cannot access one, try using Google Scholar or your university library reference catalogue. The bibliography should be presented using the Harvard referencing system.

Bibliographic search procedures are discussed in Chapter 2, pages 16–29. Referencing is discussed in Chapter 8, pages 176–178.

EXERCISE 6

Discussion Themes

Devise eight 'milestone' discussion themes for either a focus group or a series of semi-structured interviews on one of the following topics or a topic of your choice:

Luxury craftsmanship and massification
Luxury post-COVID
How effective is luxury customer relationship management?
Luxury: cultural appreciation or cultural appropriation?
The impact of social media influencers on the essence of luxury
Heritage brands and new luxury: never the twain shall meet?
Is the allure of luxury contributing to overconsumption?
The influence of brand managers and designers on the evolution of luxury
The ethics of excess
Society's relationship with the luxury logo

Focus groups and semi-structured interviews are discussed in Chapter 6, pages 115–122.

EXERCISE 7

Contextualisation

Write a 1,000-word essay on why it is important to contextualise research on luxury.
    Contextualisation is discussed in Chapter 3, page 46.

EXERCISE 8

Prepare an Executive Summary

Prepare an executive summary for one of the following:

Your Master's dissertation (if complete)
Your Master's dissertation as you anticipate it will look when complete
The dissertation you wrote for your undergraduate degree
One of the longer essays you completed for your coursework
An academic article that you feel is most influential on your own research

The executive summary should consist of a maximum of eight bullet points, each containing no more than a single sentence. The content of the executive summary may be broadly similar to the abstract – discussed in Chapter 8 – but should centre on staccato points rather than narrative prose. Imagine you are communicating your research ideas and findings to a very busy CEO. You must decide which information is essential to allow you to communicate succinctly to the reader the key elements of the dissertation/essay. We believe that the ability to produce an effective executive summary will constitute a useful transferable skill for those of you who end up working in the luxury industry.

EXERCISE 9

Research and Luxury Brand Management

Write a 1,000-word essay identifying up to eight reasons why you consider a research dissertation on luxury could be of value to the field of luxury brand management.

The interface of research and luxury management is discussed in Chapters 2 and 9.

EXERCISE 10

Correlation Analysis

Using the data provided in Table 10.1: first, undertake a correlation analysis of the following two sets of data: *luxury goods market revenue by country (2022)*[1] and *total population by country (2020)* (for this exercise, ignore the difference between these two dates). Before attempting the analysis, write a paragraph anticipating the strength and direction of this correlation and explaining the reasons behind your judgement in this regard. After completing the correlation analysis, write a further short paragraph explaining the actual outcome.

Correlation analysis is introduced in Chapter 7, pages 144–147. You should use the Pearson's r correlation test and you will also need to find a p (probability) value for the test.

Having completed the first part of the exercise, now undertake a correlation analysis for *luxury goods market revenue by country (2022)* and *gross domestic product by country (2020)*. Comment on and explain the outcome.

Finally, undertake a correlation analysis for *luxury goods market revenue by country (2022)* and *gross domestic product per capita by country (2020)*. Comment on and explain the outcome.

Write a short paragraph reflecting on demographic and economic influences on luxury consumption and some of the other factors that need to be considered when looking at these relationships.

TABLE 10.1 Data Set for Exercise 10[2]

Country	Luxury Goods Market Revenue 2022 ($ Million)	Population (2020)	GDP 2020 ($ Billion)	GDP per capita 2022 ($)
Australia	6,270.0	25.69	1,331.0	51,810
Argentina	121.2	45.38	383.1	8,442
Bangladesh	856.4	164.70	324.2	1,968
Brazil	2,730.0	212.60	1,445.0	6,797
Canada	6,250.0	38.01	1,643.0	43,225
China	48,910.0	1402.00	14,720.0	10,499
Cuba	231.1	11.33	103.1	9,100
Egypt	879.2	102.30	364.1	3,559
France	14,560.0	67.39	2,603.0	38,626
Germany	12,140.0	83.24	3,806.0	45,723
Ghana	109.0	31.07	72.4	2,329
Greece	1,040.0	10.72	189.4	17,668
India	7,520.0	1380.00	2,623.0	1,901
Indonesia	1,647.0	273.50	1,058.0	3,868
Iran	408.0	83.99	191.7	2,282
Israel	1,239.0	9.22	402.0	43,615
Italy	12,320.0	59.55	1,886.0	31,671
Jamaica	157.3	2.96	13.8	4,664
Japan	26,400.0	125.80	5,065.0	40,262
Kenya	218.8	53.77	98.9	1,840
Luxembourg	323.0	0.63	73.3	115,918
Malaysia	1,772.0	32.37	336.7	10,402
Mexico	2,990.0	128.90	1,076.0	8,348
Netherlands	3,530.0	17.44	912.2	52,305
New Zealand	1,044.0	5.08	212.5	41,798
Nigeria	394.1	206.10	432.3	2,098
Norway	1,102.0	5.38	362.0	67,299
Poland	1,300.0	37.95	594.2	15,657
Russia	1,390.0	144.10	1,483.0	10,291
Saudi Arabia	1,751.0	34.81	700.1	20,112
Singapore	3,863.0	5.69	340.0	59,796
South Africa	731.5	59.31	301.9	5,090

South Korea	6,000.0	51.78	1,631.0	31,499
Spain	6,590.0	47.35	1,281.0	27,054
Sweden	2,520.0	10.35	537.6	51,942
Switzerland	4,290.0	8.64	748.0	86,604
Thailand	4,280.0	69.80	501.8	7,189
Tunisia	148.1	11.82	39.2	3,320
Turkey	810.0	84.34	720.1	8,538
Uganda	207.7	45.74	37.4	817
UAE	2,668.0	9.89	421.1	42,578
UK	13,730.0	67.22	2,708.0	40,286
USA	69,520.5	329.50	20,940.0	63,551
Uzbekistan	112.8	34.23	57.7	1,686
Vietnam	902.4	97.34	271.2	2,786
Zambia	42.0	18.38	19.3	1,051

ADDITIONAL READING AND ELECTRONIC RESOURCES

Books and Articles

Luxury

Berghaus, Benjamin, Günter Müller-Stewens and Sven Reinecke, 2014, *The Management of Luxury: A Practitioner's Handbook*, London: Kogan Page.

Berry, Christopher J., 1994, *The Idea of Luxury: A Conceptual and Historical Investigation*, Cambridge: Cambridge University Press.

Bourdieu, Pierre, 1986, *Distinction: A Social Critique of the Judgement of Taste*, London: Routledge (translated by Richard Nice).

Chevalier, Michel and Michel Gutsatz, 2012, *Luxury Retail Management: How the World's Top Brands Provide Quality Product and Service Support*, Chichester: Wiley.

Gardetti, Miguel Angel and Ana Laura Torres, eds, 2017, *Sustainable Luxury: Managing Social and Environmental Performance in Iconic Brands*, London: Taylor & Francis.

Gardetti, Miguel Angel and Subramanian Senthilkannan Muthu, 2017, *Sustainable Luxury, Entrepreneurship, and Innovation*, Singapore: Springer.

Kapferer, Jean-Noël and Anne Michaut-Denizeau, 2014, "Is Luxury Compatible with Sustainability? Luxury Consumers' Viewpoint", *The Journal of Brand Management*, 21, 1, 1–22.

Kapferer, Jean-Noël and Vincent Bastien, 2012, *The Luxury Strategy*, London: Kogan Page (2nd edition).

Kapferer, Jean-Noël, 2015, *Kapferer on Luxury: How Luxury Brands Can Grow Yet Remain Rare*, London: Kogan Page.

McNeil, Peter and Giorgio Riello, 2016, *Luxury: A Rich History*, Oxford: Oxford University Press.

Rambourg, Erwan, 2020, *Future Luxe: What's Ahead for the Business of Luxury*, Vancouver: Figure 1 Publishing.

Thomas, Dana, 2008, *Deluxe: How Luxury Lost Its Lustre*, London: Penguin Books.

Veblen, Thorstein, 1899, *The Theory of the Leisure Class: An Economic Study of Institutions*, London: Allen & Unwin (1st edition, reprinted 1970).

Wallpach, Sylvia von, Andrea Hemetsberger, Thyra Uth Thomsen and Russel W. Belk, 2020, "Moments of Luxury: A Qualitative Account of the Experiential Essence of Luxury", *Journal of Business Research*, 116, 491–502.

Research Methods

Bell, Emma, Alan Bryman and Bill Harley, 2022, *Business Research Methods*, Oxford: Oxford University Press (6th edition).

Birkinshaw, Julian, Mary Yoko Brannen and Rosalie L. Tung, 2011, "From a Distance and Generalizable to Up Close and Grounded: Reclaiming a Place for Qualitative Methods in International Business Research", *Journal of International Business Studies*, 42, 5, 573–581.

Cassell, Catherine, Ann L. Cunliffe and Gina Grandy, eds, 2018, *The SAGE Handbook of Qualitative Business and Management Research Methods: Methods and Challenges*, London: Sage.

Coleman, Renita, 2018, *Designing Experiments for the Social Sciences: How to Plan, Create and Execute Research Using Experiments*, Los Angeles: Sage.

Cresswell, John W. and David J. Cresswell, 2023, *Research Design: Qualitative, Quantitative, and Mixed Methods Approaches*, London: Sage (6th edition).

Duignan, John, 2016, *A Dictionary of Business Research Methods*, Oxford: Oxford University Press.

Durdella, Nathan, 2019, *Qualitative Dissertation Methodology: A Guide to Research Design and Methods*, London: Sage.

Eden, Lorraine and Bo Bernhard Nielsen, 2020, "Research Methods in International Business: The Challenge of Complexity", *Journal of International Business Studies*, 51, 1609–1620.

Eriksson, Päivi and Anne Kovalainen, 2016, *Qualitative Methods in Business Research*, London: Sage.

Kozinets, Robert V., 2020, *Netnography: The Essential Guide to Qualitative Social Media Research*, London: Sage (3rd edition).

Krippendorff, Klaus, 2019, *Content Analysis: An Introduction to its Methodology*, London: Sage.

Litman, Lieb and Jonathan Robinson, 2021, *Conducting Online Research on Amazon Mechanical Turk and Beyond*, London: Sage.

Mann, Steve, 2016, *The Research Interview: Reflective Practice and Reflexivity in Research Processes*, Camden: Palgrave Macmillan.

Morgan, David L., 2019, *Basic and Advanced Focus Groups*, London: Sage.

Oates, Caroline J. and Panayiota J. Alevizou, 2018, *Conducting Focus Groups for Business and Management Students*, London: Sage.

Osbourne, Jason, 2008, *Best Practices in Quantitative Methods*, London: Sage.

Pajo, Bora, 2022, *Introduction to Research Methods: A Hands-On Approach*, London: Sage (2nd edition).

Polonsky, Michael J. and David S. Waller, 2019, *Designing and Managing a Research Project: A Business Student's Guide*, London: Sage.

Punziano, Gabriella and Angela Delli Paoli, eds, 2022, *Handbook of Research on Advanced Research Methodologies for a Digital Society*, Hershey, PA: IGI Global.

Quan-Hause, Anabel and Luke Sloan, eds, *The SAGE Handbook of Social Media Research Methods*, London: Sage (2nd edition).

Quinton, Sarah and Teresa Smallbone, 2006, *Postgraduate Research in Business*, London: Sage.

Ruel, Erin, 2019, *100 Questions (and Answers) about Survey Research*, London: Sage.

Sage Publications, 2019, *SAGE Mixed Methods Research*, London: Sage.

Wiles, Rose, 2013, *What Are Qualitative Research Ethics?* London: Bloomsbury Academic.

Williams, Malcolm, Richard D. Wiggins and W. Paul Vogt, 2021, *Beginning Quantitative Research*, London: Sage.

Wilson, Helen F. and Jonathan Darling, eds, 2020, *Research Ethics for Human Geography: A Handbook for Students*, London: Sage.

Electronic Resources

Questionnaire Design

"Questionnaire design", Galton College: www.youtube.com/watch?v=ckKYdKjJGDc

"Questionnaire Design: Parts 1–3", Graham R. Gibbs: www.youtube.com/watch?v=vjailyWAcJQ

Focus Groups

"How Do Focus Groups Work?", Hector Lanz (TED-Ed): www.youtube.com/watch?v=3TwgVQIZPsw

"Moderating Focus Groups", Richard Krueger: www.youtube.com/watch?v=xjHZsEcSqwo

Interviews

"How to Develop an Interview Guide in Qualitative Research", Research with Dr Kriukow: www.youtube.com/watch?v=HvzfpFDOYyQ

"How to do a Research Interview", Graham R Gibbs: www.youtube.com/watch?v=9t-_hYjAKww

Case Study

"Case Study Research", Dr Watson: www.youtube.com/watch?v=RPB3Q9cXmvs

"Qualitative Case Study", Embraced Wisdom Resource Group: www.youtube.com/watch?v=ey4D5kKa4VY

Observation

"Observational Methods: Research Methods", Mike Sliter: www.youtube.com/watch?v=qerp9MR7pRI

"Participant Observation", University of Colorado Boulder: www.youtube.com/watch?v=c3CaBpcytmI

Data

"Intro to Data Science: The Nature of Data", Steve Brunton: www.youtube.com/watch?v=OAB2bHsee9Y

"H-Stats: 1.2 The Nature of Data", Gregory Sager: www.youtube.com/watch?v=sdzAz3CbWcA

Content Analysis

"Conducting a Content Analysis", Dr Joe Moore: www.youtube.com/watch?v=tBbGCQnxqys

"Qualitative Content Analysis", Robin Kay: www.youtube.com/watch?v=-DsSLKQqP8k

Analysis

"Qualitative Analysis of Interview Data: A Step-by-Step Guide for Coding/Indexing", Kent Löfgren: www.youtube.com/watch?v=DRL4PF2u9XA

"Chi-Square Test [Simply Explained]", DATAtab: www.youtube.com/watch?v=rpKzq64GA9Y

"Introduction to Correlation Analysis in Excel", David Langer: www.youtube.com/watch?v=1_jeoqjHtjA

"An Introduction to Linear Regression Analysis", statisticsfun: www.youtube.com/watch?v=zPG4NjIkCjc

"Analysis of Variance (ANOVA) Overview in Statistics – Learn ANOVA and How It Works", Math and Science: www.youtube.com/watch?v=CS_BKChyPuc

"A Gentle Introduction to Structural Equation Modelling", MPlus for Dummies: www.youtube.com/watch?v=kBHzggVCYwc

NOTES

1   Essentially, how much each country spent on luxury goods in 2022.

2   Data for luxury revenue by country (URL for Zambia) is derived, under institutional licence, from Statista.com (www.statista.com/outlook/cmo/luxury-goods/zambia) (accessed 1 October 2022). Data for population size and GDP were derived from the World Bank (data.worldbank.org/) (accessed 1 October 2022). GDP per capita was calculated from these data by the authors.

References

Aguinis, Herman, Isabel Villamour and Ravi S. Ramani, 2021, "MTurk Research: Review and Recommendations", *Journal of Management*, 47, 4, 823–837.

Aliyev, Farhad, Taylan Urkmez and Ralf Wagner, 2019, "A Comprehensive Look at Luxury Brand Marketing Research from 2000 to 2016: A Bibliographic Study and Content Analysis", *Management Review Quarterly*, 69, 3, 233–264.

Atkinson, Rowland, 2020, "How the Super Rich Conquered London", *The Conversation*, 28 May 2020; https://theconversation.com/how-the-super-rich-conquered-london-138865 (accessed 3 March 2021).

Atwal, Glyn, Douglas Bryson and Maya Kaiser, 2021, "The Chopsticks Debacle: How Brand Hate Flattened Dolce & Gabbana in China", *Journal of Business Strategy*, 43, 1, 37–43.

Bacon, Sir Francis, 1902 (1620), *Novum Organum* (New Logic), edited by Joseph Devey, New York: P.F. Collier.

Balabanis, George and Anastasia Stathopoulou, 2021, "The Price of Social Status Desire and Public Self-Consciousness in Luxury Consumption", *Journal of Business Research*, 123, 463–475.

Banta, Martha, 2007, "Introduction", in: Thorstein Veblen [1899], *The Theory of the Leisure Class: An Economic Study of Institutions*, Oxford World's Classics, Oxford: Oxford University Press.

Bazeley, Pat, 2008, "Mixed Methods in Management Research", in: Richard Thorpe and Robin Holt, eds, *The Sage Dictionary of Qualitative Management Research*, London: Sage, 133–136.

Beran, Tanya and Claudio Violato, 2010, "Technical Note: Structural Equation Modeling in Medical Research: A Primer", *British Medical Council Research Notes*, 3, article number 267 (DOI:10.1186/1756-0500-3-267).

Bharti, Megha, Vivek Suneja and Ajay Kumar Chauhan, 2022, "The Role of Socio-Psychological and Personality Antecedents in Luxury Consumption: A Meta-Analytic Review", *International Marketing Review*, 39, 2, 269–308.

Cabigiosu, Anna, 2020, "An Overview of the Luxury Fashion Industry" (Chapter 2), in: Anna Cabigiosu, *Digitalization in the Luxury Fashion Industry: Strategic Branding for Millennial Consumers*, Palgrave Advances in Luxury, Camden: Palgrave Macmillan.

Camic, Charles, 2020, *Veblen: The Making of an Economist Who Unmade Economics*, Cambridge, MA: Harvard University Press.

Chen, Chaomei, 2004, "Searching for Intellectual Turning Points: Progressive Knowledge Domain Visualisation", *Proceedings of the National Academy of Sciences of the United States of America*, 101, 5303–5310.

Chen, Chaomei, 2016, *CiteSpace: A Practical Guide for Mapping Scientific Literature*, New York: Nova.

Chen, Mingliang, Zhaohan Xie, Jing Zhang and Yingying Li, 2021, "Internet Celebrities' Impact on Luxury Fashion Impulse Buying", *Journal of Theoretical Applied Electronic Commerce Research*, 16, 2470–2489.

Ciornea, Raluca, Marius D. Pop, Mihai F. Bacila and Alexandra M. Drule, 2012, "Was Luxury Little Researched? An Exploration of Studies and Research Trends in the Area of Marketing of Luxury Goods, before 2005", *Management and Marketing*, X, 2, 325–340.

Coleman, Renita, 2018, *Designing Experiments for the Social Sciences: How to Plan, Create and Execute Research Using Experiments*, Los Angeles, CA: Sage.

Collier, David and Steven Levitsky, 1997, "Democracy with Adjectives: Conceptual Innovation in Comparative Research", *World Politics*, 49, 3, 430–451.

Cooper, Donald R., 2019, *Business Research: A Guide to Planning, Conducting, and Reporting Your Study*, Thousand Oaks, CA: Sage.

D'Arpizio, Claudia, Federica Levato, Constance Gault, Joëlle de Montgolfier and Lyne Jaroudi, 2021, "From Surging Recovery to Elegant Advance: The Evolving Future of Luxury", Bain and Company, Luxury Goods Worldwide Market Study 2021, 20 December 2021.

D'Arpizio, Claudia, Federica Levato, Marc-André Kamel and Joëlle de Montgofier, 2017, "Luxury Goods Worldwide Market Study, Fall–Winter 2017: The New Luxury Consumer: Why Responding to the Millennial Mindset Will be Key", Boston, MA: Bain & Company.

Deloitte, 2021, *Global Powers of Luxury Goods, 2021: Breakthrough Luxury*, London: Deloitte Touche Tohmatsu.

Dittmar, Helga, Rod Bond, Megan Hurst and Tim Kasser, 2014, "The Relationship Between Materialism and Personal Well-Being: A Meta-Analysis", *Journal of Personality and Social Psychology*, 107, 5, 879–924.

Dorfman, Joseph, 1932, "The 'Satire' of Thorstein Veblen's Theory of the Leisure Class", *Political Science Quarterly*, 47, 3, 363–409.

Douha, N'guessan Yves-Roland, 2020, "Are You Aware of Studies That Use LinkedIn as Part of Their Data Collection Method?" www.researchgate.net/post/Are_you_aware_of_studies_that_use_Linkedin_as_part_of_their_data_collection_method/5fd0755ed2f12f6b0647ba8d/citation/download (accessed 24 September 2022).

Druckman, James N., 2022, *Experimental Thinking: A Primer on Social Science Experiments*, Cambridge: Cambridge University Press.

Eisend, Martin, Patrick Hartmann and Vanessa Apaolaza, 2017, "Who Buys Counterfeit Luxury Brands? A Meta-Analytic Synthesis of Consumers in Developing and Developed Markets", *Journal of International Marketing*, 25, 4, 89–111.

Foucault, Michel, 1970, *The Order of Things: An Archaeology of the Human Sciences*, London: Tavistock.

Foucault, Michel, 1972, *The Archaeology of Knowledge*, London: Tavistock.

Geertz, Clifford, 1973, *The Interpretation of Cultures: Selected Essays*, Hammersmith: Fontana Press.

Goodman, Douglas J. and Mirelle Cohen, 2004, *Consumer Culture: A Reference Handbook*, Santa Barbara, CA: ABC-CLIO.

Gurzki, Hannes and David Moritz Woisetschläger, 2016, "Mapping the Luxury Research Landscape: A Bibliographic Citation Analysis", *Journal of Business Research*, 77, 147–166.

Hsieh, Hsiu-Fang and Sarah E. Shannon, 2005, "Three Approaches to Qualitative Content Analysis", *Qualitative Health Research*, 15, 9, 1277–1288.

Jacoby, Russell, 1987, *The Last Intellectuals: American Culture in the Age of Academe*, New York: Basic Books.

Jebarajakirthy, Charles and Manish Das, 2021, "Uniqueness and Luxury: A Moderated Mediation Approach", *Journal of Retailing and Consumer Services*, 60, article number 102477 (DOI:10.1016/j.jretconser.2021.102477).

Kim, Angella J., 2010, "The Effects of Perceived Social Media Marketing Activities on Customer Equity and Purchase Intention: Focus on Luxury Fashion Brands", Unpublished Master's Thesis, Yonsei University.

Kim, Angella J. and Eunju Ko, 2012, "Do Social Media Marketing Activities Enhance Customer Equity? An Empirical Study of Luxury Fashion Brand", *Journal of Business Ethics*, 65, 1480–1486.

Kozinets, Robert V., 2010, *Netnography: Doing Ethnographic Research Online*, London: Sage.

Kozinets, Robert V., 2014, *Netnography: Redefined*, Los Angeles, CA: Sage.

Kozinets, Robert V., 2020, *Netnography: The Essential Guide to Qualitative Social Media Research* (3rd edition), London: Sage.

Kozinets, Robert V., Daiane Scaraboto and Marie-Angès Parmentier, 2018, "Evolving Netnography: How Brand Auto-Netnography, a Netnographic Sensibility, and More-than-Human Netnography Can Transform Your Research", *Journal of Marketing Management*, 34, 3–4, 231–242.

Kumar, Bipul, Richard P. Bagozzi, Ajay K. Manrai and Lalita A. Manrai, 2022, "Conspicuous Consumption: A Meta-Analytic Review of Its Antecedents, Consequences and Moderators", *Journal of Retailing*, 98, 3, 471–485.

Landsberger, Henry A., 1958, *Hawthorne Revisited*, Ithaca, NY: The New York State School of Industrial and Labor Relations.

Lang, Chunmin and Cosette M. Joyner Armstrong, 2018, "Collaborative Consumption: The Influence of Fashion Leadership, Need for Uniqueness, and Materialism on Female Consumers' Adoption of Clothing Rental and Swapping", *Sustainable Production and Consumption*, 1, 3, 37–47.

Likert, Rensis, 1932, "A Technique for the Measurement of Attitudes", *Archives of Psychology*, 22, No. 140.

Loranger, David and Erik Roeraas, 2022, "Transforming Luxury: Global Luxury Brand Executives' Perceptions During COVID", *Journal of Global Fashion Marketing* (DOI:10.1080/20932685.2022.209738).

LVMH Group, 2021, *2020 Social and Environmental Responsibility Report*, Paris: LVMH Group.

Ma, Jieqiang, JungHwa Hong, Boonghee Yoo and Jie Yang, 2021, "The Effects of Religious Commitment and Global Identity on Purchase Intention of Luxury Fashion Products: A Cross-Cultural Study", *Journal of Business Research*, 137, 244–254.

Mann, Steve, 2016, *The Research Interview: Reflective Practice and Reflexivity in Research Processes*, Camden: Palgrave Macmillan.

Mason, Roger, 1984, "Conspicuous Consumption: A Literature Review", *European Journal of Marketing*, 18, 3, 26–39.

McMenamin, Iain, 2006, "Process and Text: Teaching Students to Review the Literature", *Political Science and Politics*, 39, 1, 133–135.

Mirabeau, Laurent, Muriel Mignerat and Camille Grange, 2013, "The Utility of Using Social Media Networks for Data Collection in Survey Research", International Conference on Information Systems (ICIS 2013): Reshaping Society Through Information Systems Design, Milan, December 2013.

Monfared, Konjkav Amirreza, Arefeh Mansouri and Negar Jalilian, 2021, "The Influence of Personality and Social Traits on the Importance of Brand Design of Luxury Brands and Brand Loyalty", *American Journal of Business*, 36, 2, 128–149.

Moore, Niamh, Andrea Salter, Liz Stanley and Maria Tamboukou, 2020, *The Archive Project: Archival Research in the Social Sciences*, London: Routledge.

Navia, Christian Rodil, Ruskikesh Ulhas Khire and Maurice Lyver, 2021, "Investigating the Impacts of Personality Traits on Collaborative Consumption Intention of Luxury Fashion Products among Middle-Aged Women", *Independent Journal of Management and Production*, 12, 2, 506–525.

Okawa, Tomoko, 2020, "Licensing and the Mass Production of Luxury Goods", in: Pierre-Yves Douzé, Véronique Pouillard and Joanne Roberts, eds, *The Oxford Handbook of Luxury Business*, Oxford: Oxford University Press, 173–194.

Park, Jungkun, Hyowon Hyun and Toulany Thavisay, 2021, "A Study of Antecedents and Outcomes of Social Media WOM towards Luxury Brand Purchase Intention", *Journal of Retailing and Consumer Services*, 58 (DOI:10.1016/j.retconser.2020.102272).

Rathi, Rubal, Ruchi Garg, Aakanksha Kataria and Ritu Chhikara, 2022, "Evolution of Luxury Marketing Landscape: A Bibliometric Analysis and Future Directions", *Journal of Brand Management*, 29, 241–257.

Richins, Marsha L., 2004, "The Material Values Scale: Measurement Properties and Development of a Short Form", *Journal of Consumer Research*, 31, 1, 209–219.

Ritchie, Jane, Jane Lewis, Carol MacNaughton Nicholls and Rachel Ormston, eds, 2013, *Qualitative Research Practice: A Guide for Social Science Students and Researchers*, London: Sage.

Shukla, Paurav, Veronica Rosendo-Rios and Dina Khalifa, 2022, "Is Luxury Democratization Impactful? Its Moderating Effect between Value Perceptions and Consumer Purchase Intention", *Journal of Business Research*, 139, 782–793.

Skousen, Mark, 2009, *The Making of Modern Economics: The Lives and Ideas of Great Thinkers* (Chapter 10: "The Conspicuous Veblen versus the Protesting Weber: Two Critics Debate the Meaning of Capitalism", 247–270) (2nd edition), New York: Routledge.

Spencer, Stephen, 2022, *Visual Research Methods in the Social Sciences: Awakening Visions*, London: Routledge.

Statista, 2020, *Luxury Market Report*, New York: Statista Consumer Market Outlook, August 2020.

Statista, 2021, *Statista Consumer Market Outlook: Product & Methodology*, Statista September 2021; CMO-Methodik_en.pdf (accessed 26 October 2022).

Sun, Jennifer J., Silvia Bellezza and Neeru Paharia, 2021, "Buy Less, Buy Luxury: Understanding and Overcoming Product Durability Neglect for Sustainable Consumption", *Journal of Marketing*, 85, 3, 28–43.

Taleb, Nassim Nicholas, 2010, *The Black Swan: The Impact of the Highly Improbable* (2nd edition), London: Penguin.

The Museum at FIT, "Yves Saint Laurent's Rive Gauche Collection", 3 March 2015, https://exhibitions. fitnyc.edu/blog-ysl-halston/yves-saint-laurents-rive-gauche-revolution/ (accessed 8 October 2022).

Thomas, Dana, 2008, *Deluxe: How Luxury Lost Its Lustre*, London: Penguin Books.

Tien, Kelly Tepper, William O. Bearden and Gary L. Hunter, 2001, "Consumers' Need for Uniqueness: Scale Development and Validation", *Journal of Consumer Research*, 28, 1, 50–66.

Tight, Malcolm, 2019, *Documentary Research in the Social Sciences*, London: Sage.

Turner, Daniel, Hiram Ting, Mun Wai Wong, Tze-Yin Lim and Kim-Lim Tan, 2021, "Applying Qualitative Approach in Business Research", *Asian Journal of Business Research*, 11, 3, 1–13.

Veblen, Thorstein, 1899, *The Theory of the Leisure Class: An Economic Study of Institutions*, New York: Macmillan.

Veloutsou, Cleopatra, George Christodoulides and Francisco Guzman, 2021, "Charting Research on International Luxury Marketing: Where Are We Now and Where Should We Go Next?", *International Marketing Review*, October 2021 (DOI:10.1108/IMR-04–2021–0154).

Walters, Trudie and Neill Carr, 2015, "Second Homes as Sites for the Consumption of Luxury", *Tourism and Hospitality Research*, 15, 1, 131–141.

Wei, Alexander, 2022, "Is the 'Sortie du Temple' of Bottega Veneta Imminent?", *Luxury Society*, 30 March 2022.

Welch, Catherine, Eriikka Paavilainen-Mäntymäki, Rebecca Piekkari and Emmanuella Plakoyiannaki, 2022, "Reconciling Theory and Context: How the Case Study Can Set a New Agenda for International Business Research", *Journal of International Business Studies*, 53, 4–26.

Woiceshyn, Jaana and Urs Daellenbach, 2018, "Evaluating Inductive versus Deductive Research in Management Studies: Implications for Authors, Editors and Reviewers", *Qualitative Research in Organizations and Management: An International Journal*, 13, 2, 183–195.

Xiao, Bo and Izak Benbasat, 2007, "E-Commerce Product Recommendation Agents: Use, Characteristics, and Impact", *MIS Quarterly*, 31, 1, 137–209.

Zazzara, Laura, Giulio Rapetti and David Charles Tyler, 2020, "Burberry Burning Backlash", Elsevier: Social Science Research Network (SSRN).

Zici, Ayanda, Emmanuel Silva Quayle, Divaries Cosmas Jaruavaza and Yvonne Saini, 2021, "Luxury Purchase Intentions: The Role of Individualism–Collectivism and Value–Expressive Influence in South Africa", *Cogent Psychology*, 8, 1 (DOI:10.1080/ 23311908.2021.1991728).

Index

Note: **Bold** page numbers refer to tables.

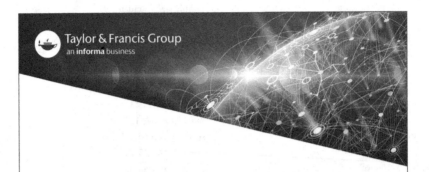

Printed in the United States
by Baker & Taylor Publisher Services